Freedom and Growth

In discussions on European pre-modern economic growth, the role of individual freedom and of the state has loomed large. This book examines whether different kinds of 'freedoms' – such as absolutist, parliamentary and republican freedoms – caused different economic outcomes, and shows the effect of different political regimes on long-term development.

S. R. Epstein's innovative approach examines political regimes as ways to facilitate economic cooperation for mutual advantage. Markets, he argues, are public goods based on cooperation, and cooperation requires enforcement. *Freedom and Growth* reveals that the most important economic consequence of the rise of centralised states between 1300 and 1750 was not whether or not they guaranteed individual liberties, but the fact that they made the growth of coordinated and competitive markets possible. Specific case studies of the late medieval 'crisis', integrated grain markets, urban hierarchies and of the use of European fair networks illustrate how states were instrumental in overcoming market failures caused by political decentralisation, and how the crisis itself represented a watershed for European political and economic integration.

This book addresses – and most importantly finds links between – two major debates in European history: the debate about the effects of political regimes on economic growth, and the debate over the late medieval social and economic 'crisis'. It offers radically new perspectives on the causes of pre-industrial growth and divergence and on the transition from feudalism to capitalism.

S. R. Epstein is Reader in Economic History at the London School of Economics and Political Science. His previous publications include *An Island for Itself: Economic Development and Social Change in Late Medieval Sicily* (1992) and he is Editor of *Town and Country in Europe, 1300–1750* (2000), and Co-Editor of *Guilds, Economy and Society* (1998).

Books published under the joint imprint of LSE/Routledge are works of high academic merit approved by the Publications Committee of the London School of Economics and Political Science. These publications are drawn from the wide range of academic studies in the social sciences for which the LSE has an international reputation.

Routledge Explorations in Economic History

Freedom and Growth

The rise of states and markets
in Europe, 1300–1750

S. R. Epstein

London and New York

First published 2000
by Routledge
2 Park Square, Milton Park, Abingdon, Oxon, OX14 4RN

Simultaneously published in the USA and Canada
by Routledge
270 Madison Ave, New York NY 10016

Routledge is an imprint of the Taylor & Francis Group

Transferred to Digital Printing 2006

Typeset in Baskerville
by Curran Publishing Services Ltd, Norwich

British Library Cataloguing in Publication Data
A catalogue record for this book is available
from the British Library.

Library of Congress Cataloging in Publication Data
Epstein, S. R., 1960-
  Freedom and growth: the rise of states and markets in Europe,
  1300–1750 / S. R. Epstein.
  240 p. 15.6 x 23.4 cm. – (Routledge explorations in modern
  history)
  Includes bibliographical references and index
  1. Europe – Economic conditions. 2. Europe – Politics and
  government. 3. Liberty–History. 4. State, The–History.
  I. Title. II. Series.
HC240 .E58 2000
330.94–dc21   00-028619

ISBN10: 0-415-15208-9 (hbk)
ISBN10: 0-415-77115-3 (pbk)

ISBN13: 978-0-415-15208-2 (hbk)
ISBN13: 978-0-415-77115-3 (pbk)

To Sean

Contents

Figures

Tables

Acknowledgements

My interest in the issues discussed in this book first arose as an under-graduate in Italy, and accordingly my debts to the many friends and colleagues in that country go back a long time. Among those who have offered advice and the fruits of their own research, while guiding me through the complexities of pre-modern Italian institutions and modern archives and libraries, I wish particularly to thank Giuliana Albini, Marco Bellabarba, Luciano Bonomi (for his easy-to-use programme of the Florentine *Catasto* of 1427), Maristella Botticini (who first told me about it), Laura De Angelis, Luisa Chiappa Mauri, Giorgio Chittolini, Nadia Covini, Lorenzo Fabbri, Franco Franceschi, Franca Leverotti, Patrizia Mainoni, Igor Mineo, Oretta Muzzi, Céline Perrol, Luciano Pezzolo, Mario Rizzo, and Andrea Zorzi. I am particularly grateful to Drs Sandra Contini, Francesca Klein and Irene Stumpo of the Archivio di Stato in Florence, who have so willingly acceded to my requests. I have also benefited from comments and information by Rita Astuti, Wim Blockmans, Marc Boone, Bruce Campbell, Bill Day, James Galloway, Richard Goldthwaite, Peter Hoppenbrouwers, Derek Keene, Meir Kohn, Marianne Kowaleski, Patrick K. O'Brien, Nick Poynder, Maarten Prak, Peter Stabel, James Thomson, Eric Thoen, Richard Unger and Chris Wickham. I am particularly thankful to Mina Moshkeri, of the LSE Cartographic and Design Unit, for her outstanding maps. I gratefully acknowledge financial support for different aspects of this project from the Molly Cotton Research Fund, the British Academy, the Nuffield Research Fund, and the Suntory and Toyota International Centres for Economics and Related Disciplines (LSE). Many of the ideas in this book have arisen from teaching graduate students at the London School of Economics, and I wish to thank them collectively for their positive responses. As always, my gratitude goes to Fernanda and Carlo Astuti for offering their home as a base for archival forays and much more, and to Rita and Sean for listening.

S. R. E.

Abbreviations

ACPc	Piacenza, Archivio comunale
AFL	Arezzo, Archivio della Fraternita dei Laici
ASAr	Arezzo, Archivio di Stato
ASCBs	Brescia, Archivio storico comunale
ASCo	Como, Archivio di Stato
ASCr	Cremona, Archivio di Stato
ASFi	Florence, Archivio di Stato
AL	Arte della lana
ARLS	Arte dei rigattieri, linaioli e sarti
CCPM	Camera del Comune, Provveditori e massari, Entrata e uscita
CRS	Corporazioni religiose soppresse dal Governo francese
DAC	Dogana di Firenze, Dogana antica e campioni (sec.XIV–1808)
PR	Provvisioni registri
SRD	Statuti, riforme, ordini e tariffe della dogana
ASMi	Milan, Archivio di Stato
ASPc	Piacenza, Archivio di Stato
ASPi	Pisa, Archivio di Stato
ASPt	Pistoia, Archivio di Stato
BA	Milan, Biblioteca Ambrosiana
BCBg	Bergamo, Biblioteca civica A. Mai
BCPv	Pavia, Biblioteca comunale
BCV	Volterra, Biblioteca comunale
BT	Milan, Biblioteca Trivulziana
ECA	Milan, Archivio delle Istituzioni pubbliche di assistenza e beneficenza (ex-E.C.A.)

1 Introduction

States and markets

Things happen when they have to, usually at the wrong time.

Nairn 1997: 16

Economic history has three major narrative themes: the transition from autarky to market society (or market integration), the development of technology or productive forces, and the extension of manufactory in a fundamentally agrarian world. Its central questions are why past growth was so slow and intermittent, and why economic performance differs between differently structured societies over time. This book addresses the question of what caused historical growth by examining the creation of markets and the consequences of market integration in late medieval and early modern Europe: pre-modern Europe for short.[1]

Until quite recently most historians would have considered such questions nonsensical. The prevailing Ricardo-Malthusian view of pre-modern societies was deeply pessimistic.[2] With static technology and little knowledge among the peasantry to control population size, pre-modern economic growth was a contradiction in terms. Diminishing returns were inescapable, and demand inevitably and regularly outran supply. In the terms popularised by the historians associated with the *Annales*, Fernand Braudel's *longue durée*, the nearly unchanging substratum of everyday life became conceptually interchangeable with Emmanuel Le Roy Ladurie's *histoire immobile*, the eternal return of the 'Malthusian cycle' of overpopulation and agrarian involution. The neo-Malthusian model derived its popularity from its theoretical parsimony, its consistency with most of the known facts, and its appeal to the nineteenth-century Romantic belief in the profoundly conservative and 'anti-capitalist' mentality of the peasantry. But the model's simplicity was also the source of its major weaknesses, namely that it could explain neither how late

---

1 The term pre-modern has no normative connotation, and is simply used to refer to the period between 1200 and 1800 as a whole.
2 For a lucid exposition, see Grantham 1999.

eighteenth- and nineteenth-century 'modernisation' could arise from such a conservative economy and society, nor why economic performance differed between countries and regions.

Criticisms of these failings came to a head in the 1970s, when four major essays appeared proposing alternative reinterpretations of the rise of European capitalism and world economic hegemony. Each model concentrated on a single, driving factor of economic growth and development. Franklin Mendels (1972) built an entire theory of social, cultural and demographic modernisation upon the centrality of industry in the countryside, Immanuel Wallerstein (1974) adopted and modified Braudel's belief in the primacy of long-distance trade, Robert Brenner (1976) emphasised class struggle and property rights to land, and Douglass North (North and Thomas 1973) focused on transaction costs and the state.

The theory of protoindustrialisation developed by Mendels, Kriedte, Medick and Schlumbohm was the most complex and also the most precise of the four. The theory was distinguished from Marxism by its emphasis on slow, cumulative change rather than on overt and subterranean conflict over property rights and resources; and it was distinguished from neo-classical models of growth by its emphasis on supply-side demographic change rather than on technology or price and income effects. Protoindustrial theory claimed that the diffusion of industry in the countryside after the mid-seventeenth century changed the incentive structure of rural labour. It drew peasants into the marketplace which they had formerly shunned; it freed them from the traditional constraints on family size posed by the limited supply of land; it undermined 'traditional' or feudal urban institutions, in particular the technologically conservative and industrially restrictive craft guilds; it created a dispossessed labour force that prefigured the industrial proletariat; and it provided the accumulation of capital needed for factory industry.

The clarity of the model's predictions made the latter easy to test and, after a quarter of a century of detailed research, little of the original theory is left standing. It is now clear that protoindustry was not always associated with a fall in the age at marriage and a rise in birth rates, and that one finds similar demographic patterns in regions with no protoindustry; that protoindustrialisation did not cause the downfall of the urban craft guilds, because the latter employed skilled labour that protoindustry lacked; and most importantly, that protoindustry was only occasionally the harbinger of modern industry. On the other hand, it is also established that protoindustry was one of the main agencies of pre-modern, market-led or Smithian growth. Protoindustry drew off excess labour from the fields while offering a reservoir of wage labour at times of peak demand at the grain and wine harvests, it supplied pre-machine economies with low-cost cloth and metalwork, and it stimulated inter-regional trade in victuals and consumer goods. But protoindustry did not fundamentally change the structure of pre-modern economies, and there was no inherent reason why it should give rise to modern factory industry if commercial or other conditions changed. Perhaps the strongest evidence to this effect is the fact that seventeenth- and eighteenth-century protoindustry was the continuation of a process of specialisation that had begun after the Black Death of 1347–50; a further reason to question the revolutionary character of protoindustry was its strong dependence on the technological and labour market externalities of 'traditional', craft-based urban industry. I discuss both points in Chapter 6 of this book.

Wallerstein's argument that a 'capitalist world system' emerged in Europe by about 1500 presupposes that the economies of Europe and its overseas colonies were part of a single, integrated system with a complex division of labour between 'centre', 'semi-periphery', and 'periphery', and that the profits from overseas trade determined the continent's economic trajectory. The thesis raises two empirical objections. The first, put forward by O'Brien, is that the volume of overseas trade in the *eighteenth* century, which was considerably larger than in the sixteenth, was still far too small to be of more than marginal relevance for the British and Continental European economies.[3] The second objection comes from evidence of medieval and early modern market integration (Chapters 3, 7), which shows that national markets in the most widely traded pre-modern commodity, wheat, did not develop for the most part before the late eighteenth century, and that the rise of an integrated European and Atlantic market occurred only after the introduction of railways and steamships in the nineteenth century.[4] To posit an integrated 'world system' already consisting of specialised national units by 1500 is therefore a 300-year anachronism.

In his original essay of 1976, which was particularly concerned with the economic consequences of the so-called 'late medieval crisis' – a period of demographic collapse and economic, social and political upheaval lasting from approximately 1300 to 1475 – Brenner made the largely untestable claim that the outcome of the crisis was determined by distributional conflicts (class struggle) between peasants and lords. Subsequently he argued that what really mattered for the pattern and outcome of the crisis in different countries were property rights to land, which set strict and near immovable constraints on market activities and technological innovation, and therefore determined contrasting growth paths.[5] Following Marc Bloch, Maurice Dobb, and Barrington Moore Jr., Brenner argued that European agriculture between 1200 and 1800 was either 'feudal' or 'capitalist'.[6] Under feudalism, the peasantry owned its

---

3 O'Brien 1982.

4 Persson 1999; Chevet 1996; Federico 1999. A national market in England emerged earlier, probably in the latter half of the seventeenth century (Kussmaul 1990; Chartres 1995).

5 Brenner 1976, 1982 and 1997.

6 See Bloch 1970; Dobb 1946; Barrington Moore 1966.

means of production, was self-sufficient for food, and was forced by military and legal force to pay a surplus to feudal lords (including state and church). The peasantry had no incentive to specialise for the market or to innovate because specialisation and innovation were excessively risky, while feudal lords increased their income by encouraging population growth and labour intensification on the land, and through warfare and pillage. Feudal property rights to land therefore created disincentives that were redistributive and anti-market. Under capitalist agrarian relations, on the other hand, the peasantry was replaced by tenants and labourers who were forced to compete productively on the market. However, agrarian capitalism emerged only in England because it was the only country where the peasantry was evicted from the land; elsewhere in Europe, the peasantry clung on and feudal property rights survived. Whether or not this constitutes an accurate account of agrarian developments in pre-modern Europe, Brenner's combination of neo-Malthusian pessimism and property-rights determinism seemed to offer a solution to the conundrum of the contrasting rates of growth of English and Continental agriculture.[7] At the same time it gave theoretical support to the widespread belief that until the end of the Middle Ages 'markets played no important part in the economic system [of Europe]; other institutional patterns prevailed'.[8]

The nature of market relations under feudalism is indeed critical to any explanation of economic change and it is on that account that Brenner's theory fails. First, Brenner argues that the reason why peasants under feudalism could resist market pressures was that they were self-sufficient for food.[9] In fact, over half the peasant population in late thirteenth-century England did not have enough land to live on and was forced to seek additional income from manufacture, trade and wage employment, and the proportion of 'self-sufficient' peasants is unlikely to have been any higher in Continental Europe, where urbanisation, markets and specialisation were equally or more advanced.[10] Second, Brenner argues that peasants were technologically less innovative than landlords but, again, evidence discussed in Chapter 3 suggests the opposite conclusion. Third, he claims that agriculture displayed economies of scale, which required the consolidation of peasant small-holdings; however, there is little empirical evidence to support this.[11]

---

7 Brenner has been challenged extensively on the matter; see Aston and Philpin 1985 for a number of criticisms of Brenner's empirical reconstruction.
8 Polanyi 1944: 55.
9 Note that self-sufficiency increases peasant welfare only if it reduces the volatility of income compared to production for the market. See p.48.
10 See Chapter 3, note 26.
11 See Gasson and Hill 1984; Hoffman 1996; Overton 1996: 127, 205; Grantham 1997b; Allen 1999.

Fourth, he predicts that if peasants were evicted from the land the productivity of labour in agriculture would rise sharply. In Italy, however, where serfdom was virtually abolished by 1300, peasant communities were weak, and 'bourgeois' ownership was prevalent – where in other words peasants had been 'evicted' from land-ownership far earlier than in England – labour productivity after 1500 stagnated.[12] Empirical studies of modern developing countries also confirm what the example of pre-modern Italy appears to imply, that systems of land ownership and the choice of agrarian contract do not directly determine agricultural performance.[13]

Brenner's interpretation suffers from the combination of a narrow form of 'property rights romanticism', whereby property rights to land determine the existence of markets and the path of technological change, and of 'typological essentialism', which defines the feudal economy in terms of only one characteristic (property rights to land) deemed to represent its essential qualities. Brenner's problems stem from his excessively narrow definition of feudal property rights – that is, of enforced rights to income streams – in terms of property to land, which excludes all the 'extra-economic' rights of lords to extract rents from transactions (production and trade), and which therefore deprives his model of an endogenous source of change and short-circuits the question of how markets in feudalism actually arose. Significantly, Brenner never discusses the emergence of markets in either feudalism *or* capitalism, appearing simply to assume that capitalist markets followed the emergence of new property rights to land with the expulsion of the peasantry.[14] These problems can be solved by identifying transactional or tributary rights as the main source of endogenous change in the feudal economy, a position I defend in Chapter 3.

The hypotheses developed by Douglass North and the New Institutional Economics school (NIE), modified to account for institutional sclerosis and rent-seeking, are both remarkably akin to classical Marxism and offer a more plausible model of institutional change.[15] By focusing on the

12 Epstein 1998b.
13 See Otsuka et al. 1992; Foster and Rosenzweig 1995; Schiff and Montenegro 1997; Botticini 1998; and in this chapter, note 7.
14 In Brenner's formulation, England escaped feudalism because, unlike elsewhere, the strongly centralised state sided with the feudal lords in evicting the peasantry after the Black Death. However, he does not explain the 300-year hiatus between the feudal crisis after 1350 and the full transition to agrarian capitalism in the seventeenth century (Brenner 1982, 1997). Brenner implies that capitalism arose in England through historical chance, a curious position for an avowed Marxist, since Marxism's main distinguishing feature compared with rival social science accounts is its brand of technological determinism (Cohen 1978). Brenner's position is more akin to that of the original 'property rights school' (Alchian and Demsetz 1973).
15 North 1981 and 1990; Droback and Nye 1997.

formal social rules and the exchange relations which allocate resources and constrain individual choice, NIE offers a synthesis between Marx's techno-institutional determinism and the neoclassical concern with the allocative functions of markets. NIE's hypothesis that formal markets arise when property rights are secured, and that they develop as transaction costs (agency problems) decline, solves the false dichotomy between feudalism and competitive markets shared by Brenner, Wallerstein and Mendels, makes the existence and nature of markets in non-capitalist societies a question to be assessed empirically rather than deductively, and offers a way of comparing the historical growth of markets across time and space.[16] Last but not least, it turns the state from a fringe actor into a major protagonist of economic growth and development.

NIE's scope and ambition have nevertheless restricted its usefulness in explaining macro-economic performance in the past. Four problems have proved to be particularly intractable. First, transaction costs can be invoked to explain both economic failure and success; to avoid circularity there is a need for a theory of institutional change that NIE has so far not provided. Second, transaction costs are hard to measure in pre-statistical societies, raising the possibility that an unmeasurable quantity is being assigned spurious causation. Third, it is not *a priori* clear what economically efficient political arrangements should look like. For example, a point frequently made in defence of democratic politics is that conditions that might be sub-optimal at one point in time may be more dynamic in the long run; equally, the claim that a strong state finds it easier to overcome rent-seeking activities seems just as plausible as the statement that a weak state finds it harder to enforce the rent seekers' claims. Fourth and most importantly, NIE consistently attributes the existence of sub-optimal or inefficient institutions to state policy, more specifically to the actions of naturally 'predatory' rulers who, by maximising revenue from their subjects, undermine property rights and incentives to investment and trade. NIE therefore assumes, as Margaret Levi has put it, that "rulers rule. That is, they stand at the head of the institutions that determine and implement state policies and regulations affecting a given polity and the state's provision of collective goods".[17]

Although this book is concerned with measuring and comparing the effects of different political institutions, my view of pre-modern states and of their economic consequences is very different from that presented by NIE theorists. The latter project backwards in time a form of centralised sovereignty and jurisdictional integration that was first achieved in Continental Europe during the nineteenth century; they therefore fundamentally misrepresent the character of pre-modern states. One basic

---

16   For an economic definition of feudalism, see pp. 49–52 in this book.
17   Levi 1988: 2.

difference between modern and pre-modern states, which had significant economic consequences, is the fact that membership of pre-modern states was not universal, or more precisely, that membership rights were distinguished by corporate status and dispensed as privileges or 'freedoms'. Because they lacked centralised, sovereign jurisdictions, pre-modern polities were also not comparable to modern federations, in which "competition among jurisdictions allows citizens to sort themselves and match their preferences with a particular menu of local public goods", because federalism, by contrast with pre-modern 'composite' states, functions through a centralised, sovereign power which binds all lower jurisdictions together and co-ordinates between them.[18] By applying an anachronistic model of the state, NIE misunderstands the main institutional causes of pre-modern economic performance.

Although Mendels, Wallerstein, Brenner and North agree that institutions, whether property rights to land, market structures, or the power of the state, mattered for economic growth, their explanations have either failed empirically or have not been put to the test. Protoindustry and property rights to land, which Mendels and Brenner identified as independent causes of growth, appear instead to be dependent variables, while Wallerstein and North project nineteenth- and twentieth-century conditions onto the pre-modern past. The purpose of this book is to consider what is lacking from previous interpretations of pre-modern economic growth, namely, an analysis of the historical and institutional preconditions of markets and the application of a standard of measurement – market integration – by which we may judge the relative economic efficiency of political institutions.

Three main assumptions guide this study. First, pre-modern growth was to a large extent 'Smithian', instigated by growth in demand which reduced transaction costs (because of economies of scale in commercial services) and increased potential gains from innovation. Second, innovation occurred mainly through the adoption of better practice from an existing repertory of unexploited techniques, and through piecemeal progress at the technical margin, rather than through major technological breakthroughs. Third, the major institutional constraints to market size were in principle two: predatory states which made property rights insecure, as argued by NIE, and coordination failures and prisoner's dilemmas which raised the costs of trade.

Chapter 2 discusses the first constraint. It asks whether the driving force of pre-modern growth was the defence and growth of individual and mercantile freedom against the autocratic powers of the state, and examines whether different kinds of political regime – absolutist,

---

18 Quian and Weingast 1997: 83. See also Weingast 1993 and 1995, which explicitly models eighteenth-century England as a proto-federation.

parliamentary and urban republican – gave rise to different economic outcomes. It finds that evidence of state depredation is in fact either negative or inconclusive, and suggests instead that the main political-regime barrier to pre-modern economic growth arose from the state's inability to enforce a unified, non-discriminatory fiscal and legal regime. The jurisdictional fragmentation and legally sanctioned monopolies that most early modern states inherited from their medieval past increased negotiation, enforcement and exaction costs and were the main source of rent seeking and high transaction costs. Limitations to, rather than excesses of, state sovereignty are what restrained the rise of competitive markets.

This book examines political regimes as ways to facilitate cooperation for mutual advantage. Its arguments follow from the simple observation that markets are public or collective goods based on cooperation, and that cooperation does not come for free. The institutional redesigning that is needed to adapt to new technologies and patterns of demand involves many different and interlocking elements, which it is difficult to replace individually without also radically modifying other components. Because of problems of collective agency, these changes are less costly if the institutions to be modified are centralised than if they are split among different actors, interest groups, or jurisdictions. A joint monopolist like the state supplies public goods including defence, law and order, and secure property rights more effectively than decentralised monopolists, because the latter give rise to multiple coordination failures (institutional arrangements which persist despite being collectively damaging because no individual actor wishes to change them and no actor wishes other actors to change them either) and prisoner's dilemmas (institutional arrangements in which rational actors do not uphold common rules of engagement because it is in their short-run interest to defect).[19]

For coordination failures to be overcome and competitive markets to be established, the constraining 'rules of the game', as North has called them, need to be changed. Changing the rules generally requires an external

19 The classic statement about the problems of providing public goods is Olson 1965. In game theory, a prisoner's dilemma arises when the dominant (e.g. invariably preferable) strategy for two players is to act 'egoistically' and to 'defect', even though they would be better off if they cooperated. The decision can be due to lack of information about the other player's actions, to linkages with other decision-making processes which condition the short-run returns from co-operation and, most frequently, to the absence of outside enforcement of consistent behaviour by interacting agents. Although the solution to the prisoner's dilemma involves some central enforcement of individual actions, it is indeterminate as to which institutional solution will be chosen. A prisoner's dilemma is more likely to arise where interaction is not repeated or the final interaction can be foreseen, when information about other individual actions is lacking, or where there are large numbers of interacting individuals. Moreover, solutions to prisoner's dilemmas are unstable because it is in the self-interest of individual agents to defect; therefore the solutions usually require a central authority to enforce them.

agent who can push the changes through and (in the case of prisoner's dilemmas) enforce the new terms of the game. However, since the imposition of new rules causes losses for claimants to income streams arising from the previous set of rules, market failures are seldom resolved without compensating the losers. The size or costs of compensation – and hence the probability of changing the rules – will differ substantially between political regimes. To the extent that institutional incentives define a society's opportunities for economic growth, the capacity to overcome distributional conflicts and solve recurring coordination failures will therefore be the principal cause of variation in economic performance.[20] The question why did economic performance differ is in fact a question about how pre-modern markets emerged.

The argument I have just outlined gives rise to two broad predictions. First, it implies that differences in state sovereignty will be reflected in formal and informal barriers to domestic trade – tolls and tariffs, fragmented measurements, legal monopolies, fiscal privileges and suchlike – which will in turn cause different rates of growth and levels of welfare. Chapter 3 applies this hypothesis to the late-medieval crisis, and shows how intensified political centralisation during the fourteenth and fifteenth centuries lowered the costs of organising new institutions and of modifying property rights and caused a form of institutional 'creative destruction' which raised the European economy to a higher growth path.

Second, the argument predicts that different institutional constellations mattered to the extent that they solved coordination failures differently and gave rise to different economic equilibria.[21] This claim is examined in Chapters 4 to 7. In Chapter 4, I analyse the rise of regional fairs across Europe as an example of state-driven institutional change that combined coordination failures arising from the necessary inter-linkages between fairs and prisoner's dilemmas caused by rent-seeking obstructions by towns and cities. In Chapters 5 to 7 I look at how local institutional arrangements shaped developments at a regional level, taking individual Italian regions as test cases. In Chapter 5, I examine regional patterns of urban growth, explain why pre-modern Italy was the only major European country with several competing metropolises rather than a single dominant one, and

---

20 Coordination failures arising from individual actions offer a more plausible micro-level explanation for the persistence of economically inefficient institutions than arguments based on collective (class) action, although it goes without saying that coordination failures are themselves caused by the prevailing macro-institutional structures to which a structural, class-based analysis applies. Acemoglu and Zilibotti 1997 and Grantham 1999 also emphasise the importance of coordination failures for pre-modern growth, but do not discuss how they were overcome.

21 In economic jargon, an equilibrium occurs when no individual agent stands to gain by moving if the other agents stick to their actions. It is the result of a feedback process that reinforces the particular actions of agents and is therefore self-enforcing.

discuss the economic consequences. In Chapter 6, I analyse the rise of protoindustrial districts in Italy after the Black Death, investigate why protoindustry was disproportionately concentrated in the Lombard plain, and discuss how successful protoindustries benefited from state action and technological externalities. In Chapter 7, I discuss the policies of marketing and market integration and examine how the prisoner's dilemmas arising from competing systems of urban grain supply were overcome after the Black Death, but also show how coordination problems raised the costs of moving from one institutional equilibrium to another.

The choice of Italy as a testing ground for the preceding hypotheses on the consequences of the Black Death and of state formation is in some ways problematic. Estimates of living standards suggest that in large parts of the country they reached a peak soon after the Black Death, which was followed after 1500 by a long phase of economic stagnation; in this Italy shared many similarities with the other major medieval growth pole, the southern Low Countries. Over the same period, comparatively poor countries like England were experiencing rapid growth that allowed them to catch up with the more advanced regions of late medieval Europe. A comparison between per caput GNP in England and Tuscany is instructive. English GNP per head *circa* 1300 was £0.78, rising to £1.52 *circa* 1470 and to £1.63 *circa* 1561; by contrast, Tuscan GNP per caput was £2.86 *circa* 1460–70 (88 per cent above England's) but only about £2.11 *circa* 1560, indicating a loss of 26 per cent in absolute terms and of nearly 60 per cent relative to England.[22] Although developments in Tuscany are not typical of post-Black Death trends across the whole Italian peninsula – some of the less developed Italian regions also experienced a phase of economic catch-up with more advanced regions like Tuscany – aggregate and regional data on urbanisation indicate that the period of regional convergence between 1350 and 1500 was followed by stagnation in most of the peninsula.[23]

Although a comparatively undynamic economy like pre-modern Italy's might seem an odd choice to study the economic consequences of state structures, the country's remarkable institutional variety at the regional

---

22 Estimates (deflated) for England from Mayhew 1995: 244; for Tuscany *circa* 1460-70 from Roscoe 1862: vol.2, Appendix XI, note 78, pp.78–80, summarised by Rutenburg 1988 (original figures in florins). For Tuscany *circa* 1560 I have converted the figures quoted in Flemish guilders by Vandenbroeke 1998: 363–4 to English sterling. English national aggregates of course also conceal considerable regional disparities; however, regional economies in late medieval England do not display similar signs of convergence as in Italy (Schofield 1974). The Tuscan economy probably peaked before 1460: the declared per caput value of real estate capitalised at 7 per cent in 1480 was 13.6 per cent lower than in 1427 (data from Molho 1994a: 363; my calculations).

23 See the new estimates by Craig and Fisher 2000: Table 6.2, which shows Italian growth rates between 1500 and 1750 consistently at the bottom of the European league.

scale offers an ideal testing ground for the kind of comparative approach pursued here. One conclusion from Chapter 2 is that institutional models based on national aggregates are misleading both because 'national' constitutions did not matter much for property rights 'on the ground', and because in most European countries before the late eighteenth century the political and administrative structures that did matter were mainly those operating at the regional level. This creates a potential problem for attempts to relate broad constitutional patterns to economic performance; in Italy, however, the fact that the political boundaries of the larger territorial states coincided closely with their regional economies makes it easier to identify political effects.[24]

With the exception of Chapter 2, which sets out the general case against a Whig approach to historical political economy, the book focuses on the era of 'crisis' between 1300 and 1550, which I argue marked a fundamental break-point in the development of an integrated European economy before the Industrial Revolution. The claim is not new – it is made by Wallerstein, Brenner and North among others, although not by the protoindustrial theorists – but has drawn more on assertion than on satisfactory proof and argumentation; this book brings more robust evidence to bear on the matter. By focusing on the late medieval crisis, this book also aims to draw together the two debates on the transition from feudalism to capitalism and on the developmental role of pre-modern states which have so far followed entirely separate paths.

---

24 For recent overviews of the literature on pre-modern economic regions, see Prak 1995; Pollard 1997; Scott 1997.

2 Freedom, freedoms and growth

Freedom and growth

It has recently become again fashionable to argue that freedom from despotic government was the main institutional prerequisite for pre-modern economic growth. The unique combination of natural liberties, parliamentary constitution, and common law entrenched by the English Glorious Revolution of 1688 and the freedoms enjoyed by republican city-states and by the Dutch United Provinces were the root causes of their economic success. Experience in countries with parliamentary and republican regimes is contrasted with that of autocratic Continental regimes like Spain and France, in which excessive taxation, redistributive economic policies, and the ruler's arbitrary whim produced political bondage and economic stagnation. In a fresh twist to the old Whig interpretation of English history, the Anglo-American legal and constitutional settlement is erected by implication into a model of the economically optimal political arrangement.[1]

These arguments share several questionable assumptions about how institutional constraints shape economic performance. One such assumption is that different political regimes or constitutions sanction different forms of individual freedom and behaviour, such as 'individualism' or 'trust', which are associated with different incentive patterns and rates of economic growth.[2] Despite the claim's apparent plausibility, however, attempts to test causal links between political regimes and

---

1 Seminal statements along these lines can be found in North and Thomas 1973; Jones 1981; Gellner 1988. See also Hall 1985: ch.5; Olson 1982; Cameron 1989; Levi 1988; Mann 1989; Landes 1997. For a discussion of constitutional history in similar terms, see van Caenegem 1995.

2 See Macfarlane 1987; Gambetta 1988; North 1995. Development is narrowly defined here as an increase in per caput income. On a broader view that incorporates general measures of well-being such as basic civic and political freedoms, a democracy (however qualified) would by definition be more conducive to development than a non-democratic regime. However, since such modern democratic freedoms are not apparent in pre-industrial settings the issue can safely be ignored.

economic performance both in past and in contemporary societies have proved inconclusive, largely for lack of a theory of individual response to social and institutional norms or 'ideology' and of a theory of how individual responses are aggregated into the collective beliefs and expectations that we commonly term 'culture'.[3]

A second problematic claim concerns the nature of pre-modern states. The view that economic growth requires secure property rights because uncertainty of title undermines trade and investment is not generally disputed. Modern Whigs accept that states are the major suppliers and enforcers of new institutions and property rights and that they therefore help reduce the costs of trade and transacting. More contentiously, however, they also claim that the main variable determining the development of markets is the incumbent rulers' desire to maximise revenues. They assume in other words that any security failures that might arise are primarily a consequence of *state* actions, and that the *rulers'* ability to unilaterally change property rights poses the most serious institutional threat to growth. The proposed solution to this developmental Catch 22 is that sovereigns commit themselves in advance to respect property rights and the 'rules of the game', the problem being that incumbents will only commit themselves if political institutions – be they parliamentary or republican – force them to do so. Simply put, the reason why pre-modern economic growth was so patchy and episodic outside post-1688 England and a handful of other European countries is the absence of republican and parliamentary institutions which constrained autocratic rule.[4]

The argument that the central issue of pre-modern polities was how to bind the predatory actions of the state raises two problems, one concerning the nature of state sovereignty before the nineteenth century, more specifically the nature of European 'absolutism', the other concerning the nature of pre-modern parliaments and republics. The argument presumes, in its strongest form, that pre-modern rulers had the power to modify property rights at will, and in its weakest form that pre-modern rulers exercised full and undivided sovereignty and full and final authority over their subjects. Since these were indeed the central claims both of absolutism and its enemies, it is not an unreasonable assumption; but it is an assumption refuted by decades of research on pre-modern political practices that has shown how 'absolutism' was a largely propagandistic device devoid of much practical substance.

---

3 The literature on the constitutional foundations of contemporary growth is summarised and tested by Hadenius 1992; Siermann 1998.
4 The theory of the predatory state, which follows from the rational choice assumptions of New Institutional Economics in both its macro and micro formulations, was first set out in Brennan and Buchanan's (1980) analysis of the 'fiscal constitution'; see also North 1981: ch.3; Levi 1988: ch.5; Barzel 1989; Eggertsson 1990. For historical applications of the theory, see North and Thomas 1973: chs.8, 10; North and Weingast 1989; Olson 1991; North 1995; Rosenthal 1998.

Outside England – 'ruled by an ancient and forceful monarchy' and endowed with an unusually centralised state – neither absolutist nor republican states achieved full jurisdictional sovereignty before the late eighteenth or in some cases the nineteenth century.[5] Previously both the legal and political foundations and the practice of absolutist rule were contested at every turn by feudal lords, town councils, corporate entities and religious institutions, many of whose privileges, prerogatives and traditional customs – known as their *liberties* and *freedoms* – had survived the growth of national monarchies from the later Middle Ages largely unscathed. Absolutism as a form of unrestricted rule appears increasingly as a mainly theoretical response devised by contemporary political thinkers to counteract the practical problems of fragmented sovereignty and the challenges that institutional fragmentation posed to a ruler's legitimacy.

The organic and piecemeal way with which European territorial states had emerged from the high Middle Ages meant that most early modern sovereigns were hemmed in by the rules, customs and rights of a motley of competing jurisdictional rights, which gave local societies considerable margins of negotiation and sometimes *de facto* fiscal and judicial independence. Local and regional representative bodies (*parlements*, estates, urban councils and suchlike) could challenge the legitimacy of princely jurisdiction, while administrative complexity and the concerted action of urban oligarchies and feudal lords raised frequently insurmountable barriers to the standardisation of law across national territories.[6] The strength of a monarch's theoretical claims to absolute rule was frequently inversely proportional to his *de facto* powers.[7] This contradiction between the political theory of absolutism and its practice produced the widespread contemporary distinction between absolutism (defined as a constitutional arrangement in which legally chartered freedoms were respected and upheld) and despotism (defined as a system in which they were not).[8]

If we define sovereignty as a bundle of 'public' or collective property rights over a given territory, the most salient feature of pre-modern political arrangements was the fact that most absolutist states did *not* have clearly defined and enforceable public property rights of taxation. On the three standard measures of a state's fiscal power – the right of assessment, the degree of compliance, and the efficiency of exaction – most pre-modern states failed to meet modern definitions of state authority. For the

---

5 The quotation is from van Caenegem 1995: 78.
6 For the moment I do not distinguish between efficiency in the sense of efficient decision-making and in the sense of establishing incentive structures which promote an efficient allocation of resources. The distinction is pursued further at a later stage.
7 Recent analyses of eighteenth-century France imply a similar conclusion, although they do not examine the institutional deadlock of French absolutism in the terms presented here. See Root 1989; Rosenthal 1992.
8 Kelley 1981: 314–22; Black 1984: ch.11.

same reason, pre-modern states could not easily enforce uncontested private property rights among their subjects, although paradoxically, as we shall see, the English monarchy came closer to achieving this goal than any of its European peers.[9] Jurisdictional fragmentation, which gave rise to multiple coordination failures, rather than autocratic rule was arguably the main source of the institutional inefficiency of 'absolutism' before the nineteenth century.

The view that pre-modern parliament is the most important measure of the civil rights of property and the person rests on the same erroneous assumption that pre-modern states exercised full sovereignty and that civil rights applied to all. Pre-modern societies did not define liberty in nine-teenth-century liberal terms as equality before the law and as freedom of conscience and of action from state encroachment, but in terms of status and inequality of "privileges, immunities, or rights enjoyed by prescription or grant".[10] Pre-modern economic freedom was consequently not an abstract condition of 'equality in law and market', but a claim to legal priv-ilege and to the income streams which privilege conferred. For this reason, pre-modern societies spoke of *freedoms* in the plural and the concrete, rather than of *freedom* in the singular and the abstract. The same legal privileges that underlay pre-modern distinctions of status – between aristocrat and bour-geois, townsman and peasant, guildsman and wandering journeyman – sustained the pre-modern feudal, urban, communal and corporate rights to hold separate law courts, claim fiscal privilege, maintain industrial monop-olies and exclude competing marketplaces that we will discuss in the following chapters. Pre-modern 'freedoms' were not a constitutional birthright and an indivisible public good as in modern liberal theory. They were socially specific, temporally contingent and frequently legally trans-ferable sources of privilege and exclusion. Whereas the liberal concept of freedom underpins the ideology of shared citizenship, pre-modern freedoms challenged the state's claim to undivided and final sovereignty.[11]

Pre-modern Europeans conceived freedoms differently from their modern counterparts, because their political and economic rights were differently defined. Pre-modern sovereignty was fragmented and contested, just as that of modern states is in principle undivided. The fact that pre-modern freedoms were defined in terms of personal and local

---

9 There was no such thing as "fiscal absolutism" in Castile' (Thompson 1994b: 182), a point that can easily be extended to early modern France (Collins 1988; Bonney 1981). For convenient summaries of recent literature on absolutism see Miller 1990, Greengrass 1991, and Henshall 1992; also Richet 1973; Sahlins 1989; Elliott 1992; Nader 1990; Thompson 1994a; Bossenga 1997. English 'fiscal absolutism' is discussed later.

10 See *Oxford English Dictionary*, 1st edn., s.v. Liberty § 7; the earliest dated usage of the term 'liberty' in this sense is by Wyclif in 1380.

11 The concept of freedom as privilege is also central to modern understandings of freedom; see Epstein 1995b.

privilege meant, paradoxically, that central parliaments with the authority to tax and wishing to establish a single, unified fiscal and legal jurisdiction could actually threaten society's legal, political and economic freedoms. It follows that the major source of economic inefficiency in societies with fragmented sovereignty was the limited extension of the state's, and on occasion of parliament's, powers over competing jurisdictional rights.[12]

This chapter examines the empirical basis for Whig arguments about the nature of pre-modern states and the causes of European economic growth. The next section discusses the effects of constitutional structure on property rights, that is, on the institutional preconditions for growth, while the section on 'Republics and growth' asks whether the allegedly more 'democratic' constitutions of republican states, ruled by urban oligarchies rather than a single monarch, improved incentives for investment and innovation. In practice, neither the presence nor the absence of a strong parliament or of a strong representative base in the cities seem to have made much difference in economic terms. What mattered instead was the extent of state sovereignty and the degree to which political and economic power were kept separate.

Monarchies and growth

North and Weingast have recently provided the clearest and best documented argument that the Glorious Revolution of 1688 gave the eighteenth-century English economy a strategic advantage that pushed the country towards industrialisation. Their proposed measure of the economic gains from revolution is based on the following narrative which I briefly summarise.[13] In the early seventeenth century the Stuart kings could no longer fund their increasing requirements with traditional sources of revenue, including the sale of royal lands, but attempts to raise taxes set them against Parliament. James I and Charles I responded in typically 'absolutist' fashion, imposing new taxes without the Commons' consent and resorting increasingly to forced loans (which they repaid, if at all, with considerable delay), to monopoly rights and patents of nobility, to rights of purveyance (whereby goods were requisitioned below market prices) and to other arbitrary exactions. The Stuart monarchy could do so because it combined executive, legislative and judicial powers and was militarily stronger than all individual opponents. Parliament's inability to check royal power allowed the Crown to renege on prior political agreements and to

---

12 In early modern Castile, Habsburg attempts to make the fiscal system less inequitable and cumbersome were resisted by the cities and by their representatives in the Cortes (parliament), which feared the loss of their privileges and immunities; when the Cortes decided to support the crown's attempts at reform, the cities refused to cooperate and blocked the proposals. Thus, Spanish 'absolutist' taxation was the principal solvent of privilege, a fact that corporate bodies were determined to resist (Thompson 1994b).
13 North and Weingast 1989; also Weingast 1997.

expropriate lenders and other subjects. The latter rose up to preserve their personal liberty, rights, and wealth in the first Civil War of 1644–6; but only the Declaration of Rights of 1689 created truly secure property rights in the country, as Parliament established sovereignty over taxation, gained the right to audit government accounts, curtailed royal prerogative powers, and established a truly independent legal process.

North and Weingast argue that constitutional certainty laid the foundations of economic freedom; security of property stimulated investment and economic growth and sustained England's rise to Great Power status in the eighteenth century. They find evidence of these changes in the development of English financial markets and state debt after 1688. The Crown's financial credibility was greatly improved by the fact that it could no longer dictate the terms of the loans and could not arbitrarily default, and by Parliament's control over taxation; consequently, interest rates fell sharply and the size of the national debt incurred to finance England's foreign wars soared. By 1720 public debt stood at over fifty times the level of 1688, while nominal interest rates more than halved from 10 to 4 per cent over the same period. The English state avoided the trap of inflationary finance and its financial activities stimulated the rise of private capital markets. Eighteenth-century England's military might is proof of the new regime's institutional and economic success.[14]

North and Weingast's claim on these grounds that constitutional differences in the role of parliament gave rise to fundamentally different incentive structures and shaped long-run economic growth rests on further, unspoken assumptions. First, they presume that interest rates on government debt accurately measure the security of property rights in the private sector also; second, they assume that absolutist states which did not develop parliamentary institutions along English lines suffered from their rulers' political and financial predation.

The comparative security of property rights helps define the relative risk of investments. If property rights are subject to despotic whim, as was allegedly the case in England before 1688 and under absolutist regimes elsewhere, investors will demand higher rates of return to compensate for the greater risk of capital loss. Since significant structural improvements in the degree of risk to private property should give rise to proportional declines in the expected rate of return on capital, that is, in the imputed rate of interest, we would expect greater institutional security after the English Glorious Revolution to have caused the rate of return to *private* capital to fall sharply.

In fact, no such shift in trend took place, and private rates of return continued to follow a trend begun during the fourteenth century.[15] Rates

---

14   The inference is nonetheless unwarranted, since there is no reason to assume that a state's military power is a function of its economic prowess (McNeill 1954; Gilpin 1981).
15   See p. 62 (Figure 3.1).

of return to the main capital input, land, and political or constitutional events in England between 1350 and 1837 show no discernible connection. "Secure private property rights existed in England at least as early as 1600, and probably much earlier. As far as most private investors were concerned, nothing special happened in 1688, or, for that matter, in any period between 1600 and 1688".[16]

If, however, North and Weingast are right to argue that the post-1688 English economy enjoyed greater institutional stability compared to its absolutist neighbours, the fact should be reflected in the interest rates paid by different states. Fortunately it is possible to verify the claims quite easily because Continental states also included a vociferous and influential republican minority. In principle, republics should have been politically and financially more reliable than monarchies, because republican rule and powers of taxation were vested in collective institutions and were subject to greater popular scrutiny. Republics should therefore have had to pay significantly lower interest rates than non-parliamentary monarchies, enjoying a premium similar to that of the British monarchy after the Glorious Revolution, when nominal rates of interest fell from 10 to 4 per cent in the space of a few years. In other words, North and Weingast's description of institutional developments in seventeenth-century England should apply equally to the transition from an autocratic regime to a more accountable republican constitution.[17] Did the most salient example of such a transition, the transformation of the Dutch Netherlands from Habsburg principality to urban-based federal republic in the 1570s, have equally momentous financial consequences? What do the interest rates paid by absolutist regimes reveal about their perceived financial reliability and how do they compare with pre- and post-1688 England?

Table 2.1 (pages 20–23) reports nominal interest rates paid by European governments between 1350 and 1750 distinguished by constitutional regime; the data are summarised graphically in Figure 2.1. With the significant exception of England before 1688, which lacked a long-term funded debt, all the figures refer to interest on long-term government debt, which measures the borrower's financial and institutional credibility more accurately than short-term money market rates.[18]

---

16   Clark 1996: 565.
17   John Hicks, who to my knowledge first associated the fall in interest rates paid by the British government after 1695 with the changes wrought by the 'Constitution' of 1689, noted that the latter gave the monarchy 'the long-term credit of a Republic' (Hicks 1969: 94). He believed however that the reason for the difference in interest rates between political regimes lay in their relative continuity: monarchies were more unstable than republics.
18   Long-term interest rates reflect both the state's fiscal fungibility (whether the discounted present value of expected income equals the present value of expected outlays) and the lenders' perception of the security of claims to future income streams. Note that all figures in Table 2.1 are nominal or coupon rates of interest paid to par value, rather than short-term market rates which were often substantially higher. Although nominal rates

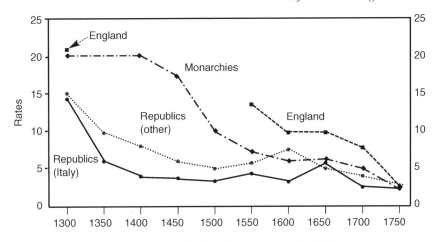

Figure 2.1 Interest rates and constitutional structure, 1300–1750

Two major patterns can be discerned regarding the contrast between monarchies and republics and between England and Continental states. First, as predicted, most urban republics paid lower coupon interest rates than monarchies; European monarchies were unable to match the interest rates of 2.25–3.25 per cent paid by Florence and of 4–5 per cent offered by Venice in the late fifteenth century before the late seventeenth or eighteenth century. Second, however, there was considerable and equally significant variation, with the most financially and administratively adept states paying the lowest interest rates of all. Florentine banking skills, the most advanced of their time, explain why Florentine rates in the late fifteenth century were over a third lower than those of Venice, despite the fact that Venice was by then politically more stable and economically more successful. Yet interest rates in urban republics outside Italy – including Geneva, many of the smaller city-states in Switzerland, southern Germany and Alsace – were *not* significantly lower than the average paid by monarchs. Nor did the Dutch Netherlands fare any better, despite the sophisticated financial system established along

do not precisely reflect interest rate levels, they had to be set at a level that lenders deemed reasonable and they demonstrate a clear long-term trend. The suggestion that states could arbitrarily set interest rates is implausible, for reasons discussed below; although both pre-modern monarchies and republics frequently raised 'forced' loans among their wealthy elites, the lack of elite opposition to such loans even though they had ample scope to resist implies that real interest rates were not considered extortionate. Since I am concerned with relative rather than absolute levels, I do not consider rates of inflation, which can plausibly be disregarded for most of the period under consideration with the possible exception of the second half of the sixteenth century; in any case, the rate of inflation defines the deviation from a country's relative purchasing power parity, which we can expect to equalise in the long run.

Table 2.1 Nominal interest rates on public debt in Europe, *c.*1270–1750*

Cities and urban republics

	Date	Rate	Source
Siena	1290–1320	15–30 (ST)	4: App. 13
	1325–40	10–20 (ST)	"
	1342–54	5–10 (ST)	"
Florence	1347–82	5	28
	1392	3.33	"
	1395	5	"
	1410	3.75	"
	1444–50	3.375	"
	1471–75	3.25	"
	1480	3	"
	1493	2.25	"
Genoa	1303–40	6–12	19: 98
	1347–95	8–10	28
	1410	7	"
	1450	4	"
	1522–49	4.37	7a
	1550–99	4.33	"
	1600–20	2.23	"
	1725–85	3–3.4	12: 22
Vicenza	1274	36	7: 239–53
	1281	25	"
	1287–1304	15–25	"
	1305	10	"
Venice	1285–1326	8–12	22: 37, 54
	1340–1530	4–5	22: 86, 93; 26
	1521	5	26: 738
	1531–6	6	27: 296
	1537–40	7.5–8	"
	1541–5	6	"
	1545–55	4–5	"
	1560–93	3	27: 296; 25: 178
	c.1600	4	20: 334
	1616–25	5	27: 296
	1645–65	5–7	"
	1672–80	2–3	"
	1725–65	1.8–1.9	12: 22
	1785	1.4	12: 22
Cologne	1351–70	10 (ST)	13: 547
	1370–92	5–5.5	"
	1450–74	3–4	"
Dortmund	late 14th c.	11–12.33 (ST)	13: 532
Mainz	1400–30	3–4	13: 552
	1430s	5	"
	1444	10 (ST)	"

Table 2.1 continued

	Date	*Rate*	*Source*
Nuremberg	1377–1427	10 (ST)	13: 548
	1427	4–5	"
	1540–50	5	17: 117
	1561	6	"
	1565	5	"
Saxony	1496–7	5	13: 523
Switzerland	18th c.	3–4	21: 536
Basle	1394–1402	6.67	13: 550
	1402–	5–5.5	"
	1424–28	10 (ST)	"
Geneva	1538	5	2: 119
	1557	6.67–7	"
	1572	8.33	"
	1613	8	"
	1648	6.67	"
	1668	5–6.67	"
	1681	5	"
Zürich	mid–14th c.	10	13: 551
	1386–1415	9–16.67 (ST)	"
	1404	5	"
	1415–	10–11 (ST)	"
Bruges	1299	14–16 (ST)	13: 538
Verviers (Liège)	1678–9	6+	15: 59
	1746–8	3	"
Netherlands	late 13th c.	12.5 (ST)	13: 532
	"	10	"
	early 15th c.	8–10 (ST)	"
	"	6.25–6.67	"
United Provinces	1572	8.33	17: 118
	1599	8.3	34: 123–4
	1606	7.15	"
	1608	6.25	"
	1640	5	"
	1655	4	"
	1660–72	3.75–4	17: 118
	1672–1700	3–3.75	"
	1709–13	4–4.5	11: 474
	1724–5	3–4	"
	1740	3.5–4	"
	1750–2	2.5–4.5	"
Monarchies			
Denmark	18th c.	4–5	21: 536
France	1415–17	25	13: 483
	1438–51	15–20	13: 488

Table 2.1 continued

	Date	Rate	Source
France	1522–43	8.33	17: 117
	1594–1601	8.33	3: 19
	1600–10	3.5–4.3	8: 73
	1630s	4–5	8: 86
	1656–61	14.5	3: 318
	1661–9	5.5–7	8: 47
	1679	5–5.875	17: 131
	1698–9	5	14: 227
	1717–18	4	35: 379
	1719	3	”
	1735	5	17: 170
	1749	5	”
Habsburg Austria	1555–79	5–10	16: 74
	1580–94	5–8	”
	late 17th c.	5–6	21: 532
	1700–40	5–6	21: 536
	1760–80	3–4	”
Habsburg Castile	1504	10	30: 14
	1515	6.7	23: 49
	1526	9	30: 14
	1540	7.5	”
	1545–50	6.25	”
	1557–75	5.7–7.6	23: 49
	1584–98	5.8	23: 49; 30: 14
	1623	5	23: 49
	1667	7	”
Habsburg Low Countries	c.1500	8–12	17: 118
	1515–43	6.25	33: 62
	1552–65	9.8	33: 94
Habsburg Milan	1598	7	9: 344
	1602–14	5.25	9: 73
	1637	5	10: 330
	1655–58	7	9: 73–6
	1659–61	2–4.5	9: 81–6
	1706–30	4	9: 108
	1725	3.3	12: 22
	1745–85	2.6–2.9	”
Habsburg Naples	1520–29	8.3–10	5: 143–5
	1530–38	9.7–11.7	”
	1540–46	8.7–10.5	”
	1550–59	8–9.4	”
	1560–75	8.8–9.3	”
	1580–98	6.8–8	”
	1663–1700	7	27: 313
	1785	3.2	12: 22
Holy Roman Empire	1312–13	15–26.67(ST)	13: 512

Table 2.1 continued

	Date	Rate	Source
Holland (county)	1320	20 (ST)	13: 499
Piedmont	1680s	5	31: 662
	1725	0.3	12: 22
	1745	1.2	"
	1765–85	1.8–1.9	"
Papal States: Bologna	1555–95	7.01	6: 131–2
	1575	7.01	"
	1595	7.03	"
	1625	7.04	"
	1655	6.18	"
Papal States: Rome	1560s	7	27: 296–7
	late 16th c.	6–8	29: 467
	early 17th c.	6	26: 740
	1656	4	27: 296–7
	1686	3	29: 466
	1725–85	1.7–1.9	12: 22
Tuscany (Duchy)	early 18th c.	4–6	21: 536
	post 1726	3.5–4	"
	1725–85	0.4–0.5	12: 22
England	1293–5	15.5 (ST)	18: 118–24
	1328–31	26 (ST)	13: 456
	1540s	18 (ST)	24: 302
	1546–58	13–14 (ST)	20: 113
	1603–24	10 (ST)	1: 155
	1624–40	8 (ST)	"
	1693	14 (ST)	17: 126
	1694	8	35: 385
	1710	8.3	17: 156
	1717	5	35: 388
	1727	3.57	17: 161
	1736	2.86	"
	1750	3	"

* Rates are the par rate of emission of long term debt, which includes consolidated debt and perpetual rents. Higher short term rates (ST) applied to floating debt and life annuities, and are reflected in the market value of long term debt which could be below par.

Sources: (1) Ashton 1960; (2) Bergier 1962; (3) Bonney 1981; (4) Bowsky 1970; (5) Calabria 1991; (6) Carboni 1995; (7) Carlotto 1993; (7a) Cipolla 1975: 269–70; (8) Collins 1988; (9) Cova 1991; (10) Dent 1973; (11) Dickson 1967; (12) Felloni 1977; (13) Fryde and Fryde 1963; (14) Goubert 1970; (15) Gutmann 1980; (16) Hildebrandt 1992; (17) Homer and Sylla 1991; (18) Kaeuper 1973; (19) Kedar 1976; (20) Kellenbenz 1986; (21) Körner 1995; (22) Luzzatto 1963; (23) Mauro and Parker 1977; (24) Outhwaite 1966; (25) Pezzolo 1990; (26) Pezzolo 1994; (27) Pezzolo 1995; (28) Pezzolo 2001; (29) Piola Caselli 1991; (30) Ruiz Martin 1975; (31) Stumpo 1988; (32) Thompson 1994; (33) Tracy 1985; (34) Veenendaal 1994; (35) van der Wee 1977.

Italian and German lines during the first half of the sixteenth century. Before the Netherlands seceded from Spain in 1579 their rates were twice as high as those of Italian city-states and on a par with Castilian *juros*, but after independence the Dutch Republic's relative position actually got *worse*: before final peace was struck in 1648 the Republic had to pay higher nominal interest rates than the Spanish Habsburgs because of the lenders' concerns that the Dutch bid for independence would be unsuccessful. On the other hand, sixteenth-century Genoa, which was formally independent but was in practice under Spanish tutelage and acted as the empire's main financial clearing house, had some of the lowest rates in Europe.

It is evident therefore that formal constitutional arrangements do not explain the interest rates paid by urban republics, and that the latter did not enjoy an automatic financial premium over monarchies. If it is true that the interest rates a state must pay reflect its political and financial credibility, the latter in pre-modern Europe was not purely a function of constitutional structure. An alternative explanation of the interest rate differentials to which I have already referred is that they convey technical rather than political disparities in the fiscal and financial institutions at the borrower's disposal, including the liquidity of local bond markets. Holding all else constant, states with more efficient fiscal, administrative and banking systems would be able to raise credit more cheaply because they honoured their debts more easily, and lenders would also be more forthcoming if the loans were easily transferable. Which of the two explanations applies?

One way to adjudicate between constitutional and financial explanations is to follow interest rate differentials over time. If structural differences in risk levels caused by constitutional factors mattered, the margin between different political regimes should have persisted over time; but if differentials were caused by mainly technical factors, the disparity should have narrowed as more advanced fiscal and financial apparatuses were more widely adopted.

Fig. 2.1 indicates that the origin of the disparities was largely technical. Between 1350 and 1750 long-term state interest rates converged. By 1750 interest rate differentials between monarchies and republics had by and large disappeared. In parallel with European financial convergence, a second secular trend saw the average nominal interest rates paid by monarchies fall over the same period by a factor of 6, with most gains being made between 1500 and 1700 (from *c.* 8–12 per cent to *c.* 4 per cent).

The single most notable exception to both patterns was England before the Glorious Revolution. Between 1500 and 1700, government interest rates in England – which were invariably short-term because the English lacked a consolidated public debt before 1694 – were consistently higher than under Continental monarchies. The English crown was still having to offer short-term rates of 10 per cent in the early 1690s, when the Dutch Republic could offer rates of 3–3.75 per cent, Venice paid 4–5 per cent, France offered 5 per cent, and Habsburg Austria 5–6 per cent. As Table 2.1 and Figure 2.1 make clear, the sharp decline in English interest rates after 1700, which North and Weingast ascribe to the benefits of a parliamentary regime, was in fact the effect of a belated catch-up with the Continental European, absolutist and republican norm, principally through the introduction of a modern financial system and of its correlate, the consolidated public debt. Having lagged in terms of financial sophistication behind the Continent since at least 1500, post-1688 England was able to adopt the most advanced techniques developed by their Dutch allies. Nonetheless, although by 1750 England had achieved some of the lowest interest rates in Europe (though not as low as the minuscule Duchy of Tuscany!), its financial edge over its main military competitors was far smaller than that which they had enjoyed over England during the preceding two centuries. The Glorious Revolution may have consolidated an English financial revolution, but its main effect on the country's cost of capital was to raise England to the Continental benchmark.[19]

A full explanation of the English anomaly requires both a detailed knowledge of the English fiscal system and a comparison with tax systems among the major European powers, two matters that are only now beginning to be addressed.[20] However, recent work on English taxation suggests some lines of interpretation.[21] While the high interest rates paid by the Stuarts may reflect a more high-handed approach to public finance than that of their Continental peers, the real puzzle is why *all* English monarchs between 1500 and 1690 had to pay a risk premium over their Continental counterparts.[22] The proximate answer is that England's fiscal system was underdeveloped; the more fundamental reason was that the country's long political and military isolation shielded the English monarchy from the main stimulus for fiscal and financial change, namely war.

By 1500 most national fiscal systems in Europe were based on a core income raised from the sovereign's demesne supplemented by one-off

19 The Glorious Revolution and the period of warfare that followed accelerated a process of reform that had its origins in the Civil War; see Braddick 1996 and Roseveare 1991.

20 The fundamental works in this area are collected in Bonney 1995a and 1999, supplemented for early modern Italy by Pezzolo 1995.

21 The following discussion of seventeenth-century developments relies on Ashton 1960; Roseveare 1991; Braddick 1994 and 1996; O'Brien 1988; O'Brien and Hunt 1999. For the Tudor and early Stuart period, see Schofield 1988; Hoyle 1998; Harriss 1963; Hurstfield 1955; Aylmer 1957a and 1957b.

22 By the 1630s the Stuarts' reputation had so deteriorated that they could no longer raise funds on international financial markets (North and Weingast 1989: 820 note 36).

'national' taxes approved by consultative bodies in case of war. Additional revenue came from the feudal prerogative, which included forced loans, concessions of monopolies, distraint, and forced requisitions to supply armies. Several states had begun to expand their tax base during the fourteenth and fifteenth centuries through more regular 'national' taxation, and this trend accelerated under the financial and administrative pressures of the sixteenth-century 'military revolution'.[23] But warfare still remained the main justification for raising taxes, and administrative arrangements for tax collection were poor; fiscal revenues were consequently irregular and rarely coincided with short-term fluctuations in expenditure. Since regular income from state demesnes was too small to smooth income through savings, there was mounting pressure to establish new sources of funding that were both predictable and regular. The most effective solution was to borrow money against future income.

Although feudal rulers had resorted to borrowing for centuries, the fact that lenders could not impose penalties above those strictly pertaining to the loan itself meant that feudal borrowers could gain by refusing to repay their debt. The rulers' inability to commit credibly to repayment therefore put strict limits to the amounts they could raise. Under the new political and military conditions which arose in the later Middle Ages, they found it increasingly difficult to fund short-run and unforeseen increases in expenditure. In response, monarchies made the radical move of appealing directly to the capital markets for loans; some, like the Castilian crown between 1495 and 1503–4, took the further step of introducing a royal or public floating (later consolidated) debt funded by regional and 'national' taxes. An early thirteenth-century invention of the Italian and German city-states, the public debt derived its success from the fact that the main lenders were also members of the political elite who were charged with raising the taxes that funded the debt. As the low interest rates on offer reveal, the system worked because it aligned the creditors' and debtors' incentives. Lenders and borrowers had a joint stake in ensuring repayment and, more broadly, in ensuring the borrowing city's political and financial stability.[24]

From the early sixteenth century, emerging national monarchies began more systematically to sell long-term bonds whose coupons were paid out of current and future tax revenues. By selling a large proportion to the elites responsible for raising the money to pay for the bonds, national rulers aligned the lenders' and the taxpayers' interests; since failure to repay the loans would have alienated the very local and

---

23   Schulze 1995.
24   For northern Europe, see Fryde and Fryde 1963; for Italy see Cammarosano 1988; Molho 1993 and 1994b.

national elites on whom monarchs relied for administrative, military and financial support, rulers were also effectively committing themselves not to repudiate the debt. By binding themselves politically to repayment – by raising the political costs to themselves of default – rulers were able to tap previously inaccessible domestic capital.[25] This, of course, was only half of the story, for in order to fund a large public debt monarchs also required a broader tax base. States' attempts to expand their revenue by overcoming feudal and corporate restrictions on 'public' and ordinary taxation lie behind most political and constitutional developments of late medieval and early modern Europe.[26]

England's self-imposed post-Reformation isolation from Continental politics between the mid-sixteenth and the late seventeenth centuries was made easier by the protection afforded by high costs of invasion, but the Channel also insulated the Crown from the pressures that drove fiscal and financial innovation on the Continent. The English consequently avoided the sixteenth- and seventeenth-century military and financial revolutions.[27] By virtue of England's military isolation, moreover, the monarchy could respond to the dwindling of ordinary income from the royal demesne and from an increasingly obsolete system of direct taxation by relying increasingly on 'extraordinary' revenue drawn from an archaic combination of royal (feudal) prerogative and forced loans and benevolences (so-called 'free' payments, effectively *ad hoc* windfall taxes on the rich). The lack of a demonstrable long-term military threat meant that English rulers had little need and less opportunity to put their tax system on a more rational footing. On the other hand, a lack of external threats also meant that when requirements for larger and more regular sources of funding arose in the early seventeenth century, parliament found it quite easy to refuse aid.[28]

The remarkable similarity and long-term decline of interest rates among the major Continental states indicates that the rulers' autocratic and predatory impulses that rulers were kept in check by military competition. Monarchs were especially restrained by the proximity of substitutes who could claim title to their throne and by the lenders' ability to defect if they considered the rulers' demands excessive: by the fact, in other words, that Continental subjects could exercise both

---

25 Conklin 1998 shows that so-called fiscal default by the Spanish, often cited as evidence of Spanish autocracy, was an accepted way of renegotiating short-term debt whereby lenders suffered no significant losses. For similar arguments that the French and Spanish financial crises and 'bankruptcies' were essentially moratoria on interest payments, see van der Wee 1977: 391; Körner 1995: 520; Velde and Weir 1992.

26 Ormrod 1995; Schulze 1995.

27 Braddick 1993.

28 This was the attempt of 1610 to draw up a Great Contract that would replace the royal prerogative with regular taxes (Braddick 1994: 6; Braddick 1996: 18). For the constitutional implications of early seventeenth-century taxation, see Holmes 1992.

'voice' and 'exit' with regard to their incumbent rulers.[29] At the death of a ruler in the sixteenth century 'there would be at least a 50 per cent chance of a disputed succession, with the immediate likelihood of foreign intervention; or of succession by a woman or a child, with a strong chance of civic strife for the control of the regency' (the calculation takes no account of the chance that a ruler be deposed through civil war or invasion). Subjects therefore had frequent opportunity to make their voice heard.[30] 'Exit' could be achieved just as easily by wealthy merchants taking their capital elsewhere, as Tilly has argued, and by the less mobile landed elites who provided essential political, military and administrative support and who could simply refuse to cooperate.[31]

England's political and military isolation had important financial consequences. Between 1544 and 1574 the English raised the bulk of their loans in Antwerp, but interest rates were 12–14 per cent and loans were never offered for more than one year. Attempts to raise money on better terms failed, and the English, who interpreted this as meaning that the markets were rigged against them rather than being a reflection of their own failings, decided in 1574 to withdraw from Continental financial markets. Elizabeth's officers drew two conclusions from the debacle: first, that the monarchy should avoid debt if possible; second, that unavoidable borrowing should be restricted to the domestic market where the crown could dictate terms with its lenders. The latter assessment proved to be correct, and of £461,000 borrowed between 1575 and 1601, only £85,000 was raised on interest, the rest being rendered as compulsory loans 'for free'.[32] Yet the benefits of financial authoritarianism were more than matched by the 50 per cent interest rate premium the Crown paid compared with Continental monarchs, by sixteenth- and seventeenth-century London's strikingly underdeveloped financial markets, and not least by the London merchants' fiscal rebellion turned revolution of the 1640s.

Paradoxically in view of Parliament's earlier opposition, England took the first steps towards a modern, post-feudal fiscal and credit system based upon regular taxation during the first civil war, when Parliament was forced to set up regular taxes to finance its war effort. The tax system established after 1641–42 evolved further during the 1660s and was established in its main outlines by the 1670s, but the development of adequate financial institutions lagged behind. The Glorious

---

29 Hirschmann 1970.
30 Koenigsberger 1995a: 160–1.
31 Tilly 1990. For evidence of how financial defection actually worked, see Conklin 1998.
32 Outhwaite 1966; Outhwaite 1971. Note that England was able to exercise more pressure on its lenders compared to Continental states precisely because of the lack of external threats to the monarchy; see note 19 in this chapter.

Revolution's main economic contribution was thus not strictly speaking fiscal or constitutional, but was to allow the country's financial institutions to begin a rapid convergence to the European fiscal norm.[33] The decline in interest rates after 1700 was the result of the country's financial revolution rather than of a revolution in political freedom and rights.

Republics and growth

The belief that the emergence of political and civil liberties was inextricably linked to economic freedom and growth also underlies the view, popular since the Enlightenment, that western Europe's break with feudalism and with associated economic stagnation owes much to the existence of independent city-states.[34] The economic and social changes associated with the transition from a traditional, corporatist, religiously-minded society, to the increasingly secularised, individualistic and mobile world of capitalism originated and developed in European towns.[35] The growing material wealth, new codes of law, religious beliefs and aesthetics, nation states and, ultimately, world expansion associated with western Europe's 'great transformation' can all be traced back to the peculiar dynamism of its urban society and to the social tensions and innovations it brought about.

Although this view that the medieval Western city is the source of modern legal and political freedoms is often credited to Max Weber, Weber also noted that the origin of those freedoms lay in an act of

33 'Nearly all that was "revolutionary" about the years following 1688 was the product of war, not of some novel ideology. . . . All the distinctive themes of constitutional evolution . . . were, in large measure, developments enforced . . . by the most expensive conflicts that England had yet fought.' Many of the techniques extended to government finance after 1688 had been developed by the Treasury in the period 1665–79 with the 'ambition to revolutionize the basis of government borrowing' (Roseveare 1988: 708). England managed to turn its relative backwardness into a latecomer's advantage by adopting and perfecting financial best practice from the allied United Provinces; thus, for example, eighteenth-century England was the only country in Europe to offer perpetual loans. The more specific benefits of late seventeenth-century fiscal reform are harder to identify. We saw previously that the reforms had little effect on base rates. Any benefits accruing from sharply lower interest rates on the national debt were probably balanced by the sharp rise in the levels of taxation after 1700; the share of national income appropriated as taxes rose from approximately 3.5 per cent in the 1670s to 11–12 per cent during the American War. While these levels were unmatched elsewhere in Europe (Mathias and O'Brien 1976), the claim that state debt crowded out private investment is disputed (Roseveare 1988: 703–7). On the other hand, the fiscal and financial reforms were at the root of England's rise to Great Power status in the eighteenth century (Brewer 1990).

34 For a classic formulation, see Smith 1976: III, iii-iv.

35 Langton and Höppe 1983; Hicks 1969.

usurpation of legitimate, feudal power by groups of burgers who acted collectively to establish their free status: that is, subject to a special and autonomous law. The emergence of free citizen status defined non-citizens as *unfree*; urban freedom was the outcome of legally sanctioned *privilege* which distinguished the town from the feudal or subject countryside.[36] This fact casts light on an interesting institutional paradox that will be pursued in later chapters. Among the most valued urban privileges or freedoms was the concession of manufacturing monopolies within a certain radius of the town walls, whose stated aim was to fetter rural freedoms by legally restraining rival rural industry; to develop, therefore, pre-modern rural manufacture required the same kind of legal immunities upon which towns built their fortunes. What is more, rural industries found it harder to develop under republican regimes than under monarchies, because republics were keener to uphold urban privileges than territorial lords who were willing to over-ride vested interests and to foster inter-urban competition if this helped to extend the rulers' sovereignty. In other words, the capacity and willingness of towns to stop autonomous 'protoindustrial' manufacture in the countryside was directly proportional to the extent of their freedoms and political independence.[37]

The second strand in the argument linking economic and political freedoms postulates an inherent hostility in pre-modern Europe between urban 'capital' and state 'coercion'. In this view, commercial cities which benefited from open travel and communication struggled against monarchs who aimed to establish full sovereignty within clear political boundaries. But the rulers' financial requirements also led them to support the towns against the feudal aristocracy in exchange for fiscal aid, and fiscal bargaining gave rise to parliamentary representation and in due course to modern democracy and freedoms. Pre-modern states therefore faced a developmental dilemma: sovereigns found towns easier to tax than the countryside, but excessive fiscal pressure nipped emergent capitalism in the bud. In practice, urban capitalism was only able to flourish beyond the reach of the more powerful monarchies. More generally, it is claimed that economic growth could only take place where towns were strong and states weak: by implication, only within urban republics.[38]

Once again the argument is hard to substantiate. In the first place, there

---

36   For towns as the originators of modern freedom, see Weber 1978: vol.2, 1212–372; Käsler 1988: 42–8, 200; Berman 1983: ch.12. For towns as islands of privilege, see Weber 1978: vol.2, 1254.

37   See note 55 and Chapter 6.

38   Tilly 1990: 52-3; Blockmans 1989: 733, 735, 752. Following Max Weber and Otto Hintze, Anderson 1974 similarly argues that the 'parcellization of sovereignty' and 'free towns' were preconditions for capitalism.

is no evidence that townspeople paid higher taxes under monarchies than republics. On the contrary, since republics were generally smaller, military and therefore fiscal costs per head were probably higher than in monarchies.[39] Neither does the evidence of interest rates discussed previously suggest that urban republics offered consistently better financial conditions than monarchies. Nor, finally, is the claim about the economic superiority of independent city-states compelling: Italian city republics lost economic leadership by the early sixteenth century, whereas the Dutch United Provinces profited from their cities' *failure* to turn into city-states at the end of the Middle Ages.[40]

Second, the claim that cities were normally aligned against rulers is implausible. Cities that faced powerful feudal competitors became the monarchies' main allies in the latter's struggle to extend sovereignty. Rulers in France, the Crown of Aragon, the southern Netherlands and Piedmont compensated their towns' support with lower transaction costs, greater domestic security, military backing in commercial ventures abroad and, last but not least, with political, commercial, industrial and financial privileges that helped turn the urban mercantile elites into *rentiers*. Towns only opposed monarchic rule when the loss of jurisdictional prerogatives outweighed potential gains from jurisdictional integration: this is the meaning of the wars waged by the *drie Steden* (Ghent, Bruges and Ypres) against Burgundian rulers in the fourteenth and fifteenth centuries and of the resistance by Castilian cities to Habsburg fiscal reform.[41]

Third, it is open to question whether republican rule offered many advantages for those lacking the rights and privileges of citizenship. If we take parliamentary representation as the main measure of political freedom, monarchies emerge as far more 'liberal' or pluralistic than towns. Parliaments were a monarchical invention that republics, which had little interest in giving subject towns and villages a political voice, never dreamt of setting up.[42] But even on more sophisticated measures, republican subjects faced several limitations to their economic and political freedoms that monarchical subjects did not. These problems arose either from the concentration of powers in the hands of a ruling oligarchy or from the inefficiency of a federal decision-making process, as a brief discussion of two paradigms of pre-modern republican rule, Florence and the Dutch United Provinces, shows.

---

39 Similarly, larger states benefited from economies of scale in warfare because they could spread their fixed costs more thinly (Bean 1973; Tilly 1990).
40 Hoppenbrouwers 2000.
41 For urban alliances with monarchs against feudal lords, see Spruyt 1994. For Flanders, see Blockmans 1997; for Castile, see Thompson 1994b.
42 Koenigsberger 1995a: 143.

Florence offers a model for the majority of republican city-states in which the ruling oligarchy jointly controlled legislative, executive and judicial powers. For about a century, between 1330 and 1434, Florence seemed to offer a historically pregnant alternative to the territorial principality, as it extended the model of the republican city-state to a region measuring more than 12,000 square kilometres. Yet in retrospect the Florentine project obviously failed, both in strictly institutional terms with the rise of the informal Medici *signoria* in the 1430s, and in economic terms as punitive fiscal, commercial and industrial policies gave rise to bitter resistance among its new subjects.[43] This was arguably a difficulty that city-states faced everywhere in their territories, although Florence faced it on an unusually large scale. The emergence in the 1430s of Cosimo de' Medici as regional *padrino* and *pater patriae* reflects the inability of the Florentine republic, and of 'city-state culture' more generally, to integrate subject cities and territories into republican structures of consent and representation.[44]

How can this political failure be explained? Why did Florence's subjects systematically resist its rule, forcing it to find political stability under the Medici? Why, more generally, did Italy's urban republics so seldom turn economic hegemony into consensual and stable territorial rule? The problem arose from a fundamental conflict of interest. Like urban republican elites elsewhere, the Florentine oligarchs were resented because they treated their new territories like the city-state's original *contado*, as a source of taxation and of personal gain for office-holders and as a market to be monopolised. Florence failed to transform its urban republic into a territorial republic because its political elites combined, on the economic front, commercial and landed power, and on the political front, legislative, executive and judicial powers. The elites did not distinguish their interests as rulers from their interests as merchants and landowners: they did not distinguish clearly between *government* and *state*. As territorial rulers, they were charged with mediating impartially between competing interests, but as political and economic elites they had a stake in the outcome.[45] As the Florentine Francesco Guicciardini explained, this was a predicament faced by all republican regimes:

> It is most desirable not to be born a subject; but if it must be so, it is
> better to be under a prince than a republic. For a republic oppresses
> all its subjects, and shares out its benefits only among its citizens;
> whereas a prince is more impartial, and gives equally to one subject

---

43 For constitutional change see Najemy 1982; Rubinstein 1966. On fiscal policy, see
    Epstein 1996a, with references. For industrial policy, see Chapter 6 of this book.
44 Epstein 2000b. For the reference to Cosimo, see Molho 1979.
45 See Chapter 5.

as to the other, so that everyone can hope to be beneficed and employed by him.[46]

David Hume later fleshed out the political economy of city-state rule:

> It may easily be observed, that though free governments have been commonly the most happy for those who partake of their freedom; yet are they the most ruinous and oppressive to their provinces. . . . When a monarch extends his dominions by conquest, he soon learns to consider his old and his new subjects as on the same footing; because, in reality, all his subjects are to him the same. . . . He does not, therefore, make any distinction between them in his *general* laws; and, at the same time, is careful to prevent all *particular* acts of oppression on the one as well as the other. But a free state necessarily makes a great distinction, and must always do so, till men learn to love their neighbours as well as themselves. The conquerors, in such a government, are all legislators, and will be sure to contrive matters, by restrictions on trade, and by taxes, so as to draw some private, as well as public advantage from their conquests. Provincial governors have also a better chance, in a republic, to escape with their plunder, by means of bribery or intrigue; and their fellow-citizens, who find their own state to be enriched by the spoils of the subject provinces, will be the more inclined to tolerate such abuses. Not to mention, that it is a necessary precaution in a free state to change the governors frequently; which obliges these temporary tyrants to be more expeditious and rapacious, that they may accumulate sufficient wealth before they give place to their successors.[47]

In sum, whereas sovereigns maximise revenue by taxing everyone proportionally, republics maximise revenue by taxing some disproportionally. The benefits of greater political and economic participation in the dominant city were more than counterbalanced by the costs to the remaining subjects of one-city rule. Just a few decades after the formal abolition of the Florentine Republic, the Dutch Republic made one of the most notable attempts to overcome the city-state's traditional limitations by constituting a federation of fifty-eight independent city-states that became a unique political experiment and model.[48] Although the history of the Dutch

46 Guicciardini 1951, note CVII: 'È da desiderare non nascere suddito; e pure avendo a essere, è meglio essere di principe che di repubblica; perché la repubblica deprime tutti e sudditi; e non fa parte alcuna della sua grandezza se non a' suoi cittadini; el principe è più commune a tutti, e ha equalmente per suddito l'uno come l'altro; però ognuno può sperare di essere e beneficiato e adoperato da lui.' See also Brown 1991: 108–9.
47 Hume 1993c: 17.
48 The North European Hansa, some members of which joined the Dutch republic, was a

Republic seems to offer strong support to the view that political freedom gives rise to economic success, the country's constitutional framework was arguably a major cause of the Netherland's relative decline from the 1680s.[49] When the Dutch political settlement emerged in the late 1570s, it was decided to require unanimity on issues of national concern like war, peace and taxation so as to avoid any individual city gaining the upper hand. However, the decision entrenched a permanently weak national leadership and subjected decision-making to debilitating bargaining and stultifying compromise between towns. Before the Peace of Westphalia in 1648, the all-out war of independence against Spain supplied the cities with a common enemy and helped paper over their main differences, but once the threat to political survival receded local sectional interests came to the fore. The lack of a coordinating federal authority, the dispersal of sovereignty among competing centres, and the requirement for unanimity slowed decision-making over issues of taxation and foreign policy where urban interests diverged most sharply. The same factors inhibited attempts to abolish urban commercial, industrial and legal restrictions and privileges, which raised production costs and undermined international competitiveness. Whereas economic success enabled the Dutch to finance an eighty-year war of independence against the world's most powerful empire, the Netherlands preserved its urban freedoms at the cost of relative economic decline; the political preconditions of the Dutch cities' economic success turned into institutional fetters to further growth. In practical terms, both the federal Dutch Republic and absolutist monarchies lacked the kind of clear and unambiguous political coordination that came from unified and uncontested territorial sovereignty.[50]

Constitutions and growth

Having begun with the hypothesis that political freedom was essential for economic success, we are being led to conclude that the two may be either incompatible or unconnected. The answer to the question whether systems of governance determined economic performance is at first sight negative. The Whig dichotomy between 'parliamentary' or 'free', and 'absolutist' or 'arbitrary' rule must be rejected for confusing constitutional form with practical content, and English insularity with institutional uniqueness.

The theory that derives positive economic incentives from political

---

much looser association of independent city-states which lacked a political 'centre' and whose main weakness was its consequent political unaccountability; see Spruyt 1994: ch.6.

49 For the argument that democracy causes faster economic growth, see Olson 1991; North 1995.

50 This paragraph follows 't Hart 1989; 't Hart 2000; van Zanden 1993: ch.7.

freedom is in any case probably mis-specified. Although it is in principle true that an autocratic government not subject to constitutional checks cannot credibly commit itself to existing property rights, there is a priori no reason why a democratic polity will *more* credibly bind itself to constitutional rules.[51] Democratic freedoms may equally threaten economic growth, for two reasons. First, democracies fall prey to pressure groups whose elected representatives pursue the particularistic goals of their constituencies rather than collective interests; this favours policies aimed at economic redistribution rather than growth. Second, democracies can overturn past laws and decisions, if a qualified majority decides so and in the absence of binding constitutional constraints; this causes uncertainty and inhibits strategic planning and investment. The tyranny of particularism and the lack of pre-commitment in democratic societies would seem to make it essential to insulate the state's decision-making processes and the constitution from the pressure of competing interests.[52]

Democracy's main economic limitation is therefore one that I have also imputed to absolutism and to the Dutch urban federation, namely the excessive and debilitating hold of particular interests. Although the analogy should not be pushed too far (whereas liberal democracy is based on universal equality before the law, *ancien régime* liberties were premised on legal inequality), it also indicates why differences in pre-modern constitutional rights were not critical for economic performance. Whereas constitutions defined political and normative issues of freedom, what mattered in economic terms was a state's pre-commitment to rights and rules and the extent of its jurisdiction over rival claims. Yet, on the evidence of interest rates, pre-commitment to rules was by and large universal, for reasons that Hume once again spells out:

> Private property seems to me almost as secure in a civilised European monarchy as in a republic; nor is danger much apprehended, in such a government, from the violence of the sovereign, more than we commonly dread harm from thunder, or earthquakes, or any accident the most unusual and extraordinary. Avarice, the spur of industry, is so obstinate a passion, and works its way through so many dangers and difficulties, that it is not likely to be scared by an imaginary danger, which is so small that it scarcely admits of calculation. (. . .) It may now be affirmed of civilized monarchies, what was formerly said in praise of

51 This applies only if we follow a middle-of-the-road liberal definition of democracy and avoid arguing like Hayek that a democracy may be illiberal and a dictator liberal, where liberalism is defined as a system of individual freedom under the rule of law with wide scope for free-market activity (Hayek 1973; Arneson 1993: 145–6).

52 Democratic inefficiencies underlie the claim that authoritarian rule is a prerequisite for long-term growth. See Przeworski and Limongi 1993; Olson 1982; Becker 1983; Elster and Slagstad 1988; Scully 1992.

republics alone, *that they are a government of Laws, not of Men.* (. . .) The source of degeneracy which may be remarked in free governments, consists in the practice of contracting debt, and mortgaging the public revenues, by which taxes may, in time, become altogether intolerable, and all the property of the state be brought into the hands of the public. (. . .) Absolute princes have also contracted debt; but as an absolute prince may make a bankruptcy when he pleases, his people can never be oppressed by his debts.[53]

The main institutional bottleneck in pre-modern states did not arise from a lack of concern with contractual rules, despotic insouciance or parliamentary weakness, but from the coordination failures caused by the *absence of undivided sovereignty* over the political and economic spheres. Multiple sovereignty was a source of both economic and political inefficiency. Because the state did not have a monopoly of power within its borders, feudal lords, cities, corporations, and other 'public' or chartered bodies derived income from jurisdictional rights that constrained Smithian growth and challenged the theory and practices of the sovereign state.

The main thrust of recent historical research is to view pre-modern state formation as a slow and non-linear process of expanding sovereignty rather than as the 'rise of modern political liberty'. Full state sovereignty is a prerequisite of modern liberty; but modern liberty is not a precondition for the sovereign state.[54] From this vantage point the connection between institutional structure and economic change becomes clear. The most important source of pre-modern institutional inefficiency was the near-ubiquitous parcellization of sovereignty, which restricted states' ability to coordinate or curtail competing political and economic claims. Jurisdictional fragmentation was the result of a surfeit of sanctioned liberties and a fragmented system of law, of a body of conflicting traditions and rights that arose from the organic and additive nature of state formation on the European Continent. Jurisdictional parcellization posed three fundamental constraints on pre-modern growth: it confused and raised the costs of fiscal exaction, it raised tariff and other barriers to trade, and it became a source of ubiquitous prisoner's dilemmas and market failures discussed in subsequent chapters.[55]

---

53 Hume 1993b: 53–5. Hume appears to be arguing that public debt in a constitutional system is subject to moral hazard (behaviour opposite to that intended) because the probability of default is remote, whereas an absolutist ruler's greater nominal freedom forces him to incur more binding commitments in order to attract funds.

54 See, from slightly different viewpoints, Rosenberg 1994 and Spruyt 1994.

55 The explanation for the positive correlation between absolutist regimes and low rates of urban growth (taken as a proxy for economic growth), identified by De Long and Shleifer 1992, is therefore more likely to be absolutism's inability to enforce a unified jurisdiction rather than the pursuit of autocratic policies.

Pre-modern states could extend their sovereignty in two ways. They could usurp or restrict feudal or corporate rights, usually in wartime under cover of fiscal necessity and by right of territorial conquest, but also by returning rights to the state on the death of a feudal incumbent. Or, they could bypass existing jurisdictional claims by granting new, countervailing freedoms which restricted the old.[56] Both solutions were circuitous and fraught with danger. The first solution, which gave rise to accusations of autocratic oppression and breach of existing constitutional freedoms, and could therefore be challenged politically and in the courts, was the negative side of the competitive constraint on rulers' actions discussed previously in the context of public debt. The second solution created new sectional interests and coordination failures which could restrain market integration further and take further effort to abolish.[57] The resulting tension between attempts to streamline and rationalise financial and administrative operations, and states' continued dependence on support from privileged corporate groups, defined the parameters of 'institutional efficiency' among pre-modern states.[58] While an efficient state was necessarily also a strong and centralised (albeit not autocratic) state, its political and economic efficiency depended on the *relative* speed and cost with which it gained sovereignty over collective income streams compared to its competitors. The European polity that consistently outdid all rivals in this context before the late eighteenth century was England – not by virtue of the country's unique individual liberties, but of the country's precocious institutional unification;[59] although it may well be that the comparative weakness in England of corporate freedoms made it easier to conceive of individual freedom.[60]

56 "In a society organised on a corporative basis personal initiative could only flourish under the protection given by exemption and privileges" (Deyon and Guignet 1980: 626). For a detailed discussion and application of this principle, see Bossenga 1991.

57 The latter appears to have been the consequence of the many urban privileges granted by the Habsburgs in sixteenth-century Castile (Sanchez León 2000).

58 Bossenga 1991: 13.

59 Koenigsberger 1978; Brewer 1990: chs.1, 4. It is for this reason that England achieved national market integration a century before the rest of Europe (Reed 1973; Kussmaul 1990; Chartres 1995).

60 Brewer and Staves 1995.

3 The late medieval crisis as an 'integration crisis'

During the 1950s and 1960s a distinguished generation of scholars led by M. M. Postan, Wilhelm Abel, Ernest Labrousse, Fernand Braudel, Emmanuel Le Roy Ladurie, Maurice Dobb and Rodney Hilton, established the view – subsequently enshrined in the so-called 'Brenner debate' – that pre-modern, 'traditional' societies did not experience growth in per caput incomes for lack of technological innovation.[1] This view is now under challenge, from two directions. First, earlier claims that pre-industrial agrarian technology was incapable of keeping food output in step with rising population are now considered too pessimistic, in the light of a growing body of archaeological and archival evidence which shows that the available agricultural technology was significantly more productive than was formerly believed. Second, historians have become more aware of developments in rural by-employment and 'protoindustry' and of improvements in market organisation and trade that earlier generations had largely ignored.

Perhaps the most significant aspect of current revisionism is the suggestion that pre-modern societies were operating significantly below their technological and productive potential. This proposition implies that pre-modern technology did not pose the fundamental constraint that earlier scholars assumed. It also offers an elegant solution to the difficulty that 'stagnationist' models have in explaining why the pre-modern European population kept increasing over the long term even though the pool of agrarian technology underwent little change. Food production could grow in line with population because there existed considerable technological and organisational slack: towards 1300 agriculture in only a handful of European regions – including parts of Essex and Kent, of Flanders and northern France, of the southern Rhineland, and of Lombardy, Tuscany and possibly Valencia – was approaching the technological frontier, and agricultural systems elsewhere had still to introduce the most significant medieval innovations.

---

1 See Postan 1973; Abel 1980; Labrousse 1933; Braudel 1982; Le Roy Ladurie 1966; Hilton 1975; Bois 1984; Aston and Philpin 1985.

A major implication of this research is therefore that the decisions to innovate were not made on the basis of a simple dichotomy (adoption or non-adoption) as the stagnationist literature on the inherently 'non-adoptive' peasantry assumes, but were situated along a continuum in which the significant variable was the *intensity* of innovation.[2] The limits to pre-modern growth were not due to the absence of technology that could be applied, but to constraints on its application. Technological and organisational innovation arising from commercial improvements stimulated specialisation, but a complex array of institutional barriers to trade and frequent commercial setbacks caused by warfare made specialisation aleatory and reversible. As a result, towards 1800 many parts of Europe had still not fully caught up with productive techniques developed elsewhere since the late Middle Ages; the mechanisation of agriculture and the introduction of chemical fertilisers replaced a bundle of ancient and medieval technology that had still to be fully exploited.[3] In the light of these discoveries, the history of European agriculture between 1300 and 1800 has become a tale of the slow diffusion of best practice from more advanced to more backward regions, rather than the story of structural immobility and rustic *longue durée* evoked by historians in the tradition of the French *Annales*.

The fact that pre-industrial societies could undergo intensive growth raises the question why comparatively few regions did so. While both Ricardo-Malthusian and Marxist historians were happy to tar all pre-industrial economies with the same stagnationist brush (with early modern England and Holland presented as unexplained exceptions to the rule), regional diversity has become *the* central issue of recent research. The latter suggests new answers to the old debate on the late medieval 'crisis' and the transition from feudalism to capitalism, which are the topic of this chapter. I begin by discussing current models of the 'feudal' economy that appeal to exogenous sources of change, and propose an alternative model of endogenous development in which long-run intensive growth is one of several alternative outcomes. I then address the nature and causes of the demographic slowdown that occurred in many parts of western Europe from the late thirteenth century. Was it a systemic crisis, as Ricardo-Malthusian and neo-Marxist historians claim, or was it a series of short-term difficulties or bottlenecks to production that could have been overcome had the catastrophe of the Black Death – which killed no less than a third of the European population in the space of two years – not struck? In other words, are claims about a 'general crisis' in the fourteenth

---

2 See Feder, Just and Zilberman 1985.
3 See especially Grantham 1997a and 1999. For evidence of high levels of productivity in pre-modern agriculture, see Allen 1995; Overton 1996; Hoffman 1996; de Vries and van der Woude 1997.

century an instance of *post hoc* rationalisation based on the social, economic and political upheaval which followed the Black Death? I conclude by proposing a new model of the crisis that emphasises general patterns of development but also addresses the question why long-run intensive growth was so rhapsodic across time and space.

Much of the debate on the late medieval crisis has confused long-term, general economic trends with localised, short-term economic cycles, and has inferred structural shifts in the economy from cyclical shocks caused by warfare, commercial disruption and epidemics. While the pessimists' emphasis on cyclical contractions is understandable, not least because these are what contemporaries were most concerned with in their writings, more optimistic historians have also muddied the waters by focusing on patterns of consumption and demand rather than on changes in supply structures. Here I discuss only the long-term, structural changes in the economy that are most readily identified by comparing conditions towards 1300 and 1500, and I do not consider cyclical contractions and expansions.[4] I also pay only cursory attention to the dynamics of regional divergence, which are examined in more detail in the following chapters.

The pessimists' case

Despite significant ideological and theoretical differences, post-war historians agreed that the period between the 1280s and the 1340s marked a watershed for the European economy, and many considered it to be a 'general' crisis. The arguments are well known and can be sketched out quite briefly. The feudal economy was a one-good Ricardian economy devoted to the subsistence production of grain with no significant agricultural or manufacturing alternatives. Primitive technology and low rates of investment meant that food output was unable to keep up with population growth except by bringing new land into cultivation, subject to rapidly diminishing returns. Low investments were a consequence of the prevailing property rights and incentive structures.[5] Since feudal lords obtained their income through military and legal ('extra-economic') coercion, they had little incentive to produce for, and compete in, the market; conversely, the lack of competitive markets gave them few incentives to innovate. The peasantry's native risk-aversion and preference for self-sufficiency over 'dependence' on the market was strengthened by the absence of competitive 'capitalist' markets. The consequences of declining land productivity before 1300 were intensified by rising expenditure on feudal warfare. Because the total size of the economic pie was not increasing, lords could only meet their escalating military costs by

---

4 See e.g. Hatcher 1996 for a discussion of such cycles in fifteenth-century England.
5 Desai 1991; Hilton 1965; Postan 1967.

capturing a larger share of the social surplus, which they achieved by imposing increasingly harsh demands upon the peasantry. The contraction of the peasants' share cut into the latter's capital investments and accelerated the fall in agricultural output. Increasingly frequent famines pushed the peasantry and the poor urban wage-earners to their physiological limits. Food deprivation increased rates of mortality and prepared the ground for the Black Death. The feudal economy entered a period of involution, and the Black Death brought the crisis of a whole society to a head.

The Ricardo-Malthusian claim that the population by 1300 was outstripping available resources arose from three assumptions: first, that the marginal productivity of land was in long-run decline; second, that lower levels of food consumption, and particularly the greater incidence of harvest crises from the 1280s onwards, increased levels of background and crisis mortality and caused population to fall; and third, that medieval societies were incapable of applying preventive checks to nuptiality and natality that could mitigate the pressure on resources. However, the first and the third of these propositions are not borne out empirically, while the second is open to a different interpretation.

The only statistical evidence of a long-term decline in grain yields before the Black Death comes from a famous study by Postan and Titow of the Winchester lands between the mid-thirteenth and mid-fourteenth century. Contrary to their claims, however, the Winchester yields between 1250 and 1350 display no statistically significant trend.[6] On the other hand, recent findings for other parts of England and Continental Europe suggest that average output in some regions was still rising before the Black Death.[7] Evidence of demographic hardship is equally ambiguous, with places showing demographic stagnation or contraction appearing side by side with areas of continued growth in England, in Iberia (where Catalonia and Castile were relatively underpopulated, Aragon and Navarre less so), in Italy (where Tuscan and southern Italian stagnation or decline contrasted with continued growth in Lombardy), in parts of France, and in Flanders.[8] The main indirect evidence for changes in the pattern of food

6 Postan and Titow 1958–9; Desai 1991. It has recently been suggested that yields on English lordly demesnes of the kind assessed by Postan and Titow were lower than on peasant lands (Campbell 1997b: 238, 244–5); Winchester yields were in any case low by contemporary standards (Campbell 1995: 555–7). The lack of a clear trend in demesne yields cannot therefore be extrapolated to trends in output from peasant lands. For the suggestion that peasants were frequently more innovative than lords, see Derville 1987; Bentzien 1990: 129–31; Campbell 1997b; note 20 in this chapter.

7 Reinicke 1989; Mate 1991; Campbell 1995: 555; Cortonesi 1995.

8 B. F. Harvey 1991; Smith 1991; Dufourcq and Gaultier Dalché 1976: 122–3; Bisson 1986: 163; Zulaica Palacios 1994; Berthe 1984; Pinto 1995b: 46–54; Chiappa Mauri 1997; Epstein 1992: ch.2; Sakellariou 1996: ch.2; Dubois 1988: 242–63; Sivéry 1976: 607; Baratier 1961; Thoen and Devos 1999.

production (yields) and consumption (population) is therefore ambiguous. While it would be wrong to extrapolate broad trends from these findings, there is clearly little evidence of a *generalised* European crisis in the decades before the Black Death.

The argument that background and crisis mortality increased from the late thirteenth century faces similar objections. Direct evidence of mortality is poor and hard to interpret; even less is known about its causes. Most estimates are culled from tax records which are largely urban in origin and pose major problems of interpretation. The sporadic fiscal estimates seldom reveal the causes of demographic loss, making it hard to verify if they were caused by rising mortality or by other factors like migration. The best available studies of pre-Black Death demography in Navarre and Provence show that demographic volatility in both town and country was greatly amplified by significant levels of migration caused by pestilence, warfare and other unknown factors.[9] Although peasant mobility may have been more constrained in regions where serfdom (bondage to the land) still had a significant presence, even areas with large serf populations included large numbers of freeholders and landless individuals who had the option of migrating.

Faced with these difficulties in interpretation, Ricardo-Malthusian pessimists have searched for evidence of increased hardship elsewhere. They have focused in particular on the apparent increase in the levels of volatility of urban grain prices (rural prices are mostly unknown), which have been taken as evidence of declining harvests that caused rising mortality by hunger among the urban poor. This interpretation is not straightforward. Price volatility is strictly speaking a function of the efficiency of urban supply structures and of the elasticity of demand rather than of harvest output *per se*. Price volatility would accurately measure the volatility of harvests only if the latter were identical across very large regions, if no food substitutes were available, or if high transport costs made it impossible to import outside supplies. But there is little evidence to support these assumptions. The ecological and technological determinants of output were extremely localised, food substitutes (other grains, pulses, chestnuts, roots etc.) were generally available, and by the thirteenth century grain was actively traded over long distances.[10]

Given the lack of evidence that aggregate food *output* was declining before the Black Death, we may reasonably conclude that the rising price volatility of wheat from the 1280s reflected growing constraints on food *distribution*. Long-run developments in price volatility in European towns

9 Berthe 1984; Baratier 1961.
10 For evidence of highly localised differences in output, see Tits-Dieuaide 1975: 117–30; Ladero Quesada and Gonzalez Jimenez 1979. For the long-distance grain trade, see Bautier 1967: 9–13.

support this hypothesis.[11] Volatility was clearly not caused by excess population driven onto marginal and increasingly unproductive land, because it remained high for decades after the Black Death despite the collapse of rural populations. The instability of grain prices during the under-populated fifteenth century, and the long term decline in volatility even as population growth resumed after 1450, prove that price volatility had mainly social and institutional causes.[12] This is not to deny that climatic disorders might occasionally be so severe and affect such a wide area as to make the cost of storing and transporting food prohibitive. The most notorious example of a crisis of this kind was the Great Famine of 1315–17, whose immediate cause was a cycle of unusually high rainfall and cold weather which lasted over several years and extended across much of northern Europe; but although it is often considered the archetypal 'Malthusian' crisis because it was associated with rising mortality, it was in fact the result of atypical weather patterns that did not affect more densely populated Mediterranean Europe.[13]

While famine and mortality often coincided chronologically, modern research does not support the existence of a consistent and direct link between famine and mortality or even malnutrition and disease. Individuals seldom die of starvation and consistently low levels of food intake do not generally raise susceptibility to crisis mortality. On the other hand, strong fluctuations in food intake associated with high price variation do increase susceptibility to infectious disease, which explains why in pre-modern Europe high price volatility was associated with high pressure demographic regimes and low rates of population growth. However, price volatility is essentially a measure of *organisational* efficiency, that is, of the efficiency with which distribution and welfare systems cope with periods of dearth, rather than of a society's inability to produce food.[14] Consequently, the huge price volatility in Europe before the Black Death reflects that society's poor organisational and commercial structures rather than its technological backwardness. One salient example of these inefficiencies

11 See Chapter 7, Fig. 7.3.

12 Tits-Dieuaide 1987: 534-6 makes the same point for the period after 1400. However, her data do not include any figures prior to the Black Death and have not been de-trended; her conclusions are therefore based on incorrect estimates. See Chapter 7 of this book.

13 Jordan 1996. Postan 1973: 213 took the crisis of 1315–17 as marking the beginnings of late medieval economic decline. A recent analysis of the impact of weather on agricultural output in late nineteenth-century England, France and Germany shows that cross-country effects differed significantly; the use of aggregate national output statistics underestimates the inter-regional differences within countries (Solomou and Wu 1999).

14 For the biological consequences of famines, see e.g. Mosley 1978; Cotts Watkins and Menken 1985; Livi Bacci 1990. For their institutional mediation, see Sen 1981; Ravallion 1987; Walter and Schofield 1989a; de Waal 1990; Fogel 1994. For links between price variation, mortality and rates of demographic and economic growth, see Galloway 1988, 1993 and 1994.

was the bundle of social, economic and institutional inequalities that caused food supplies to be concentrated disproportionately in towns, a fact which in the event of a supply crisis attracted large numbers of temporary rural immigrants who spread diseases and put their hosts' food and labour markets and proto-sanitary systems under intolerable stress.[15]

The broader Ricardo-Malthusian model of the feudal economy raises similar objections. The model makes three crucial claims: first, the population periodically overshot its resource base or output 'ceiling' and had to be kept in check by rising mortality; second, available technology was incapable of increasing output in step with the long-term rise in population; and third, the agrarian sector was wholly employed producing grain for human consumption.

The belief that medieval peasants were unable to adapt their reproductive strategy to changing economic circumstances assumes that they ignored basic contraceptive and abortifacient techniques and did not calibrate nuptiality to economic opportunity.[16] This contradicts attestations from medieval medical texts and church moralists that contraceptives and abortifacients were well known during the high and late Middle Ages.[17] It also runs counter to the widely recognised positive correlation between peasant wealth and family size, which indicates that the poorer sections of the population in particular were using active and passive methods of birth control (including infanticide, exposure, differential nutrition and regulation of the age of first marriage) to restrict household size.[18] Migration, discussed previously, was also used to adapt to changing environmental

---

15 For peasant distress migrations to Italian cities in the early fourteenth century, see Pinto 1995b: 49–50. For the different impact of famine across social groups before the Black Death, see Berthe 1984: 272–3, 315–17, 320–1; Razi 1993: 38; Schofield 1997; Dyer 1998. Postan and Titow 1958–9 tried to prove a direct link between food shortages and mortality by correlating the rising number of heriots (entry fines to peasant tenures which they believed to be exacted only on a peasant's death) with grain prices, particularly during the great famine of 1315–17; heriots however were also levied on distress sales of land, so they are more accurately seen as evidence of a failure in entitlements (B. F. Harvey 1991; Smith 1991).

16 Malthus's argument about the role of preventive checks in maintaining a homeostatic balance between population and resources was forgotten by most post-war economic historians. Homeostatic models are notably neutral as to the precise equilibrium point between population and resources that will be maintained. The revisionist argument sketched out previously suggests that pre-modern populations left a significant margin between the resources they could theoretically produce with the technology at their disposal, and what they actually required for demographic survival and reproduction.

17 Biller 1980; Riddle 1991.

18 See Razi 1980; Herlihy 1965 and 1982; Leverotti 1989. Razi 1993 has also linked the extent of kinship ties among English peasants to levels of commercialisation, implying a similarly positive feedback between economic incentives and demographic behaviour. In early modern Rouen, the poor responded to price increases in wheat (which are a close proxy of short-term living standards) by sharply lowering fertility rates; the fertility of the urban wealthy was virtually unaffected. On the other hand, there was little difference in

constraints and opportunities for individuals not legally tied to the land. By the thirteenth century at the latest, European peasants disposed of a range of social, biological and medical controls over fertility and nuptiality that could theoretically maintain a homeostatic equilibrium between population and resources. The weight of the circumstantial evidence (including our preceding criticism of the existence of 'overpopulation') suggests that medieval populations did in fact apply preventive checks, but that underdeveloped market and welfare institutions could still do little to mitigate the brunt of exogenous, natural and man-made shocks.

The second string to the Ricardo-Malthusian bow, technological pessimism, was founded upon early estimates of pre-modern agricultural productivity that relied on crude measures of yield per unit of seed or tithing returns, and on the lack of major crop and machine innovations before the eighteenth century. Recently more sophisticated measurements of output and capital efficiency have substantially raised estimates of productivity, and have also suggested that the lack of major technical change before 1750 was not a significant constraint upon output at prevailing levels of population. Significant productivity gains supporting larger populations could still be made in eighteenth-century Europe by using available factors of production more efficiently and by introducing low cost innovations (better drainage, new crop rotations, increased fertiliser, enclosure, etc.) based on a backlog of un- or under-exploited practical and technical knowledge that had been available since the thirteenth century or before.

By the 1320s Norfolk and Kentish peasants had achieved levels of land productivity that would be reached again only during the eighteenth century. In thirteenth-century Tuscany, average agricultural productivity may have increased by 0.25 per cent per annum thanks to investments in drainage, reorganisation of plots, the planting of higher value crops, and improvements in transport and distribution that required no major technical change; such gains were associated with a rough doubling of the total population and a tripling of the proportion of urban residents in the region. Tuscany also only achieved similar levels of population density and urbanisation again after 1800. Derville, Thoen, Reinicke and others have identified similar performances for medieval northern France, Flanders and the lower Rhineland; Valencia's irrigated *huerta* also achieved high levels

---

the magnitude and timing of positive checks associated with sharp increases in prices (Galloway 1986). These results contrast with Herlihy's speculation that positive checks applied more to the poor, whereas the wealthy applied preventive checks via fertility rates (Herlihy 1987). Smith 1991: 60–5 discusses evidence for the operation of nuptiality and natality, rather than mortality, as the main check on population growth before the Black Death. While evidence of preventive checks among medieval peasants is not yet conclusive, the claim that they responded rationally to price signals implies also that they were aware of the opportunity costs of excess births.

of productivity. Grantham has calculated that pre-modern levels of urbanisation were 40–60 per cent lower than what the available technology could sustain, concluding from this that the state of agricultural technology was not a binding constraint on the size of the non-agricultural workforce in pre-industrial times. Allen has suggested that the introduction by early modern peasant landowners of small-scale improvements to drainage in the heavy Midland clays fuelled a 'yeoman' revolution in agricultural productivity, and Hoffman has documented similar patterns of growth in central and northern France. Tits-Dieuaide has shown how the near doubling of output per hectare in Flanders between the thirteenth and eighteenth centuries depended on a long and slow process of crop and technical innovation rather than a rapid eighteenth-century agrarian revolution.[19]

The research I have just summarised suggests that the rate of peasant and landlord innovation was principally determined by the prevailing rate of interest and by the transaction costs defining the opportunity costs of trade.[20] Since real interest rates in the long run are a function of investment risk and investment opportunity (market size), both of which are determined by search, enforcement and transport costs (in addition to technological change, which in this case however was a dependent variable), we can conclude that the main reason for the low rates of investment in pre-modern agriculture and of frequent setbacks in agricultural productivity was the disincentive posed by inordinately high transactions costs.[21] Most of the latter arose from the coordination failures and lack of investment in public goods (transport and commercial systems, credible and predictable justice, financial and political stability) caused by pre-modern political and jurisdictional fragmentation and warfare.[22] It also follows that, in the longer term, population density was positively correlated with agricultural productivity. As might be expected given the high cost of transporting bulk foods and the benefits from higher population densities in terms of specialisation and scale economies in

---

19 See Campbell and Overton 1993; Campbell 1995: 555; Persson 1991; W. R. Day 1999; Reinicke 1989; Derville 1987; Thoen 1997; Glick 1970; Allen 1995; Hoffman 1996; Grantham 1993 and 1997; Tits-Dieuaide 1984.

20 John Langdon has shown that English smallholders who faced higher average rents than large peasants substituted horses for oxen more rapidly than large-scale tenant farmers and feudal landlords. Smallholders also engaged proportionally more in trade, where the horse's higher maintenance costs were outweighed by its greater strength and speed (Langdon 1986: 172–253). Interest rates are discussed below.

21 'The central problem of medieval agriculture was not that methods of raising and maintaining productivity levels were unknown but, rather, that there were insufficient incentives to encourage their adoption outside a few favoured localities' (Campbell 1995: 544).

22 For the effect of public goods on agricultural supply elasticity, see Schiff and Montenegro 1997.

infrastructure.[23] Consequently, the highest rates of medieval agricultural productivity were found in regions such as north-central Italy, Flanders, Île-de-France, Artois, and Norfolk that also had the highest population density in Europe at the time.

None of these criticisms can be taken to imply that bottlenecks to production leading to demographic slowdown could *not* arise, and it is in fact clear that many European regional economies were experiencing a slowdown during the late thirteenth century. However, the criticisms shift the explanatory focus from the balance between population and resources (as in the Ricardo-Malthusian model) and the structure of land ownership (as in Brenner's version of that model) to the complex relations between agrarian production and markets.

Among the Ricardo-Malthusian model's most misleading features is its overwhelming focus on grain production. While cereals were evidently the most salient pre-modern product in terms of volume, their importance by value and rate of commercialisation (which was always less than output since a large proportion was consumed directly by the producers) decreased steadily over time. By 1300, the cereal share of GNP even in a relatively underdeveloped economy like England's was probably less than 40 per cent.[24] Until quite recently, however, the sectorial bias in favour of agricultural staples ignored the substantial occupational alternatives faced by rural producers, which included pastoral activities for wool (which may have accounted for up to a third of rural GNP in early fourteenth-century England), meat, dairy and leather, Mediterranean tree crops and especially various forms of by-employment in manufactures and services.[25] It could be argued that the bias reinforced the belief in a 'general crisis', because it led historians to ignore the perceptible increase in parts of Europe of rural and small town by-employment in the decades before the Black Death, an increase that implies that the price of staple foods was stable or declining relative to low-quality manufactures and raw materials like wool. Opportunities for non-agrarian employment were presumably among the causes of the increased peasant land fragmentation observed during the period.[26]

---

23 Boserup 1965. Tits-Dieuaide 1981 and 1984 states this explicitly with regard to pre-modern Flanders.

24 Estimates extrapolated from Campbell 2000.

25 Hymer and Resnick 1969. Kitsikopoulos 2000 estimates that an average 5-person family farm in fourteenth-century England had 20 per cent of full workdays per annum available for outside employment.

26 Smith 1984: 22–38 estimates that between 40 and 70 per cent of peasant holdings were too small to absorb the full labour of their resident households; see also note 25 of this chapter. The figure contradicts Brenner's claim that the basic economic unit in the feudal economy was the self-sufficient, autonomous peasant farm (this book, Chapter 1). Although much of the surplus labour was employed as wage and servant labour, evidence of other forms of rural

By excluding activities that raised the peasants' disposable incomes and stimulated agrarian specialisation, the post-war models of the feudal economy overestimated the welfare effects of harvest and supply crises before the Black Death. Single-minded concentration on cereal production also led historians to ignore or misunderstand the importance of domestic trade and markets, and to assume that since 'average' peasants owned their means of production and could meet their food consumption needs off the land, they would only trade under 'extra-economic' compulsion.[27] In the prevailing view, markets were foisted on the peasantry by feudal lords, Church and state who needed to monetise their agricultural surplus; medieval towns were at the same time rentier consumers of peasant surpluses and 'islands in a feudal sea'; and peasants under normal circumstances avoided markets because commercial production was subject to greater risk, that is, to greater income volatility. These arguments are wrong in both theory and fact. Product markets (and to a lesser extent land, labour and credit markets) were ubiquitous under feudalism and peasants were frequently at the forefront in demanding them, while towns played an important role as centres of consumption, industry and trade in stimulating agrarian and manufacturing specialisation; in more developed regions like Lombardy, Tuscany and Flanders the urban share of the population approached 30 per cent. The claim that income volatility can be overcome by diversifying output is correct, but ignores the fact that diversification is best accomplished through markets which pool the output of many farms and stimulate specialisation and productivity. In principle, there is no reason why peasants should avoid markets, although the degree of involvement will be tempered by market inefficiencies, susceptibility to exogenous shocks like warfare, access to credit, information costs and the like.[28]

by-employment is extensive. See Watts 1967; Birrell 1969; Hatcher 1973: 84, 152–6; Bridbury 1982: ch.1; Bailey 1988; Campbell 1998: 21; Miller and Hatcher 1995: 410–11; Sutton 1989; Sivéry 1976: 607; Comba 1988c; Mainoni 1994a: ch.1; Wolff 1976; Fourquin 1964: 115 and note 289; Gual Camarena 1976. The importance of the wool sector for the pre-Black Death English economy, emphasised by Silver 1983 and Desai 1991, is confirmed by Campbell's recent estimate of 40 million sheep circa 1304–9 (Campbell 2000).

27 The neglect of domestic trade and markets is visible in Postan 1973 and in the insistence by Brenner 1982 that towns were merely centres for the organisation of the long distance luxury trade and for the consumption of the feudal surplus. Dobb (1946: ch.2), who had far less historical material at his disposal, took a more sophisticated position. His intuitions on the role of 'petty commodity production' have been developed by Rodney Hilton (1985, 1992), who has had an important influence on the recent revival of interest in small towns, markets and commercialisation in medieval England.

28 While long accepted for the more urbanised and less feudal regions of Europe like Flanders, parts of Iberia, southern France and Italy, similar patterns have also been described recently for less developed countries like England, which between *c.*1086 and 1348 experienced a tripling of the rate of urbanisation and perhaps a tenfold increase in per caput coinage in circulation, with all the trappings of increased commercialisation (Miller and Hatcher 1995; Britnell 1993).

Post-war historians thus underestimated the productive potential and the actual performance of medieval or 'feudal' agriculture. Agrarian practices developed for the most part before the mid-fourteenth century could raise output and productivity considerably above the demographic 'ceiling' achieved towards 1300. Many of the potential gains in productivity from that technology had still to be exhausted by the eighteenth century. The major influence on the rate of innovation was the cost of trade. Ease of access to structured, stable and competitive markets was the main precondition for growth. Most medieval societies, which appear to have regulated their size in response to economic opportunities, did not exploit their technological knowledge to the full before the Black Death for lack of adequate incentives. In most cases, the barriers to trade and therefore the opportunity costs of innovation were simply too high.[29]

The feudal economy and the crisis

A new model of the feudal economy must incorporate the recent findings I have summarised; it must avoid the tautological appeal to trade that causes trade; and it must offer a parsimonious explanation of why regional economies performed differently for long stretches of time.[30] What follows is a brief sketch of what such a model might look like.

In the feudal-tributary mode of production, most rural producers owned their means of production and sold a proportion of their produce on the market.[31] Feudal lords (which included the ruling elites in towns

---

29 These conclusions appear to follow in the tracks of recent 'commercialisation' or neo-Smithian revisionism, which has been particularly influential among Anglo-American medievalists. This group of scholars tends to maximise the cumulative impact of commercial change, to suggest that welfare levels were not severely eroded by 1300, and to imply that the early fourteenth-century mortality crises were temporary and reversible setbacks. However, the commercialisation thesis has two weaknesses. First, the assumption that medieval peasants behaved like modern Kansas farmers glosses over the more interesting question of how incentive structures changed over time. Second, a strictly Smithian model of growth which abstracts from the institutional context is unable to explain why some areas were more commercialised and technologically advanced than others. Significantly, attempts to address these differences within the 'commercialisation' framework appeal to exogenous institutional factors like the extent of seigniorial controls. The recent reformulation of Pirenne's thesis that growth was driven by urbanisation and access to water transport (Grantham 1997a) raises the question of what drove urbanisation in the first place. There are enough examples of successful towns that did not have direct access to water transport, and conversely of coastal areas that did not develop strong commercial emporia, to suggest that simple opportunities for trade did not inevitably give rise to to commercial success. The commercialisation model describes growth, but does not explain it.

30 On tautological appeals to trade, see note 29.

31 Following Haldon 1993, I employ the term 'tributary' to emphasize that feudal incomes were obtained just as much through tax and tribute as through labour services and economic rent. Analyses of the feudal mode of production exclusively in terms of labour

with jurisdictional prerogatives over the hinterland) extracted a surplus from the peasantry by means of a decentralised system of legal compulsion backed by military threat; the surplus was received directly as rent in cash, kind or labour, and indirectly through levies on trade and the provision of justice. Although the relative share of income from different sources varied over time and space, the share from rights of jurisdiction (which included compulsory labour services) was always substantial. The principal threat to feudalism therefore did not come from trade; up to a point feudalism thrived on trade.[32] But although feudal lords did not exclude markets, they regulated and taxed them for income. Moreover, because feudal lords were less directly exposed to market pressures than peasant producers – at the end of the thirteenth century the demesne sector in England accounted for perhaps 5 per cent of the lords' income and 0.5 per cent of GNP – they were also less likely to encourage agricultural innovations, although they adopted them when they occurred.[33]

The main obstacle to growth in the feudal economy was thus the cost of trade, which was defined mainly by institutional regulation and tariffs, by political and military stability (the warfare so prevalent in this society disrupted trade), and to a lesser extent by developments in transport technology. Within the boundaries of a lord's or city's jurisdiction, markets were by and large competitive, with the exception of the market in food

relations and property rights to land (see Bois 1984; Brenner 1982 and 1997) with no regard to market structure lead to a theoretical and empirical dead end. The definition of the peasantry as a class producing jointly for subsistence and for the market is also preferable to essentially arbitrary definitions based on farm size, tenurial relations, imputed behavioural patterns, and so forth.

32   The point was made by Dobb 1946: 39–42, 70–81; see also Wolf 1983; Haldon 1993. The main long-term threats to the feudal mode of surplus extraction lay elsewhere. Firstly, the development of a class of wage labourers no longer tied to its means of production undermined feudal coercion because it could credibly threaten to migrate; it forced lords to compete on the market for labour rather than rely on compulsory labour services. Second, state centralisation – the transfer of sovereignty over feudal means of coercion from subordinate lords to superior territorial authorities – transformed feudal rights of jurisdiction, which sanctioned the decentralised feudal mode of coercion, into fiscal or property rights over commercial transactions. The transformation of decentralised feudal immunities into state-defined and redeemable claims to fiscal rights turned the legal and economic base of the feudal class into a tradable commodity. Financial capital rather than social status became the elites' new coin of exchange, while the state's decision whether to sell income streams to the highest bidder or to abolish them altogether became increasingly subject to financial rather than political considerations. Early modern 'absolutism' was not simply a form of state feudalism (Anderson 1974). By embarking on the road to centralised, monopolistic jurisdiction, early modern states were laying the institutional basis of modern capitalism; see Chapter 8 in this book.

33   Estimates are based on data kindly provided by Bruce Campbell and Nicholas Poynder of Belfast University. For the greater rate of innovation among peasants than lords, see notes 6, 20 and 112 in this chapter.

supplies which towns frequently tried to regulate; up to a point, feudal decentralisation could support both extensive and intensive types of growth.[34] Yet the lords' and towns' main purpose in stimulating trade was to maximise rent streams from their fiscal and jurisdictional rights. Since those rights were also a fundamental aspect of their social and political powers, the introduction of jurisdictionally 'free' trade would have reduced feudal and urban revenue and challenged the jurisdictional superiority of lord over peasant and town over country. Consequently, strong feudal and urban jurisdiction was incompatible with long-run economic growth. Not surprisingly, agricultural innovation appears to have been inversely correlated with the intensity of seigniorial rights, and rural industrial growth was inversely correlated with the jurisdictional powers of towns and lords.[35] The fundamental constraints in the feudal economy came from the market monopolies and other coordination failures arising from political and jurisdictional parcellization, rather than from technological inertia.

In principle, therefore, pre-modern feudal economies could develop along two opposite lines. They could either maintain and intensify the parcellization of sovereignty – a direction taken for example by the Polish Commonwealth, the German territorial states and Spanish Naples after the mid-seventeenth century – or evolve into more centralised and politically integrated states as occurred elsewhere. In most of western Europe, the use by feudal lords of their powers of coercion to tax and monopolise trade, which maintained the feudal economy permanently below its productive potential, was counterbalanced by the same elites' strategy of territorial expansion through war. Warfare was as much a part of the internal logic of feudalism as jurisdictional exploitation. Although the main goal of feudal territorial expansion through warfare was to broaden the lord's political and economic resource base, it also benefited the wider economy by increasing jurisdictional integration and reducing transaction costs within the new territory.[36] As we shall see, state formation also reduced the costs of modifying existing property rights and introducing new institutions: it lowered seigniorial dues, abolished or seriously weakened rival feudal and urban monopolies (prisoner's dilemmas), systematised and territorialised fragmented legal codes and legislation, weights and measures (coordination failures), limited opportunities for pillage and warfare, and

34 Capitalism is defined here by contrast as an economic system in which the majority of producers work for a wage, which is set competitively through markets, and the owners of capital stock compete on the market for profits based on marginal cost rather than for politically sanctioned rents. On this definition, the economy of pre-modern Europe at least up to the seventeenth century was largely feudal-tributary and not capitalist.

35 For agricultural innovation, see Campbell 1997b: 244–5; Verhulst 1985; Verhulst 1990: 25. For rural manufacture, see this book, Chapter 6.

36 See Contamine 1980. For jurisdictional integration, see Olson 1982: ch.5.

reduced rulers' opportunities to act as autocratic 'stationary bandits' against their subjects. State formation was thus a major cause – possibly *the* major driving force – of market integration and Smithian growth before the nineteenth century.

To sum up: economic development in the feudal system was the outcome of two countervailing forces, the one pressing for military and jurisdictional decentralisation, the other pushing for increased political and jurisdictional centralisation. In the long run, the latter won out, lowering transaction costs and stimulating commercialisation and specialisation. The 'prime mover' and 'contradiction' within the feudal mode of production lay in relations between lords, peasants, markets and the state.

'Creative destruction' and institutional integration

If we take population growth as an approximate measure of economic growth, as the research I have summarised implies, the evidence of an economic slowdown in many parts of early fourteenth-century western Europe is hard to gainsay.[37] But if as has been suggested demographic stagnation was a consequence primarily of preventive rather than positive checks, what was causing economic opportunities to contract?

I pointed out previously that neither the demographic slowdown nor the increasing incidence of famines prove that the population was outstripping available resources, and I suggested that the increased volatility of grain prices, the socially unequal exposure to famine, and the highly variable patterns of demographic change observed around the turn of the fourteenth century were caused by institutional bottlenecks to specialisation through trade.[38] Where opportunities for agricultural intensification and specialisation were being foreclosed and the costs of transporting grain to meet local shortages increased, the incidence of famines and price volatility rose also; vice versa, because peasants respond only to price changes they expect to be permanent, higher price volatility led them to defer investments and to 'retreat' from the market.[39] The rising incidence of feudal warfare from the 1280s and 1290s – which has been connected to a more generalised 'late medieval crisis of order' – was particularly disruptive, not so much because of the destruction wrought, which was localised, but because it

---

37 See Galloway 1988 for evidence of the positive link between demographic and economic growth in early modern Europe.

38 An institutional interpretation of this kind explains better than technological factors the marked regional and local differences in demographic performance, because institutional frameworks were subject to greater local variation than technology.

39 Nerlove 1958: 82–6, 210–15. Peasants or farmers expect prices to follow a 'random walk', where any change of price, if any, is random; see Persson 1999 for explicit modelling of pre-modern grain prices along these lines.

gave rise to heavier taxation, to distraint and purveyance of commodities to supply armies, to commercial upheaval, and to higher and more volatile prices.[40] Societies responded to hardship by deferring marriage and procreation or, if serfdom did not tie peasants to the land, by migrating. On the other hand, where institutional and market conditions were more stable, the population continued to expand. Thus in central and southern Castile the thirteenth-century *reconquista* opened up unsettled lands for which the number of immigrants was too *small* and, not surprisingly, the alleged symptoms of a Ricardo-Malthusian crisis (stagnant or declining population, volatile and rising prices and land fragmentation) in this region were muted; Castile's principal economic constraint arose from a *lack* rather than an *excess* of population.[41]

Elsewhere the economic slowdown resulted from growing competitive rent-seeking by feudal lords – including towns which possessed significant jurisdictional rights over the countryside, as in parts of Italy, Flanders and possibly Catalonia – in pursuit of the profits of trade, stable food supplies, and for territorial enlargement. In sum, the slow build-up of royal, seigniorial and urban levies and the increased incidence of warfare from the last two decades of the thirteenth century raised the risk threshold of specialisation and reduced incentives for agricultural innovation. The fact that these bottlenecks were not present everywhere to the same extent explains why the population in some regions kept on growing. Where and when an economic slowdown did occur, it was less a technologically-determined 'agrarian crisis' than an institutionally induced 'crisis of distribution'.[42]

Although there is considerable disagreement over the effects of the

40 On the late medieval crisis of order, see Kaeuper 1988: 170–83. The economic conse-
    quences of late thirteenth- and early fourteenth-century warfare are particularly well
    studied for England, where however, by contrast with most other European countries,
    the higher nobility sided with the monarchy rather than against it. See Maddicott 1975
    (who on pp.70–5 qualifies the 'Postan thesis' along the lines sketched here); Prestwich
    1972; Harriss 1975; Miller 1975; Kaeuper 1988 (with extensive bibliography) also dis-
    cusses France. Mate 1982 suggests that large landowners could protect themselves more
    easily against military-induced pressures than smallholders. Bailey 1998a links high price
    volatility in pre-Black Death England to inefficient markets and frequent disruptions to
    food distribution; see also Zulaica Palacios 1994: 39, 44, 81–2; Epstein 2000c. On the
    other hand, the very nature of these disruptions to trade would have tended to keep
    supply crises localised (Berthe 1984: 240 for Navarre).
41 Valdeon Baruque 1971; Mackay 1977; see also Sesma Muñoz 1995 for economic expan-
    sion in southern Aragon between 1250 and 1350. The demographic consequences of the
    Black Death were equally muted; the Castilian population had already begun to recover
    in the early fifteenth century (Yun 1994).
42 For urban lordship as a source of profit, see Miller and Hatcher 1995: 285–90; Nicholas
    1971; and this book, Chapters 4–7. For a regional example of the intensification of rural
    conflicts over access to land, pastoral rights and water scarce resources and of increased
    rural banditry from the early fourteenth century, see Berthe 1984: 258–65.

crisis and of the pandemic shock caused by the Black Death, it is generally agreed that it marked a watershed in the transition to capitalism.[43] For Brenner, the development of agrarian capitalism required the expulsion of the self-sufficient and market-averse peasantry from the land. This however only occurred in England; elsewhere, the 'crisis' actually reinforced the feudal mode of production based on an independent peasantry or on serfdom. According to Wallerstein and, more ambiguously, to Braudel, the crisis set the stage for the transition to 'merchant capitalism' and to a 'capitalist world system' with parts of western Europe at its core.[44] Both interpretations assume that the transition to capitalism was set in motion by factors external to feudalism itself, as indeed follows logically from the assumption that feudalism possessed no internal dynamic for growth. Brenner sees the *deus ex machina* as the balance of class power determined by historically contingent national characteristics ('the peculiarity of the English'); for Braudel and Wallerstein, the overseas discoveries offered the necessary markets to pull the medieval economy out of stagnation. The most frequently heard answer to Dobb's old question whether there was a 'prime mover' within feudalism bringing about the transition to the capitalist mode of production is a clear and resounding no.[45]

In view of the foregoing discussion, however, the economic dynamic of feudalism is better explained in terms of two positive endogenous forces, market production and political centralisation. The Black Death emerges as an exogenous event which contributed to the feudal economy's transition from a low-level 'equilibrium trap' to a higher growth path by sharply intensifying pressures that had been building up over centuries.[46] Since the late eleventh century, increasingly powerful political and economic forces had been pressing for territorial and jurisdictional simplification, thereby reducing transaction costs and increasing the influence of the market. Pressures towards integration had come to a head during the last decades of the thirteenth century, as 'state warfare' broke out across the British Isles, France, Flanders, southern Germany, Prussia, Italy and Iberia; the two Hundred Years Wars between England and France and between Catalonia-Aragon, Sicily and Naples were its most salient manifestations. War required taxation, and taxation required forms of political consensus building, of state sovereignty, and of administrative resources that were quantitatively and

---

43 The views of Le Roy Ladurie (1966), who observed no fundamental discontinuity between the economy of 1300 and that of 1550, are in a clear minority.

44 Brenner 1982; Wallerstein 1974; Braudel 1982. Their position is hard to distinguish from that of Sweezy 1950.

45 Dobb 1946: ch.2.

46 See B. F. Harvey 1991 and Herlihy 1997 for the suggestion that the Black Death was the sole cause of the transition. The Black Death was exogenous in a non-trivial sense because it was unpredictable.

qualitatively new.[47] Even without the shock of the Black Death, in other words, pressures for political centralisation generated within feudal society itself would, over time, have lowered transaction costs, improved incentives for trade and specialisation, and slowly raised the economy to a higher growth path. By shifting the bargaining power between land and labour so rapidly, however, the fourteenth-century pandemic turned a comparatively smooth evolutionary process into a wave of Schumpeterian 'creative destruction' driven by heightened political and economic struggle.[48]

Supported by a wealthier peasant elite whose bargaining powers were inflated by the shortage of labour, and by many urban elites who stood to gain from weaker feudal rights and levies, aspiring rulers increased the jurisdictional integration of their territories, making markets more competitive, stimulating commercialisation and setting the stage for the long sixteenth-century boom.[49] The extent of jurisdictional integration was, however, defined by institutional and political factors which differed between states and which also established the parameters for further integration. To the extent that jurisdictional integration defined the basic incentive structures for specialisation and trade, the late medieval crisis caused greater economic integration *within* politically bounded regions at the same time that it defined the institutional parameters for subsequent divergence *between* regions.

Much of the debate on the late medieval economy has focused on the demand side, especially on the extent to which changes in the bargaining power of lords and labourers improved the standard of living of the poor. It is indeed clear that, despite significant regional differences in the extent of income distribution and in patterns of consumption, personal welfare did for the most part increase after the Black Death. Rising levels

---

47 Genet 1995. For a succinct discussion of the institutional, economic and legal causes of the Anglo-French war, see Allmand 1988: 6–12. For the effects of increased warfare after 1282 on long distance, mainly maritime trade, see Munro 1997: 65–87. For the growth of late medieval taxation, see Ormrod 1995; Bonney 1999; Pezzolo 2000.

48 Bois 1984 also integrates warfare in his model of the feudal economy, but only emphasises its destructive consequences while disregarding the benefits of political consolidation. The many urban and rural insurrections after 1350 still await a modern comparative examination; see Mollat and Wolff 1970; Fourquin 1972; Hilton and Aston 1984 for references. These eruptions were one aspect of far broader and more long-lasting struggles over the limits, prerogatives and duties of the state over the issues of justice, taxation and political representation, which can only be touched upon briefly here. For recent discussions of late medieval state formation along these lines, see Spruyt 1994; Ertman 1997. The concession of charters of incorporation, of the status of county corporate, and of other privileges and liberties to English towns after the Black Death was an important aspect of royal bargaining for taxes (Ormrod 1990: chs. 6, 9; Palliser 2000).

49 There is no need to labour the point that the economic consequences of political integration were largely unintentional. For a discussion of the fundamentally political objectives of market integration, see Chapter 4 of this book.

of consumption are well attested for meat, cheese, butter and beer (the latter in central and northern Europe) and, in Mediterranean countries, for wine, olive oil, fruit and vegetables, while probate inventories, dowries, and archaeological excavations show marked increases in the use of cheap cloth, crockery, wooden utensils and suchlike. These changes are rarely quantifiable, but an example from the unusually well-documented Genoese tolls on consumer goods demonstrate the shift very clearly. Between 1341 and 1398, the city's population fell from 60,000–65,000 to 36,000–40,000 (a loss of 40 per cent), tolls on foreign cloth imports collapsed by 61 per cent, but tolls on local cloth consumption rose by 3 per cent and those on wine consumption fell by only 25 per cent.[50]

It has recently been suggested that relative changes in living standards in pre-statistical societies can be estimated as the difference between the annual rate of growth in urbanisation and in total population.[51] Applying this method to late medieval Italy results in average improvements to living standards of 30 per cent between 1300 and 1500, albeit with most of the gains concentrated in the South, a conclusion in keeping with the narrative literature. A similar calculation applied to England suggests average gains of 60–70 per cent between the 1330s and the 1520s and supports Mayhew's recent estimate of a near doubling in per caput income between 1300 and 1470. England's considerably larger gains than Italy are due to the fact that England was still a much poorer country which was entering a long phase of catch-up growth.[52] The oft-quoted description of the late Middle Ages as the 'golden age of the peasant and labourer' appears on the whole to be correct.[53]

---

50 Day 1963: xxviii–xxx.
51 The method assumes that the rate of urbanisation is a relative measure of specialisation and productivity; if urbanisation rises relative to the total population, average living standards also increase (Craig and Fisher 2000: ch.6).
52 Mayhew 1995: 241. The quantity of currency per caput rose 50–100 per cent between the early fourteenth century and the mid-fifteenth, despite which payments in kind and barter also increased (Britnell 1993: 183–5). My estimates are based on the relative share of urban wealth as revealed in the tax assessments of 1334 and 1524 (listed in Bridbury 1962: 111), and on populations of 5 and 2.3 million at the two dates. In the subsequent debate Bridbury successfully defended his use of the tax assessments to estimate changes in the relative wealth of town and country (Rigby 1986; Bridbury 1986). Calculations for Italy are based on data in Malanima 1998. For a discussion of the productivity gap between early fourteenth-century England and northern Italy, see Persson 1993.
53 Abel 1980; Dyer 1989a and 1989b. For a contrasting view (based on trends in Flemish and English building wages in the period 1350–1400), see Munro 1997: 72–4, discussed further in Chapter 6, note 1. While Postan (1973) accepted that the bargaining power of peasants and wage earners improved after the Black Death, he suggested that this caused a decrease in work effort as low earners could achieve their target incomes more easily. The hypothesis of a 'backward bending supply curve of labour' also seems to underlie Wallerstein's argument that the economic crisis required the discovery of new external markets, and Brenner's claim that peasants had to be deprived of land ownership to get 'agrarian capitalism' on its feet.

The past focus on grain production has however diverted attention from more significant developments in the structures of supply that led to the deepening (an increase in the volume, number and quality of commodities exchanged) and widening (an increase in geographical size) of the market. Market deepening entailed three related phenomena: first, the previously mentioned increase in per caput *consumption* of already commercialised goods with higher elasticity of demand; second, an increase in the traded *proportion* of total output (greater 'commercialisation'), reflected for example in the development across late medieval Europe of rural cloth and metal industries; third, an increase in the traded *range* of consumer goods. These processes, which were the outcome of major social, technological and institutional change, show striking structural similarities with the 'industrious revolution' of the seventeenth century, whose most distinctive feature was the increase in labour inputs in response to a growing range of consumer goods.[54]

One reason why real demand appears to have increased during the late Middle Ages is that the Black Death reduced the proportion of un- or under-employed in the population and increased labour participation.[55] The widespread commutation after 1350 of servile labour dues to market-based tenancy contracts, occurred in response to increased peasant resistance against coerced labour, but it also aligned the tenant's incentives more closely with those of the landlord and increased the quality and intensity of peasant labour. Weaker seigniorial control over peasant labour and land markets made the peasantry more responsive to commercial stimuli.[56] The diffusion of crops like rice, sugarcane, olive oil and wine in southern Europe, hops in north-central Europe, and woad, madder and flax helped distribute labour inputs more evenly during the year so that the same amount of land could produce more with less labour.[57] It is also possible that more unmarried women were employed in the urban service sector, particularly in the

54 de Vries 1994; see also Goldthwaite 1993.
55 See Hatcher 1994: 26–7; Penn and Dyer 1990. De Vries 1992: 62 suggests on the basis of stricter definitions of religious festivities that the length of the work year diminished in the fifteenth-century Netherlands owing to the labourers' stronger bargaining powers; see also Persson 1984. Elsewhere, however, no change in the length of the working year has been detected after the Black Death (see e.g Roncière 1976 for Florence), suggesting that the changes identified by de Vries were part of a more determined campaign by the late medieval Church to enforce religious festivities rather than of worker mobilization.
56 The economic as opposed to the social gains from the late medieval commutation of servile labour have not attracted much attention; see however Dyer 1989a: 130–1; Britnell 1993: 223. For a demonstration of the lower productivity of servile compared to wage labour, see Stone 1997. Clark 1987 addresses the role of labour intensity for pre-modern agricultural productivity.
57 Bautier 1967: 13–16; Watson 1983; Tits-Dieuaide 1981; Sivéry 1973: 327.

production and petty trade of clothing and food, and that the growth of rural manufacture required greater labour inputs by children and women. Both developments may explain the apparent increase after the Black Death of restrictions to female craft labour in towns.[58]

Gains in labour productivity and increased labour force participation were matched by institutional and technical changes that increased regional specialisation.[59] If the average per caput value of trade increased after the Black Death, as the preceding argument implies, transaction costs at the margin must also have risen. Conversely, since a large proportion of trading costs was fixed, there were economies of scale to be exploited through more efficient distribution systems. The latter were expressed at the micro-level in a sharp increase in service and supply trades such as butchers, brewers, corn chandlers, and bakers, and at the macro-level by the growing integration of territorial states. At its simplest, the jurisdictional integration of a territory – technically a form of customs union – reduced feudal and urban tariffs, raised domestic competition, and intensified deflationary pressures on the price of cheaper, bulk commodities on which the marginal effect of tariffs was high.[60]

The late Middle Ages witnessed some of the most wide-ranging attempts in Europe before the eighteenth-century and Napoleonic reforms to overcome coordination problems by integrating money and coinage and standardising measurements at the regional or national level. While monetary agreements between independent lords and towns had been common during the twelfth and particularly the thirteenth century, the pace of development quickened during the later Middle Ages. Monetary unions flourished after 1350 in Alsace, Swabia, Franconia, in the Upper Rhineland and the Netherlands, and elsewhere in south-western and western Germany, in reaction to the political and monetary disintegration that followed the fall of the Hohenstaufen.[61] In the regional states of Italy, coinage by individual city-states was supplanted by the mintings of the dominant city, Milan, Florence or Venice. In France, the royal silver *blanc* engaged in a struggle for hegemony over monetary regions that had themselves only recently emerged from feudal fragmentation. Inasmuch as political fragmentation gave rise to coordination

---

58   Goldberg 1992; Poos 1991; Howell 1986;Wiesner 1986; Knotter 1994. See however Bailey 1996 and 1998b: 300 for doubts concerning the English evidence.

59   The argument here follows the model of endogenous innovation proposed by Young 1993, in which the growth in market size and improved skills (knowledge) stimulate invention and innovation by raising the rate of return to investment. See note 87 of this chapter.

60   For examples of tariff reductions, see Daviso di Charvensod 1961; Bergier 1963a: 175–80; Bergier 1975; Zulaica Palacios 1994: 45, 56. For the stricter enforcement of political frontiers, see MacKay 1987.

61   Wielandt 1971: 664, with references; Scott 1997: ch.6.

failures and to competitive devaluation, political integration may also have reduced the frequency of, and incentives for, monetary debasement.[62]

The growing internationalisation of large coins also helped to lower commercial transaction costs. The use of gold coinage mainly for large internal and international payments, which made it less susceptible to local abuse, became more common; in the Hansa area of influence gold coins account for one-fifth of all hoards in the fourteenth century, but the proportion rises to four-fifths in the fifteenth.[63] In the course of the four-teenth century the Florentine florin and the Venetian ducat established international benchmarks for national gold currencies; only England, the fifteenth-century Rhineland principalities, and briefly France minted gold coins of a different standard.[64]

The proliferation of local measurements typical of post-Carolingian Europe was not simply a time-consuming nuisance and a constant cause of commercial friction; it was also an important source of fraud. Measurements, moreover, were one of the most visible signs of sovereignty; their regulation and simplification was thus an important symbol of the growing reach of the state. While the extreme localisation and fragmen-tation of measures made unification hard to police and enforce, efforts to establish common 'regional' or 'national' measurements intensified after the Black Death. Even in England, where the monarchy had been attempting to unify the country's measures for centuries, the enforcement of common national standards became a matter of growing concern during the fourteenth century.[65]

Lower trading costs and states' ability to enforce contracts more effec-tively and over larger areas as a consequence of changes in the institutions of justice also contributed to a sharp rise after 1350 in seasonal and annual fairs specialising in regional and inter-regional trade. These fairs, which reduced search costs for traders and producers and which may have contributed to the emergence of a Transalpine network of petty traders, provided institutional backing for market inte-gration.[66] Localised demographic shocks stimulated the rise of more integrated labour markets for unskilled labour, particularly for seasonal migrants between uplands and lowlands and between differently specialised lowland regions; it seems likely that rural hiring fairs emerged

---

62 Cipolla 1963b. Kindleberger 1991: 167-9 makes the similar point, that political frag-mentation and the lack of effective central authority in the Holy Roman Empire exacerbated monetary devaluation during the *Kipper und Wipperzeit* of 1619–23. The implication that political centralisation was making late medieval states financially more reliable is supported by the developments in interest rates discussed later.

63 Sprandel 1971: 354.

64 Spufford 1988: 319–21.

65 Zupko 1977: ch.2. See also Held 1918; Wielandt 1971: 678; Le Mené 1982: 33–48; Epstein 1992: ch.3.

66 Fontaine 1996; this book, Chapter 4.

or were developed further to coordinate these labour flows.[67] The period also witnessed regional and inter-regional agreements between towns and specialised master artisans, the development of journeymen associations, and the establishment of technical entry tests for masters who were not locally trained, all with the aim of improving the quality and market for skilled labour.[68] In Germany, territorial lords acted increasingly as mediators between iron miners, and brokered industrial alliances that benefited from economies of scale in production.[69]

A well-established though more circuitous way to lower tariffs and the associated customs formalities that was extremely popular among towns and large trading companies like the *Ravensburger Gesellschaft* and the Augsburg Walser was to seek toll exemptions from their main commercial counterparts. These agreements differed from standard mercantile franchises by being restricted to specific communities within a state rather than applying indiscriminately to an entire country, possibly because states were increasingly loath to jeopardise valuable taxes, but also because patterns of trade between towns were becoming more settled and predictable.[70] Of equal importance was the disappearance during the fifteenth century of the law of reprisal, whereby governments granted creditors the right to seize the goods of a debtor or of the latter's countrymen on the basis of the principle of collective liability. Reprisals and collective liability were not merely ineffective and highly damaging to trade, but constituted a practical admission of political and judicial failure. As legal systems became more formalised, commercial laws more sophisticated, and state jurisdictions less contested, individual responsibility replaced collective liability and the costs and benefits of trade could be more clearly apportioned.[71]

Evidence that markets were becoming safer and more integrated comes in the first place from grain prices, which became more homogeneous and less volatile as barriers to trade within territorial states came down.[72] Equally strong proof of improvements in market structures comes from trends in investment, productivity and technological innovation. Probably the most remarkable evidence of structural improvements after the Black Death comes from the collapse in public and private interest rates. The

---

67 Viazzo 1989; Epstein 1998b; Penn and Dyer 1990.
68 Reininghaus 1981; Sortor 1993: 1494; Fourquin 1979: 286; Epstein 1998a.
69 Sprandel 1969: 310.
70 Bergier 1963a: 176; Epstein 1992: ch.3; Kleineke 1997. Toll immunities were nothing new (Masschaele 1997: 111–13); what changed was the geographical scale at which they were applied. Changing patterns of trade are revealed by the stabilisation of urban hierarchies; see this book, Chapter 5.
71 The rise and fall of the medieval laws of reprisal lack a modern, comparative study. The law of reprisal attracted the interest of nineteenth-century legal historians; see de Mas-Latrie 1866; Astorri 1993: 70–2 (reprisals were being phased out by Florence in the early fifteenth century); Timbal 1958: 137 (reprisals fell out of use in France in the early sixteenth century).
72 See Chapter 7 of this book; also Unger 1983; Tits-Dieuaide 1975: 255–6; Poehlmann 1993.

decades after the Black Death saw a major change of trend in European interest rates, which set in motion a gradual decline in the real cost of capital that lasted up to the eighteenth century. Interest rates paid by larger monarchies dropped from 20–30 per cent before the Black Death to 8–10 per cent in the early sixteenth century, and from 15 to 4 per cent in the more advanced Italian, German and Netherlands cities over the same period. The development is particularly striking because it took place at a time of increasing warfare and of increased political and commercial insecurity. In Italy, for example, official interest rates in Florence, Venice and Genoa fell at the same time as their combined consolidated debts soared from 2 to 9.5 million florins in the space of two generations (c.1340–80). Heightened military risk was evidently more than compensated by improved contract enforcement, which raised the reliability of borrowers and reduced the probability of default, and by the growing sophistication of local, national and international financial markets. As we discussed in the previous chapter, the major force driving fiscal and financial convergence among Continental states was the growth of international military competition.[73]

The fall in the expected rates of return and cost of capital for individuals was nearly as impressive.[74] The cost of capital in England declined from a rate of 9.5–11 per cent which had prevailed between 1150 and 1350, to 7 per cent in the half century after the Black Death and to only 4.5 per cent by the late fifteenth century; proportionally similar gains occurred elsewhere in Europe. By the second half of the fifteenth century, Europeans were enjoying a huge 'free lunch' consisting of a more than doubling in the amount of capital available per person. The effect will have been a massive substitution of capital for labour (Figure 3.1).[75] Although the reasons for the decline in interest rates have not attracted much discussion, several of the factors examined previously played a role. They included a sharp decline in commercial and institutional risk as state authorities became more reliable and their judicial apparatuses improved;

73 See Chapter 2 and Figure 2.1.
74 For rates to approximate the cost of capital, credit markets have to be capable of assessing risk and exact interest rates accordingly. Few historians would argue that risk was not assessed in this way by the later middle ages, although the extent of market power (competition) and institutional efficiency (integration) in pre-modern credit markets has still to be examined in detail.
75 Identification of interest rates (based on perpetual rents on land) with national boundaries does not imply that pre-modern credit markets were integrated, and in fact it is unlikely that they were (Buchinsky and Polak 1993); our concern is with the long-run trend. The interest rate charged in England for more risky investments like grain storage declined proportionally, from 12–13 per cent in 1260–1400 (Brunt and Cannon 1999) to 7.23 per cent in London in 1770–1800 (Clark 1988: 275–6). Clark's figures for perpetual rents in France between 1400 and 1600 are probably too high, as implied by Rosenthal 1993: 134, who reports significantly lower rates for the seventeenth century.

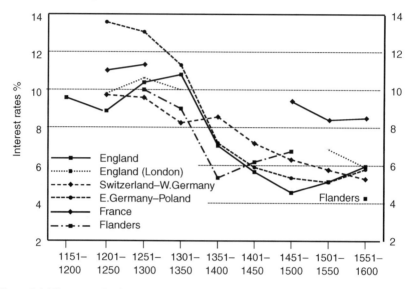

Figure 3.1 The cost of private capital in Europe, 1200–1600 (interest rates)

Sources: Clark 1988: 273–4 (figures for England are the average of perpetual rent changes and the rent/price ratio on land); Keene and Harding 1987; Thoen 1988 vol.2: 911–12; Neumann 1865: 266–73

increased opportunities for investment as market barriers declined; and a growing range of consumer goods which raised the individual propensity to save. Investments after the Black Death became safer, more easily available, and more valuable because profits could be spent on a broader array of goods.

The lower cost of capital made a vital contribution to the most significant long-term effect of market integration, which is to increase investment and specialisation. These effects can best be traced through changing patterns of urbanisation, which reflect both the division of labour between 'town' (where the industrial and service sectors were concentrated) and 'country' (where the primary sector predominated), and the degree of specialisation among towns.

Rates of urbanisation generally increased after the Black Death as marketing and distribution systems improved: more people lived in towns because they could be supplied more easily with food, and because more efficient labour markets made it easier to respond to short-term fluctuations in rural demand for agricultural labour at harvest time.[76] However, most gains in urbanisation occurred in the less advanced regions of southern and north-western Italy, and in other comparatively backward

---

76   For rising urbanisation, see de Vries 1984: 41–3; for general constraints on premodern urbanisation, see Grantham 1993 and 1997a.

economies like Castile, Portugal, Holland, northern and southern Germany, Bohemia, Poland and, possibly, England. By contrast, after 1350 urbanisation in the more developed economies of Flanders, Tuscany, Sicily and Catalonia stagnated or declined, perhaps indicating that these regions were facing structural barriers to further growth.[77]

The growing proportion of town dwellers was matched by the rise of more clearly defined regional urban hierarchies; due to its high degree of political centralisation, England was the first country to develop a rudimentary national urban system.[78] Although urban hierarchies at the beginning of the sixteenth century appear retrospectively to be strictly regional and 'medieval', they were in fact largely the outcome of the late medieval crisis. As with the development of national urban hierarchies in the seventeenth century, the rise of regional hierarchies during the fourteenth and fifteenth centuries was hastened by political centralisation, which weakened traditional urban economic prerogatives, reduced barriers to trade between towns, and concentrated an unprecedented volume of administrative and fiscal resources within newly designated regional and national capitals. The economies of scale and agglomeration brought about by growing urban competition and larger markets were also reflected in the growing concentration in towns of more specialised cloth industries and in the increased specialisation of craft guilds on the one hand, and in the development of regional 'protoindustrial' clusters on the other.[79]

Market deepening and widening also intensified Ricardian specialisation based on comparative advantage. A salient instance of this was the development of a pan-European cattle trade after 1400, and similar albeit less far-flung trade networks developed for metals (copper, iron, tin and silver), salt and grain.[80] The latter were probably the result of growing intra-industry trade between diversifying countries. Industrial and agricultural regions and industrial districts specialising in cheap and medium

---

77 See Chapter 5, note 11.
78 Chittolini 1987; de Vries 1984; Chevalier 1982: ch.2; Lesger 1994; Galloway 2000; this book, Chapter 5. Urban hierarchies are measured against a benchmark consisting of the 'rank-size rule', in which the population of a city with rank R equals the population of the largest city divided by its rank; thus, the population of the third largest city will be one third of that of the largest city in the hierarchy. Since urban size reflects the concentration (specialisation) of activities and functions, market integration (which increases specialisation) will increase differences in size and rank between cities. The actual 'rank-size distribution' should therefore more closely approximate the theoretical 'rank-size rule' as markets become more integrated.
79 For industrial concentration and craft specialisation, see Fourquin 1979: 282–3; Persson 1988. Greater division of labour *within* crafts is evidence of external economies reaped through larger markets rather than of internal industrial economies, which were not large. For regional clustering, see below, Chapter 6.
80 For the cattle trade, see Blanchard 1986; Sivéry 1976: 604–5; Scott 1996: 8–9. For the metals, salt and grain, see Kellenbenz 1986; Bridbury 1955.

quality cloth-making, mining and metal-working, glass and timber, silk, olive oil and livestock arose across Europe, becoming in many cases the direct precursors of early modern 'protoindustries'.[81]

None the less, pervasive fiscal, monetary and linguistic barriers to trade and factor mobility between states, along with rising jurisdictional integration within states, made domestic specialisation the less costly option. Political integration diverted trade towards domestic markets.[82] The weaker synchronicity of epidemics across Europe during the fifteenth century compared with the second half of the fourteenth, and the considerable discrepancies in the timing of demographic recovery, which range from the late fourteenth century or early 1400s in Castile and Flanders to the 1440s in Italy and southern France, and to the last quarter of the fifteenth century in parts of central Europe and England, also imply that the European economy was becoming more regionalised.[83] Despite the rise of proto-national states in Castile, Burgundy and France, the economic landscape of Renaissance Europe remained obstinately regional as a result of the 'late medieval contraction and concentration of political power'.[84]

The strong growth throughout Europe after the mid-fourteenth century of rural and small town manufacture, particularly of the textile industries, after the mid-fourteenth century which bears a striking resemblance to seventeenth-century 'protoindustrialisation', will be discussed more fully in Chapter 6. Briefly put, the common opinion that the 'ruralisation' of industry was simply a response by urban merchants and manufacturers to the increased wage costs and restrictive practices of craft manufacturers in the towns is too simplistic. Late medieval 'protoindustrialisation' was not a zero-sum game in which gains by one party matched equivalent losses by the other; nor, in most cases, was the spread of manufacture beyond the town walls simply a form of by-employment in marginal, upland regions where agricultural returns were too low for peasant survival, as established models of protoindustrialisation argue. The spread of country crafts gave rise to a more complex and sophisticated regional division of labour. It was a central element in the reorganisation of rural and urban industry and agriculture described in this chapter, whose consequences would be felt for centuries. It was also, however, the

---

81 For regional specialisation, see Bautier 1967; Epstein 1991. For late medieval protoindustry, see Chapter 6.

82 Carus-Wilson 1950–51 implies the same in arguing that England's cloth industry benefited after the 1320s from the temporary interruption of trade with Flanders, and was later able to capture foreign markets owing to the political upheavals among its major rivals, the north Italian and Flemish towns.

83 For the weaker synchronicity of epidemics, see Del Panta 1980: 118.

84 Bautier 1967. Regional economies diverged strongly after the Black Death even in a relatively more integrated economy like England's; see Schofield 1965. On 'contraction and concentration', see Scott 1997: 175.

scene of extensive and vigorous conflicts between the established urban producers and the up-and-coming small towns and rural communities. More than any other sector of the economy (with the possible exception of the market for grain), late medieval regional crafts became a focus of lively contestation in the arena of the territorial state. Crucially, the success of regional crafts was inversely proportional to the concentration of economic and institutional power in the hands of a dominant city. Inter-urban rivalry, frequently reinforced by princes sympathetic to the endeavours of small towns and villages, was a condition for the new industries' success. The balance of power between princes, chartered towns, and the territory therefore played a critical role in late medieval 'protoindustrial' success.[85]

Growing regional trade and labour market integration, and particularly the increasing mobility of masters and tramping journeymen, more than compensated for declining population by stimulating technological diffusion.[86] By exposing a larger proportion of the population to new technology, market integration may also have increased the rate of invention.[87] Higher rates of investment spurred by rising demand and declining real interest rates fostered the diffusion and refinement of existing products and the development of new ones. Improvements to consumer goods include the mass diffusion of linen underwear [88](which raised standards of cleanliness with unquantifiable benefits for public health and created a source of cheap linen rags for the kind of higher quality, more durable paper needed for movable type printing);[89] the diffusion of 4- and 5-needle knitting, which created a new stocking and cap industry from scratch;[90] the creation of transportable hard cheese (*caciocavallo* and Parmesan) and of *maccheroni* pasta in Italy;[91] the

---

85 See Epstein 2000a: ch. 1.

86 Between 1380 and 1480, no less than 20 per cent of Florentine weavers came from outside Tuscany. Between 1430 and 1455, 55 per cent of weavers came from an area including Holland, Flanders, Brabant, northern France, and northern and southern Germany. This *Italienische Reise* also took in other Tuscan cities in addition to Venice, Milan, Vicenza and Rome. Significantly, 'German' workers, who appear to have replaced Florentine labourers who left the city following the Ciompi revolt of 1378, were given the better quality cloths to weave (Franceschi 1993: 119–35). Stromer 1978: 140–1 speculates on how by decimating the rural craft base and destroying inherited technical know-how, the Black Death speeded the adoption in Swabia of the new techniques of fustian weaving brought by Lombard immigrants. For the effects of German immigration to France, see Sprandel 1964.

87 For historical and theoretical models of endogenous technological change, see Persson 1988; Sokoloff 1988; Romer 1990 and 1994; Young 1993 and 1998.

88 Heers 1976.

89 Paper manufacturing reached Germany in the last decades of the fourteenth century (Boorsch and Orenstein 1997: 4).

90 Turnau 1983.

91 Epstein 1992: 174; Miani 1964: 578 note 2; Sereni 1981: 323–5.

increased use of barrels for transporting wine, olive oil and other perishable products;[92] the development through selective cross-breeding of the Castilian *merino* sheep, which laid the base for the Spanish woollen industry's success in the fifteenth and sixteenth centuries;[93] the invention in the Low Countries and south-western England of ways of processing and preserving herring and pilchard directly on board fishing boats;[94] the transformation of glass into a middle-class commodity (glass panes became a common sight in the homes of the wealthier bourgeois, and the first glass-house for plants made its appearance in the Low Countries during the fifteenth century);[95] and the production of quality wines identified by their place of origin.[96]

Other better known inventions and innovations include, in the financial and commercial sectors, the development of an international market for state loans in Nuremberg;[97] the creation of the first chartered public banks in Barcelona (1401) and Genoa (1407); the diffusion of maritime insurance contracts and of bills of exchange, and the late fourteenth-century invention of double-entry book-keeping, and of the 'multinational' merchant company thanks to the invention of commercial correspondence that enabled merchants to sedentarise;[98] and the introduction of the compass, the invention by the Portuguese of nautical astronomy, and the rediscovery of the astrolabe.[99] Among the better known industrial innovations can be found the invention of the wire-drawing mill in southern Germany, which tripled productivity;[100] increases in the size and efficiency of traditional furnaces, which turned ceramics from a luxury good into a commodity; the invention of pure crystal glass in early fifteenth-century Venice;[101] the diffusion of the 'indirect method' of smelting, the invention of the blast furnace in the fifteenth century, and the improvements in underground drainage that made deep-shaft mining possible;[102] technical improvements to water locks for inland navigation and the introduction in 1407–8 of windmills for land drainage in Holland;[103] and the industrial production of gunpowder, portable guns and movable cannon.

---

92 Zug Tucci 1978.
93 Lopez 1953; Munro 1997: 46–8, 97 note 27; Iradiel Murugarren 1974.
94 Unger 1978; Kowaleski 2000.
95 Antoni 1982; Fourquin 1979: 293.
96 Melis 1984; Fourquin 1964: 89–90.
97 Stromer 1976.
98 De Roover 1953, 1956 and 1963; Melis 1991: 161–79, 239–53.
99 Kreutz 1973; Waters 1968.
100 Stromer 1977.
101 Jacoby 1993.
102 Sprandel 1969: 311–12 estimates that iron output increased from 25–30,000 tons in 1400 to 40,000 tons in 1500.
103 On water locks, see Henning 1991: 457; on windmills, see Hoppenbrouwers 1997: 106.

Social, political and economic upheaval and increased artisan mobility accelerated cross-fertilisation between industrial sectors and economic regions. Examples include the transmission of quality glass production from Venice to Bohemia; the sectorial (from the Italian cotton fustian industry to the woollen industry) and geographical diffusion and improvement of the great or Saxon spinning wheel, which hastened the replacement of combed with carded wool and allowed for productivity gains of up to 80 per cent;[104] the transmission via the Venetian and Florentine fleets of Mediterranean shipping technology to northern Europe, including the galley and, more significantly, the two- and three-masted carrack and caravel which gave rise by the late fifteenth century to 'the first truly European vessel, ending a major division in the Continent's maritime technology that had persisted since the early Middle Ages';[105] the adaptation of small fishing and river boats to short-haul coastal transport and the invention of the north Atlantic barge;[106] the 'cartographic revolution' that brought together the distinct traditions of portulan charts, 'imaginary' world maps, and 'empirical' local and regional maps to radically transform Europeans' knowledge and perceptions of their space;[107] the technical cross-fertilisation between metallurgy, goldsmithing and engraving that produced spring-driven clocks and watches and movable type; the increased application of water power for metalworking, for spinning wool (in fifteenth-century Cologne) and silk (particularly in Bologna, where it would make the fortunes of the city's early modern silk industry), and for grinding raw materials like woad and Sicilian sugar cane;[108] and the combination of European and Arab dyeing techniques, including the increased use of alum mordant.[109] Last but far from least, the fifteenth century witnessed the 'invention' by the Florentines and Venetians of the technological patent, a momentous development brought about by the increased mobility of 'secret'-bearing craftsmen, which sealed the final step in the cognitive shift from an impersonal to a personal view of technological progress.[110]

Although technical diffusion and integration were more easily achieved

104 For productivity gains see Chorley 1997: 10 (my estimate), who notes that spinning accounted for the highest proportion of the production costs of wool cloth. The council of Tortosa awarded a prize of ten florins in 1457 to the 'inventor' of a spinning wheel which 'did the work of three women' (Riu 1983: 227). For the transfer of the spinning wheel and carding from the fustian to the woollen industry, see Munro 1997: 53.
105 See Friel 1995: 169 and Unger 1980 for the carrack; Tranchant 1993: 14–23 for the galley.
106 Tranchant 1993: 11–12, 45–7.
107 P. D. A. Harvey 1991.
108 Endrei and Stromer 1974; Poni 1990; Epstein 1992.
109 Ploss 1973: 35, 42.
110 Long 1991.

in manufacture and trade than in agriculture, whose technologies tend to be location specific and require local adaptation to be successfully transferred, there was also a notable diffusion of agricultural best practice in the Upper and Lower Rhineland, the County of Flanders and the Low Countries, England (which introduced Flemish hops in the fifteenth century), and Lombardy and Tuscany. Peripheral regions like Zeeland, Poland and Russia introduced high medieval innovations like the heavy plough. In many cases innovation was instigated by the peasantry, possibly in response to the falling cost of capital.[111] Plants of Islamic origin like indigo, rice, spinach, sugarcane, artichokes, and probably eggplant, which had been little more than garden curiosities before the Black Death, became more widely accepted and spread across the western Mediterranean.[112]

The quickening pace of innovation in production and trade was reflected in the development of written and spoken languages. This was the period during which dominant 'national' or regional dialects began to emerge, with London English and Parisian *langue d'oil* leading the way. The creation of regional *linguae francae* in place of Latin marked the triumph of secular commercial, administrative and popular forces, and brought the languages of elites and masses closer to each other.[113] While impossible to quantify, the gradual standardisation of regional and national languages made communication for trade, for the settling of disputes in court (in 1362 English became the official language of legal proceedings), for the enforcement of legislation, or simply for travel, easier and more effective.

The process we have described bears more than a passing resemblance to the accelerated circulation of practices and ideas which historians traditionally term the Renaissance. This is not the place to address the recently revived debate on the relationship between the world of ideas and their material context during the later Middle Ages;[114] it is nonetheless significant that the metaphors of commerce, circulation and consumption are increasingly used to describe a phenomenon that was previously defined in strictly idealistic terms. The evidence reviewed suggests that the worlds of production and ideas were facing similar stimuli and pressures to open up to the new, the unusual and the unexpected, and that they responded in equally dynamic and innovative fashion.

---

111 Reinicke 1989: 327–34; Bentzien 1990: 105–31; Thoen 1990; Hoppenbrouwers 1997: 103–4; Langdon 1986; Postles 1989; Epstein 1998b; Watson1981: 76. For an analysis of agrarian technological diffusion which emphasises human capital and knowledge spillovers, see Foster and Rosenzweig 1995.
112 Watson 1983.
113 See Millward 1989: 122–4 and McIntosh 1986 for the insurgence of London and Chancery English.
114 Goldthwaite 1993; Jardine 1996; Grafton 1997.

Conclusion

The late medieval crisis was, as in the original meaning of the term 'crisis', a turning point. Unusually, a period of rapid and traumatic demographic collapse unleashed a process of 'creative destruction' which raised the west European economies to higher growth paths.[115] The crisis brought them closer to their technological frontier and established a new dynamic equilibrium. The acceleration in population growth rates across Europe after 1450 compared to the previous era of expansion before 1300 indicates that the late medieval crisis, which impelled state formation in western Europe, may have marked the most decisive step in the continent's long trajectory to capitalism and world hegemony.[116]

Development (structural change) combined with growth (rising income per head). Higher disposable income among the lower classes increased demand for a more varied diet and better made manufactured goods; higher levels of taxation to fund warfare may also have raised aggregate demand, although it is unclear to what extent states were simply appropriating a larger share of a stable or contracting feudal surplus.[117] But the demographic shock's most significant effects were institutional, because it sharply accelerated the process of political centralisation inherent to the feudal-tributary mode of production and intensified the competitive struggle between states and between institutional 'systems' (monarchical, republican and mixed) that had arisen in the eleventh and twelfth centuries. The reason why economic growth occurred despite demographic collapse was the dynamic force of the state.

Centralisation underlies all the major institutional changes to market structures previously described. It lowered domestic transport costs, made it easier to enforce contracts and to match demand and supply, intensified economic competition between towns and strengthened urban hierarchies, weakened urban monopolies over the countryside, and stimulated labour mobility and technological diffusion. Centralisation and territorial integration were nonetheless strongly contested by the more powerful feudal lords and towns; the extent of territorial integration was therefore determined by the balance of power between the four major political coalitions: central rulers, feudal lords, and urban and rural elites. As the following chapters show, the key to the different economic performances

---

115 For the standard argument that positive institutional and technological change occurs at times of rapid population *growth*, see North and Thomas 1973; North 1981; Persson 1988.

116 Compare the compound annual rate of demographic growth of 0.18 per cent between 1000 and 1300 with the near doubling of the rate to 0.34 per cent in 1400–1600 (calculated from Gunder Frank 1998: 168, 170). Although the figures' precision is spurious, their orders of magnitude are plausible.

117 Ormrod 1995: 157–9.

in late medieval and early modern regions can be found in the political economy of state formation and markets.

Although maritime trade and the overseas discoveries have often loomed large in explanations of the late medieval recovery, their effects appear on the whole rather marginal. Maritime exploration and discoveries played virtually no role in bringing the demographic crisis to an end. With the exception of England, where the population did not begin to recover before the 1490s, demographic recovery between the late fourteenth century in Flanders and the mid-fifteenth century in Italy, France, Iberia and Germany began several decades before the significance of the Portuguese expeditions of the 1430s was fully appreciated. In any case, the maritime discoveries of the 1490s are better seen as a continuation and syncretism of technology and information that evolved between the Mediterranean and North Sea areas during the previous decades, rather than a radical break with an inward-looking and depressed medieval world. Contrary, moreover, to the suggestion that a fifteenth-century 'bullion famine' caused "appalling direct effects on trade" by restricting the supply of credit, the sharp secular decline in interest rates between 1350 and 1500 proves that capital was not in short supply, and implies furthermore that American bullion, which only began to augment European silver supplies significantly from the 1530s, was neither necessary nor sufficient to sustain the recovery.[118]

Similar comments apply to the effects of maritime trade within Europe. Long-distance maritime trade during the demographic crisis contracted relative to trade overland or by sea within individual regions and began to expand significantly only after population had begun once more to expand.[119] The disruption of foreign trade by warfare may have accelerated a process of import substitution in the cloth industry and forced established urban industries like those of Flanders and Lombardy to specialise in higher value-added products with smaller overseas markets.[120] While the comparative buoyancy of medium-range shipping during the century after the Black Death was aided by the emergence of

118 See Spufford 1988: ch.15 for a summary of the literature on the 'bullion famine' (p.358 for the quotation); Day 1999: 23 and passim, claims that falling mine production and bullion imports between 1375 and 1475 caused a late medieval economic depression. However, Europe could not suffer a balance-of-payments deficit with the Near East (which is documented) and bullion shortage simultaneously, and money supply conditions varied significantly between regions (Sussman 1998). If, as the latter implies, the European bullion market was not integrated, arguments about a 'general bullion famine' are moot.

119 Postan 1952: 191–222; Kellenbenz 1986: 272–5. In the debate between Cipolla, Lopez and Miskimin (1964) on the late medieval 'crisis', the latter were concerned with long distance trade and were therefore more pessimistic, whereas the former based his more optimistic assessment on the rising volume of shorter-range trade.

120 van der Wee and Peters 1970; Munro 1991 and 1997: 65–87; also Chapter 6 of this book.

larger transport ships and of insurance based on value rather than weight, which reduced transport costs for bulk goods, the volume of longer-distance trade remained minuscule compared with that of domestic trade.[121] In fifteenth- and sixteenth-century Sicily, whose exports of grain, silk, sugar and lesser agricultural products made it one of the most open economies of pre-modern Europe, foreign trade accounted for no more than 15 per cent of GNP. In England, another major exporting nation, the proportion was less than 8 per cent.[122]

Finally, one may question Braudel and Wallerstein's opinion that merchant capitalism associated with long-distance trade and urban entrepôts constituted the main exogenous source of growth. Two examples, Tuscany and Holland, can illustrate the point. Tuscany before the Black Death was among the most developed economies in Europe, testified by a population density of 60 inhabitants/km², a rate of urbanisation close to 40 per cent, and the presence of an industrial, commercial and financial metropolis of 120,000 inhabitants. Holland by comparison was an under-populated and under-urbanised backwater. A century later, the economy of Tuscany was stagnating and Florence was quickly sliding down the urban ranks, whereas Holland was being transformed into one of the most advanced, urbanised and commercialised economies of Europe.[123]

Holland's main advantage over Tuscany was not its ease of access to the sea. The relative decline during the later Middle Ages of advanced maritime economies like Catalonia and Flanders goes to show that easy access to maritime trade and well-established mercantile and industrial communities did not provide a permanent comparative advantage. What allowed late medieval Holland to respond so effectively to the new opportunities at the cross-roads of the North Sea economies was an unusual degree of institutional flexibility born of weak seigniorial and urban jurisdictional powers. New towns could spring up and rural manufacture could flourish under weak monopolies and rent-seeking. The twin ecological challenges of sea and marshlands entrenched habits and institutions supporting collective cooperation. During the fifteenth century, Holland's urban ratio increased by a factor of two or three. In Tuscany, by contrast, Florence gained direct access to the sea in 1406, but the city's elites deployed their unrivalled authority to divert rent streams and to de-industrialise the region to their short-term benefit, with the result that territory's economy never reclaimed its medieval heights.[124]

---

121 On ships and insurance, see Unger 1980; Melis 1964.
122 Epstein 1992; Campbell 2000 (based upon the author's estimates for *c.*1300).
123 Epstein 1996b and also Chapter 6 of this book; Jansen 1978; Blockmans 1993; Hoppenbrouwers 2000; TeBrake 1988.
124 See Chapters 5 and 6.

The preceding discussion raises the broader question of what caused pre-modern economies to diverge. The pessimistic answer is that the long-run stability in per caput cereal consumption everywhere in pre-modern Europe outside England proves that, in fact, economic stagnation was the norm, and that early modern England is the one exception that proves the rule. The pessimists presume that pre-modern European economies outside England were fundamentally similar and imply that political, social and institutional differences did not much matter, thus leaving the English 'exception' an unexplained mystery. The more optimistic line pursued here is that measures of economic growth based strictly on cereal consumption underestimate per caput and GNP growth. They do not allow for increased consumer utility caused by better and more diverse food and by declining price volatility, to which the rise of more integrated markets during the later Middle Ages made a major contribution. Moreover, they ignore the fact that most pre-modern growth occurred in the manufacturing and service sectors rather than in cereal production, even though the precise gains cannot be measured very accurately.

The optimists therefore take evidence of some pre-modern growth to ask why there was not more. They emphasise regional diversity and consider its causes a puzzle to be explained. While this chapter has dwelt mainly on the common features of the late medieval crisis, it has also indicated how the political economy of the crisis could set regional economies on different paths. The answer does not lie, as Brenner has claimed, in whether the peasants or the landlords could claim full ownership of the land. Peasants were quite capable of raising land and labour productivity if they had the opportunity; on the other hand, landlords were quite happy *not* to embark on capitalist specialisation if faced with insufficient commercial incentives, as pre-modern Italy's 'failed transition' clearly shows.[125] Market structures rather than property rights to land determined regional growth paths; but market structures were the institutionalised outcome of complex social, economic and political struggles between sovereigns, feudal lords, cities and rural communities, and could therefore differ significantly between regions. The balance of power determined the extent to which income was redistributed, domestic transactions costs were reduced, gains from specialisation could be captured, low cost rural industries could develop, and the price of food supplies could be stabilised. Thus, although inter-regional trade and migration stimulated some degree of economic convergence, domestic political and market structures were fundamental for economic performance in the longer run.

125 See Epstein 1998b.

4   States and fairs

The late medieval crisis and institutional change

I argued in Chapter 3 that as shifts in income distribution, declining trans-action costs and rising labour productivity in the century after the Black Death increased market integration and regional specialisation, per caput trade must by implication have increased as well. However, the lack of quantitative sources means that the claim must be tested against more oblique indices of trade. Two such measures are used in this book: market integration, which figures more extensively in Chapter 7, and institutional changes aimed at reducing the cost of trade discussed here.

Had trade grown along the lines previously hypothesised, we would expect transaction costs to increase in two ways. As the average distance travelled by each unit rose, the average cost to transport, market, and exact payment for a unit of produce would also increase. Moreover, as peasants became more commercially oriented and specialised, the oppor-tunity costs of trade would also rise, as time spent taking produce to the market could be employed more profitably on the farm.[1] Consequently, rising transaction costs restricting the potential gains from trade would create strong incentives to organise markets more efficiently.

This chapter examines the proliferation of 'regional' fairs across Europe after the Black Death as an especially salient institutional response to increasingly complex patterns of trade and to the associated escalation of costs.[2] Regional fairs developed for the most part in the small towns and burgeoning villages which benefited particularly from late medieval

---

1   D. W. Jones 1978. Bois 1984: 365–7 claims in contrast that peasants spent more time on marketing when their surpluses were larger. For productivity gains from organisational change that reduces the proportion of a peasant household's labour devoted to non-agricultural activities ('Z-goods'), see Hymer and Resnick 1969.

2   I define 'regional' fairs as those with neither strictly local nor purely 'international' functions, occurring only a few times a year, lasting usually more than one day, and often having toll exemptions and other privileges that daily and weekly markets lacked.

political and economic upheavals.[3] The fairs provided the organisational backbone to an emerging continental trading system which connected local, regional and continental markets, and they challenged the trading privileges and monopolies of the established cities and towns. The economic and the political aspects of fair foundations were therefore strongly related.

Purpose

Most studies of the late medieval economy have ignored the rise of the new fairs on the grounds that they were a defensive measure taken by communities and feudal lords to protect a dwindling volume of trade, and thus unworthy of detailed attention.[4] However, interest in domestic fairs has also been overshadowed by the widespread mercantilist belief in the primacy of long-distance trade in pre-modern economies, and by Max Weber's hypothesis that by the late Middle Ages international fairs had been replaced by more sophisticated, permanent urban trading networks.[5]

In fact, local and regional fairs were the backbone of the pre-modern economy, acting as vital relay posts for conveying the high-value, exotic goods that entered long-distance trade, and as nodes in the complex marketing networks that linked the countryside to Europe's hierarchies of towns.[6] Yet a

---

3 See Chapters 5–6 of this book. See also Britnell 1993: 170–1; Stabel 1997.

4 On the mercantilist belief, see Verlinden 1963: 150–3; see Lombard-Jourdan 1984 for a recent overview. On the replacement of fairs by trading networks, see Pirenne 1963: 8–9, 80–1; Gilissen 1953: 324; Verlinden 1963: 150–1; Coornaert 1957: 363; also Pounds 1974: 354.

5 For the concept of the 'permanent fair', see Weber 1961: 219; see also Allix 1922: 544–5 and Prou 1926: 279; Luzzatto 1958: 149–50; Luzzatto 1955; Lopez 1971: 88; Cassandro 1978: 243. Weber's view that economic 'modernisation' caused a decline in periodic markets is widely shared; see Pounds 1973: 406; Lopez 1971: 87–9; Grohmann 1969: 207–9; Glasscock 1976: 174; Moore 1985: 217, 222; Britnell 1993: 90; Lombard-Jourdan 1970. For evidence that fairs prospered in early modern Europe see note 67 of this chapter. The suggestion by Verlinden 1963: 137–8 and Pounds 1974: 354–61 that the new international fairs arose in the 'pioneer' regions of central and eastern Europe, where towns were less developed, is disproved by the large number of international fairs established after 1350 in the Low Countries, France, southern Germany, Italy, and Spain (listed in note 6).

6 The daily and weekly markets where most small-scale retailing took place, and the international fairs (which nonetheless underwent a remarkable expansion in numbers after the Black Death) have been disregarded. Even at the height of population expansion before the Black Death, the volume of international trade was too small to support more than a handful of specialised fairs, and under conditions prevailing after the Black Death new international fairs took on increasingly hybrid functions. For international fairs in England (Stourbridge, Bartholomew), see Walford 1883: 59 ff., 175, 180; Dyer 1989b: 324. For France and western Switzerland (Montagnac, Pézenas, Chalon, Geneva, Lyon, Caen, Rouen), see Combes 1958; Dubois 1976; Braunstein 1979; Bergier 1963a, 1963b, 1980; Gandilhon 1940: 217–39; Bresard 1914. For the Low Countries (Bruges,

simple increase in the number of fairs, as occurred after the mid-fourteenth century, does not prove in itself that regional trade was expanding. New fairs could have been simply a triumph of hope over caution, or a protectionist response to dwindling trade that could not survive in the face of relentless demographic and economic contraction. Or they could merely have been a means for princes to establish jurisdiction over regalian rights (markets and fairs had to be authorised by a sovereign authority), which did not reflect changing patterns of trade.

One test of institutional efficiency is institutional persistence. A fair had to meet both set-up and permanent running costs; commercial failure spelled disappearance. If fairs had simply been the result of a protectionist move in a period of economic contraction, few would have survived. The evidence on this count is reassuring: most late medieval fairs survived successfully into the sixteenth century and frequently well beyond, indicating that conditions for founding new fairs and the profits from trade improved after the Black Death. In other words, late medieval regional fairs responded to the need for more specialised fora of exchange.[7] The proliferation of fairs was one aspect of a process of reorganisation which saw the incorporation of localised networks of exchange within more complex and geographically extensive patterns of trade, and which was reflected in growing market integration and in the rise of consumer markets with higher elasticities of demand.

Animal husbandry, which had a strongly seasonal pattern of production and was located in upland areas far from urban markets and served by poor road networks, suffered particularly from inadequate trading structures. As depopulated uplands converted to animal husbandry, and demand for meat, wool, dairy produce and leather increased after the mid-fourteenth century, the problems caused by the lack of a cheap and flexible system of distribution became more acute.[8] The most commonly

Antwerp, Bergen-op-Zoom, Deventer, Utrecht), see Coornaert 1961; van der Wee 1963; Sneller 1936; van Houtte 1940; van Houtte 1966: 62–3, 93–4, 105–9; van Houtte 1977; Pounds 1974: 359–61; Feenstra 1953. For German-speaking Central Europe (Friedberg, Nördlingen, Zurzach, Linz, Frankfurt, Leipzig, Regensburg), see Ammann 1950–1, 1953, 1955; Hasse 1885; Irsigler 1971; Koppe 1952; Lerner 1971; Mitterauer 1967: 288–301; Rausch 1969. For Poland (Warsaw, Poznan, Gnézno and Lublin), see Samsonowicz 1971. For Italy (Bolzano, Como, Cesena, Senigallia, Lanciano and Salerno among others), see Bückling 1907; Mira 1955; Franceschini 1948-9; Pini 1984; Marcucci 1906; Sapori 1955; Grohmann 1969; Seneca 1967; also Ammann 1970: 13 on fifteenth-century German merchants travelling between fairs at Parma, Forlì, Ravenna, Recanati, Ancona, Rimini and Florence. For Spain (Valladolid, Medina del Campo), see Gual 1982; Rucquoi 1987: 399–402; Espejo and Paz 1908; Ladero Quesada 1982: 315–22. For the decline of the international fairs of Champagne in the late thirteenth and early fourteenth centuries, see Bautier 1953; Pouzol 1968; Bur 1978. For decline elsewhere, see Usher 1953; Moore 1985: 204–17; Titow 1987; Farmer 1991: 345–6; van Houtte 1977: 45.

7   Mira 1955: 27, 110; Ladero Quesada 1982: 323; Martinez Sopena 1996: 62.
8   Bautier 1967: 17–27.

devised solution was to create fairs where uplands and lowlands overlapped so as to channel pastoral products from the mountains towards the grain-growing, urbanised plains at minimal cost.[9] In northern Lombardy, for example, a circuit of half a dozen new fairs attracted livestock- and horse-merchants from the inner Swiss Cantons, Piedmont, the Veneto, and the southern Lombard plain.[10] The fairs of Lanciano in the central Italian Abruzzi were the region's main trading event for pigs, cattle, and sheep for slaughter and for export abroad.[11] In hilly and grain-deficient north-eastern Sicily, the fairs of Randazzo and Nicosia redistributed livestock throughout the eastern half of the island and towards the southern mainland regions of Calabria and Puglia.[12] Outside Italy a complex system of rural and urban fairs governed the cattle trade in the Low Countries and in west-central Germany, and in the region of Sologne, in the duchy of Orléans, the expanding pastoral economy was served by at least five distinct fairs.[13]

Livestock fairs were also often set up at the foot of major mountain passes. The three fairs of Briançon below the Mont Genèvre pass compensated for falling demand from Avignon after the papacy's return to Rome in 1378 by capturing part of the booming trade with Piedmont, Genoa, and western Lombardy; from the 1380s Briançon alone was sending 7000 sheep each year across the Alps. The Briançon fairs declined after the 1440s because of competition from a dozen or so lesser fairs, which had developed first in the early fifteenth century to service Briançon's hinterland to the south, but were better situated along the roads into Italy and slowly gained more extensive toll franchises.[14] The small town of Sisteron, near Digne in the Basse-Alpes, which was granted three fairs in 1352, 1378 and 1400 to trade livestock with neighbouring regions, was also following a pattern typical of the entire Haute-Provence.[15]

Other regional fairs, like those of Mons in Hainaut, of Romorantin, Courmesmin and Chalon in France, of Petronell in Austria, and of Colchester and Coventry in England, were instead better known for

---

9   Many such regional markets developed between 1470 and 1520 into transcontinental networks that transferred cattle from Scandinavia and east-central Europe to metropolitan markets in the Low Countries, west Germany and northern Italy (Blanchard 1986: 428–31). For a broader discussion of livestock fairs, see Allix 1922: 546–57; for England, see Campbell and Overton 1993: 76.

10   Mira 1955: 96-9; Mira 1958: 296.

11   Marciani 1965; Grohmann 1969: 119, 327, 330, 333, 336, 339. The Abruzzi had smaller livestock fairs at Albe, Celano, Pescina, Tagliacozzo, and Castel di Sangro (Grohmann 1969: 101, 125).

12   Epstein 1992: ch. 4.

13   Blanchard 1986: 429; Guérin 1960: 85–98.

14   Sclafert 1926: 622–6; Chanaud 1980, 1983, 1984. For the Piedmontese end of this trade, see Comba and Sergi 1977.

15   Sclafert 1959: 93–4.

medium-quality wool or linen cloth.[16] But no fair ever specialised entirely in one commodity. Large quantities of wool and hemp cloth, metal ore and salt were traded at the livestock fairs of Briançon; the two fairs of Reims dealt extensively in cattle and wine; the cattle fair in Randazzo was a major regional market for cheap linen and fustian cloth; and the fairs of Lanciano also dealt in saffron, cloth, leather, metalwork, and luxury goods imported by Venetians.[17] Even at the main international fairs the largest trade by volume was done in agricultural goods and cheaper manufactures.[18]

Like most services, fair networks underwritten by the legal jurisdiction and security offered by territorial rulers displayed economies of scale in carriage and handling, so the volume of trade increased more than proportionally with the size of the market. Traders could buy up livestock and other commodities wholesale at one fair for shipment elsewhere, dispose of manufactures to local intermediaries, and settle accounts at a neighbouring fair later on in the season. Fair networks also lowered the costs of search and co-ordination, improved information about commodity and financial markets, and made it easier to develop credit relations.[19] The marginal cost of acquiring market information declined. Membership of a network increased a fair's likelihood of success and helps explain why so many survived for centuries, sometimes even to this day.[20]

Although fair networks emerged through a slow process of accretion and trial and error rather than through a single, co-ordinated decision, the trade flows and commercial expertise associated with established circuits exerted a strong gravitational pull. Fairs bred more fairs.[21] Contemporaries understood this clustering process very well, but their immediate concern was to stop new fairs from diverting trade from commercial incumbents. Indeed, it was universally held that the rights of incumbent fairs and markets prevailed over new ones, and that it was the

---

16 For other livestock fairs see Britnell 1986: 142; Feenstra 1953: 225; Fournial 1967: 169–75, 392–9; Desportes 1979: 375–6, 391, 669–70; Mitterauer 1967: 127; Heers 1961: 194–5. For cloth fairs, see Bruwier 1983; Guérin 1960: 94–5; Dubois 1976; Mitterauer 1967: 301–15; Britnell 1986: 68, 80; Pelham 1945–6.

17 Sclafert 1926: 626–30; Chanaud 1983; Desportes 1979: 669–70; Epstein 1992: 118; Grohmann 1969: 117.

18 Braunstein 1979: 174; DeSoignie 1976; Coornaert 1957: 366–7; Moore 1985: pt. II.

19 Reed 1973: 180–2; Mira 1955: 104–6; Samsonowycz 1971: 251–3. Körner 1993-4: 18–29 studies a sixteenth-century merchant's activities across a fair network covering over 20,000km[2] in southern Germany and Switzerland.

20 Masschaele 1997: ch.3 discusses the legal and commercial constraints on market concessions.

21 Mira 1955 is an excellent case study of this process. The prevalence of feudal lords or communities among petitioners depended upon the strength of seigniorialism; thus feudal requests prevailed in north-western France where seigniorialism was widespread, whereas community-inspired fairs were dominant in southern France (Thomas 1996: 179). For fairs founded by feudal lords see also Michaud-Fréjaville 1996; Blasquez 1996: 115–17.

authorities' duty to avoid inappropriate competition. The rule advantaged existing fairs, but it also increased the external benefits (or externalities, in economic jargon) of fair networks by reducing duplication and directing effort towards filling the gaps in a trade circuit. There are many examples of the apparently spontaneous, but in fact institutionally guided, emergence of commercial order. In medieval Castile, Ladero Quesada distinguishes four major zones, each possessing a distinct system of connected fairs: Galicia and the Cantabrian mountains, Castile and Léon, New Castile and Estremadura, and Andalusia and Murcia. Most fairs were granted in two distinct periods, the first lasting from *c.*1150 to 1310, the second stretching from the late fourteenth to the end of the fifteenth century after a half-century hiatus, when the number of royal concessions increased markedly. Eighty-eight new grants were made between 1350 and 1499 (of which forty were before 1450) compared with only sixty-seven during the preceding two-and-a-half centuries.[22] Even allowing for gaps in the evidence for earlier periods, the intensification of trade networks after the mid-fourteenth century is indisputable.

Like Castile, southern Italy was composed of several major economic regions – Sicily, the Abruzzi-Molise, Puglia, Calabria, and Lucania, and the Tyrrhenian coast north of Calabria – each with its own fair system. Sicily recorded fifty new fair franchises and sixty–nine first attestations of fairs between 1392 and 1499, compared with only twelve new franchises and twenty-seven first attestations in the century and a half before the Black Death; the mainland kingdom of Naples recorded twenty-nine new fair franchises and 113 first attestations for the fifteenth century, compared with thirty-five and thirty respectively before the Black Death. Most new fairs arose in the economically most dynamic areas in southern Italy: the north-eastern val Demone in Sicily, and Puglia, Abruzzi-Molise, and the Tyrrhenian coast on the mainland.[23]

Developments in the central Italian region of Umbria, dominated by the commune of Perugia, contrast with patterns in Castile and southern Italy. Two of the only six new fairs identified were held in Perugia itself. A third livestock fair was set up by Perugia in the subject community of Castiglione del Chiusi in 1366 to supply the city and its hinterland with meat; in 1380 the fair was moved close to Perugia for security reasons. The remaining fairs in the small towns of Assisi, Gubbio, and Rieti were tolerated only because they did not pose a commercial threat to Perugia's own fair.[24]

Developments in Lombardy were more similar to southern Italian and Spanish patterns.[25] Most of the fourteen fairs strung across the Alpine

22 Ladero Quesada 1982.
23 Epstein 1992: 117–20; Grohmann 1969.
24 Mira 1961.
25 Mira 1955, 1958.

lowlands to the north, in the area between Lakes Como and Maggiore, were established after 1400 to serve the growing Transalpine trade.[26] This frontier area was also an important transit zone between Lombardy and German-speaking central Europe, and the dukes of Lombardy fought bitterly for its control against the Swiss Cantons for much of the fifteenth century. The fairs seem to have been highly specialised, possibly because of their unusually large catchment area that included south-western Germany and the Swiss Alpine cantons: nearly half served the cattle and horse trades, Roveredo traded mostly in local cloth, Arona specialised in metalwork, while the fair at Chiavenna was the collecting point for the popular wines of the Valtellina. The rest of the duchy of Milan, which included the Lombard plain to the south and the eastern reaches of Piedmont, was less well-served, with most fairs being situated in the large cities (Como, Bergamo, Brescia, Milan, Novara, Vercelli, Pavia, Lodi, Crema, Cremona and Piacenza), although between 1450 and 1500 smaller towns received ten or so concessions. By the 1550s the duchy numbered nearly thirty fairs, the vast majority of which were established after the mid-fourteenth century.[27]

Between the late thirteenth and the mid-fourteenth century the six fairs of Pézenas and Montagnac in southern Languedoc held a near monopoly over regional trade, especially in the growing cloth-export industry. The two town councils successfully scotched attempts in the early fourteenth century to set up competing fairs at Nîmes, Saint-Thibéry, Caux, Villemagne, and Lodève.[28] After 1350, however, the fact that a growing number of new fairs was able to bypass Pézenas' and Montagnac's restrictions suggests that regional trade was on the rise and that political circumstances were also changing.[29] In the same years regional fairs were emerging around neighbouring Toulouse; elsewhere in France fairs increased in Forez after the 1330s and in Brittany and Burgundy after 1400.[30] In Flanders, new fairs were established in the 1360s under Count Louis of Male and then again during the fifteenth century; in the northern Low Countries they proliferated in the late fourteenth and early fifteenth centuries under the counts of Holland.[31] Similar developments took place in fifteenth-century Switzerland and Germany and in Poland.[32]

---

26 Bergier 1975.

27 Mira 1955: 96–9, which omits the toll-free fair of Viadana established in 1374–92, possibly because the town was not part of the duchy of Milan (Cavalcabò 1952–3: 179). See this book, p. 156, Figure 7.2.

28 DeSoignie 1976; Combes 1958: 239–40.

29 Combes 1958: 250–9.

30 For the Toulouse region, see Wolff 1954: 201, 518. For Forez, Brittany and Burgandy, see Fournial 1967: 392–9; Fournial 1982; Duval 1981: 336; and Richard 1983, integrating Huvelin 1897 and Gandilhon 1940: 217–39.

31 Poignant 1932: 36–58; Feenstra 1953: 221–6.

32 Radeff 1991: 335–7; Cohn 1965: 174–5; also note 6 of this chapter.

Creation

Despite certain differences in chronology and geographical distribution, to which we shall return, regional fair networks developed in very similar ways across Europe. The claim however that changes in regional fairs reflect broader improvements in market structures raises two objections that still need to be addressed. In the first place, the claim seems to be suggesting that institutional innovation responded 'efficiently' to changes in the relative price of labour and land caused by demographic decline, or in other words, that rising demand for better quality 'mass' consumer goods produced a spontaneous and frictionless change in the way trade was organised. This ignores the fact that institutional change has both distributive and allocative effects. Since major institutional changes produce both winners and losers, they will be resisted by those who stand to lose the most and who also often happen to be the incumbent elites. Significant institutional change is therefore frequently hard to achieve. When institutions do change systematically and in similar ways notwithstanding different local circumstances, as in the case of late medieval fairs, this raises two puzzles. First, what made change possible? Second, why did societies resort to fairs rather than to other commercial institutions? Were fairs introduced because they were less threatening to the political status quo, implying that other institutions have performed the same function at less cost?

The second objection to a purely economic rationale for the rise of regional fairs is that it seems unable to explain regional differences in the number and chronology of fairs. The most significant anomaly is that of England, where developments differed from the Continental experience on two main counts. First, fairs were much more numerous in England before the Black Death than anywhere else in Europe, with English kings granting possibly 1,800 fairs between 1200 and 1349.[33] The discrepancy is even more remarkable in the light of medieval England's small population, which was about 5 million around 1300 compared to eleven to thirteen million in Italy and perhaps twenty million in France at the same date. Second, after the mid-fourteenth century hundreds of English fairs disappeared without trace.[34] In contrast with Continental Europe, new fairs were seldom granted in England after 1350 and a large proportion of the new concessions went to already established market-places, the larger towns and boroughs.[35] In Essex, for example, twenty-three fairs were granted in 1200–49, thirty-eight in 1250-99 and twenty-one in 1300-

---

33 Not all the markets were active at the same time (Masschaele 1997: chs.3, 8).
34 Everitt 1967: 468–75.
35 Fourteen new borough fairs were granted in 1350–99, sixteen in 1400–49 and sixteen in 1450–99 (Weinbaum 1943).

49, but only nine between 1350 and 1499, and Derbyshire, Lancashire, Northamptonshire, Nottinghamshire, Stafford-shire, Yorkshire and Suffolk show a similar chronological pattern.[36] On the other hand, there is mounting evidence that regional and inter-regional trade, particularly in livestock but also in cereals, wool, cloth, fuel, and building materials increased in late medieval England.[37] How then do we explain the rise of fairs on the Continent and their decline in England as divergent effects of a similar cause?

Politics

The answer to both sets of questions is to be found in the political and institutional arena. Institutional or supply-side explanations of the proliferation of fairs take the polity, rather than the economy, as the crucial explanatory variable. In this view, fairs were a consequence of the rise of more powerful territorial and national states, although the precise purpose of establishing state authority over marketing rights is disputed. Some historians suggest that late medieval rulers consciously strove to expand the domestic economy through trade.[38] This may be true with respect to some of the larger international events, as Louis XI's campaign to divert trade from the fairs of Geneva towards Lyon implies, but it is unlikely to be the case for the vast majority of regional fairs that were initiated by the communities concerned.[39] In any case, governments could not establish fairs by fiat if there was no trade to support them, and for the most part central authorities left the new fairs to their own devices once a founding charter had been granted. A less naive version of this argument states that official charters provided *ex post* legal support for long-standing commercial events that had arisen under very different economic circumstances, and that changing rates of recognition stand in no strict relation to changes in commercial activity. To take concessions of fairs as an index of trade therefore confuses the legal with the economic aspect of marketing. But the hypothesis finds little support in the conceding charters, which on the few occasions they mentioned a reason for the concession state very clearly that the initiative came from the recipient and not the state.[40]

Government support for the new fairs was mainly political in intent.[41]

---

36 Walker 1981; Coates 1965; Tupling 1936; Goodfellow 1987; Unwin 1981; Palliser and Pinnock 1971; McCutcheon 1939; Waites 1982; Scarfe 1965.
37 See Astill and Grant 1988; Bailey 1989; Britnell 1986: 131–2, 246; Britnell 1993: 158, 160–71; Hatcher 1970; Miller 1991: 27–30; Palliser 1988: 15–18; Pelham 1945–6; Kowaleski 1995.
38 Grohmann 1969: 261–72; Gandilhon 1940: 85–104, 217–22.
39 For Louis XI's intervention, see Gandilhon 1940: 223–34; Bresard 1914; Bergier 1980.
40 See Epstein 1992: 107 for examples.
41 Gandilhon 1940: 217–22; Grohmann 1969: 261–72.

Grants were part of a broader strategy that aimed to assert the state's legal, fiscal and political prerogatives over regalian rights, which included the right to hold markets through its territory. Most states first established a monopoly over marketing rights during the fourteenth and early fifteenth centuries.[42] Concessions of fairs were also financially appealing because grants were bought and trade was taxed, but economic motives were not paramount. Conversely, the judicial support, military protection and tax benefits that states could offer in exchange for a formal licence offered a package of rights that no community could wilfully forgo within the increasingly complex regional and interregional markets that emerged after the mid-fourteenth century.

Late medieval states were neither enlightened despots nor belated notaries of economic change. They were the willing suppliers of legal, military and fiscal support that enabled complex, regional and supra-regional fair networks to develop and survive. The state provided the political security needed for trade to occur, enforced contracts in the courts, granted toll franchises which gave the fairs significant cost margins over urban markets, and helped spread commercial infor-mation, like the fifteenth-century dukes of Milan who had bans read throughout their lands in support of their new fairs.[43] Although lesser feudal lords and cities would have offered similar services previously, late medieval states were larger and politically more effective, and their ability to coordinate, police and enforce commercial rights was corre-spondingly more valued. Last but not least, the increased power and size of late medieval states made it easier to overcome political opposition to new fairs by their competitors.

Efficiency

It might seem reasonable at this point to strike a compromise between political and economic explanations by combining the supply of, and demand for, institutional change in a two-way causal model.[44] But this still leaves some important questions unanswered. Why were fairs such a popular means of commercial innovation? Why could states act as they

---

42 Huvelin 1897: 21, 185–8, 241–2; Epstein 1992: 113. A summary of the French king's spe-cial powers of 1372 included the granting of permission to hold fairs and markets (Lot and Fawtier 1958: vol.2, 40–2). For earlier periods see Lombard-Jourdan 1970, 1982; Endemann 1964; Mitterauer 1967, 1973.

43 Franceschini 1948-9; Motta 1892: 32–3, 40; Mira 1955: 93–4.

44 See for example Mira 1955: 110–11, and the analogous argument for the rise of long-dis-tance trade in North 1991. I do not think that the problem can be solved by arguing that late medieval states expanded in response to changes in interregional trade, be it con-tracting (North and Thomas 1973: 87, 88) or expanding (Friedman 1977: 63-5; Braudel 1982: 515). See this book, Chapters 1 and 2.

did? Did the proliferation of fairs have broader institutional consequences? How can we explain differences in the rate of innovation, in particular the English anomaly?

We already noted that the fact that fairs did lower trading costs does not prove that they were the most efficient means to do so. It is not immediately clear why fairs should have been the preferred response to rising transaction costs. The most obvious alternative to fairs were towns. If towns, with their well established service sector, *had* had significant advantages of scale over the new fairs, trading in towns would have cost less and the rise of fairs outside the urban sector would have led to a *loss* of efficiency. In that case, the main purpose of non-urban fairs would have been to redistribute the gains from trade to the lords and communities concerned. But in practice, the cost advantages of town markets over new, out-of-town fairs are hard to discern. Fairs required low capital investment, little more than an open space and some trestles, tables and canopies that were set up for the duration and then removed; the smaller size of the communities hosting the new fairs kept administrative overhead costs low, so the value-added taxes (gate tolls etc.) that towns levied to cover their overheads could be kept at a minimum; and living costs for visiting traders were lower.

However, the fairs' main advantage lay in their ability to respond more flexibly than towns to changes in the pattern and intensity of trade.[45] New fairs could reduce transport and information costs by locating close to rural pastoralists and protoindustries, which were mostly situated at some distance from the larger towns.[46] As the nature of commercial information about creditworthiness, credibility and the quality of goods changed under the impulses following the Black Death, the comparative advantage of existing urban networks was probably challenged.[47] But the proof of the pudding is the fact that most new fairs survived. Traders could vote with their feet and would have avoided the new venues if they had been more costly than the old towns.[48]

There are therefore good reasons to believe that periodic rural fairs offered a more efficient response to changing patterns of trade than permanent markets in towns. The fair was also an unusually well-tested commercial institution. The late Middle Ages had been preceded by two similar periods of fair expansion during the ninth century and then during

---

45 See Smith 1976: 15–16. The efficiency of periodic marketing is discussed in Smith 1979: 21.
46 'Protoindustrial' manufacture was generally located where urban jurisdiction was weak, which was a function of distance from the more powerful towns. See Chapter 6 of this book.
47 See Chapter 5 of this book.
48 Note that the point that fair survival proves its relative efficiency over competing institutions tells us nothing about the charter recipient's motive, which could be purely defensive or redistributive. In that case, any commercial and welfare benefits would be the unintended consequence of myopic self-interest.

the eleventh and twelfth, so the post-Black Death response followed a well-trodden path.[49] In Sugden's terminology, fairs were 'prominent' or salient solutions to the problem of co-ordinating competing social and economic claims, and the costs of learning how to organise and run them were correspondingly low.[50]

A fair's success depended on economic circumstances beyond any one person's or group's control and on local and central political support. One reason why fairs were so popular is that their potential range of support was typically very broad. The backers included everyone – lord, burgess or peasant – who stood to gain from rising trade. With a single notable exception, opponents were restricted to small neighbouring communities such as Pézenas and Montagnac in Languedoc who stood to lose their trading monopolies. But although pressure to lower transaction costs, low set-up and operating costs, institutional salience, and breadth of political support explain why fairs were so popular, they do not explain why the rate of innovation differed so markedly between regions. Two explanations spring to mind. On the one hand, the lack of fairs in some areas could reflect a lack of supporting trade, that is of demand; however, the absence of an independent measure of trade besides the fairs themselves makes this argument circular and unverifiable.[51] On the other hand, the absence of fairs could be evidence of a lack of institutional supply. Since late medieval chanceries did not record unsuccessful requests for fairs, the absence of grants in a certain region could be evidence either that rulers offered tepid political support (a hypothesis which for reasons discussed previously can be safely dismissed) or that competitors with established trade fairs and markets were managing to stop institutional change.

The most hostile and most effective opponents of institutional innovation were the privileged cities and towns. The rise of independent fairs threatened the profits and authority stemming from the jurisdictional monopolies that most European towns could claim over their hinterland. The towns also had to come to terms with the states' political aims, which included a willingness to offer small towns and petty feudal lords rights or freedoms in order to challenge the larger towns' power base.[52] Although in the longer run most urban centres benefited from the increased trading activity, in the shorter term their hostility towards the new fairs was uncompromising, as instances of unsuccessful opposition due to changing political circumstances reveal.

The need for a favourable political framework to counteract strong

---

49 Endemann 1964; Musset 1976; Dubois 1982. See also Verlinden 1963: 119–26; Sawyer 1981 and 1986; Lombard-Jourdan 1970; Mitterauer 1967: 315–21 and 1973.

50 Sugden 1986: 47–52, 91–9.

51 The argument is untestable, but could still be true, in which case it would support our view that new fairs indicate commercial expansion.

52 See Chapters 5–6.

urban hostility was a determining factor for the chronology and geographical distribution of new fairs. In fifteenth-century Lombardy, new fairs proliferated only after the balance of power shifted decisively from the former city-states to the territorial prince with Francesco Sforza's victory in 1447. Even so, the cities' abiding power can be seen from the fact that most new non-urban fairs in Lombardy were established in frontier zones where urban jurisdiction was at its weakest.[53] Flemish rural fairs grew especially rapidly in the 1360s, when Count Louis of Male was vigorously supporting the countryside against attempts to expand territorial lordship by Ghent, Bruges and Ypres.[54] In Switzerland, the rise of late medieval fairs was a result of the loss of jurisdictional independence by the larger cities.[55] In fifteenth-century Castile, new seigniorial fairs and markets spread despite strong adverse lobbying by royal towns, for the Castilian monarchy was then in no position to alienate the aristocracy.[56] Market privileges also grew in the fourteenth-, fifteenth- and sixteenth-century Netherlands despite 'strenuous' protestations by the cities.[57] In contrast, the ease with which new fairs were established in Sicily and on the southern mainland can probably be explained by the unusually weak urban jurisdiction in these regions.[58] The less easily proven claim that low numbers of fairs in some regions were caused by the towns' political strength finds support in the Umbrian example, where Perugia's strict tutelage ensured the concession of only a nominal number of new fairs.

Institutional circumstances can also explain the anomalous decline in the number of fairs in late medieval England. Whereas most European states established royal prerogatives over fairs only during the fourteenth and early fifteenth centuries, the English monarchy had done so by the end of the twelfth century at the latest.[59] A combination of early political centralisation and comparatively weak urban jurisdictions allowed feudal lords and communities who wished to establish a new fair to negotiate directly with the sovereign and bypass opposition.[60] Low set-up costs explain the extraordinary expansion of fairs over the century and a half

53 Chittolini 1978: 677–8; notes 25–7 of this chapter.
54 Note 31 of this chapter; Nicholas 1971: 12, 333–4. It has been suggested that late medieval Holland lacked fairs because of its proximity to the sea (Feenstra 1953; but see Hoppenbrouwers 2000).
55 Radeff 1991: 336, 345 links the growth of late medieval fairs with the rise of small chartered boroughs in the Swiss canton Vaud.
56 Ladero Quesada 1982: 312. See also Nader 1990 for 'anti-urban' Castilian policies.
57 Noordegraaf 1992: 13–19; de Vries 1974: 155–6 (citation), 161.
58 See Chapter 5. For strong urban hostility towards new fairs in Italy, see Zdekauer 1920: 13.
59 Britnell 1978, 1979, 1981; Cate 1938. However, not all periodic markets received an official charter (Masschaele 1997: ch.3).
60 See Reynolds 1977: 102–17 for the powers of English towns. However, Masschaele 1997: chs.4, 7, 10 and *passim* shows that what he terms regional towns, numbering on average

before the Black Death, and why by the late thirteenth century supply of probably exceeded strictly commercial needs.[61]

Comparison with the Continent casts new light on recent debates on whether the contracting number of English fairs after 1350 is evidence of general economic decline or of increased marketing efficiency.[62] Before the Black Death, England's combination of weak urban jurisdiction, a strong monarchy and extensive manorialism had given rise to an unusually dense network of rural fairs that partially compensated for the country's low rate of urbanisation.[63] However, the greater number and density of fairs in pre-Black Death England limited their catchment area; compared to the regional fairs established in Continental Europe after 1350, most English fairs before the Black Death were little more than glorified local markets. After 1350, as the more recently established and commercially fragile events disappeared, the remaining fairs began to resemble their Continental counterparts in terms of size and specialisation.[64] Since the main purpose of the oversupply of fairs before the Black Death was to bolster the profits of feudal lords, declining seigniorial power after 1350 also made commercial rationalisation easier, although it is significant that free access to rural markets was among the peasants' requests in the Revolt of 1381.[65]

On the other hand, the lack of strong institutional opposition to changes in marketing practices, the fact that change occurred through loss from, rather than addition to, existing trade networks, and the English monarchy's greater ease in co-ordinating competing commercial interests and in helping to distribute commercial information across the country probably enabled England to adapt more flexibly to changing economic

---

one per county, exercised a *de facto* jurisdictional monopoly over higher order (regional, inter-regional and international) trade within their counties and went to considerable lengths to enforce it. In Castile the monarchy was also precociously powerful and had exercised jurisdiction over markets and fairs since the tenth century (Martinez Sopena 1996: 58, 63–4), but a combination of strong towns and weak seigniorialism kept the growth of markets and fairs in check.

61 Britnell 1981: 219–20. This was presumably possible because of the seigniorial 'restrictions on free buying and selling' whose abolition Wat Tyler requested in 1381 (Oman 1906: 64).

62 For arguments as to economic decline, see Britnell 1981: 217–21; Britnell 1993: 160, 184. On the case for marketing efficiency, see Dyer 1990: 18–19; Wood 1974. This explanation does not contradict the suggestion that after the mid-fourteenth century trade took new forms (Postles 1987: 22; Farmer 1991: 339) or moved outside formal markets (Hilton 1985: 9–11).

63 Britnell 1989.

64 Farmer 1991: 346–7 also suggests that fairs survived better than daily or weekly markets. A similar process of 'reorganization and rationalization of the marketing network' in England and Wales occurred after 1640 (Clark 1981: 31), in parallel with a rapid increase in inter-regional market integration (Kussmaul 1990).

65 See note 62 of this chapter.

circumstances than more urbanised Continental regions. Although England's fragmented market system compared to areas with more powerful towns may have contributed to the country's lower rate of urbanisation before 1350, the towns' institutional weakness stood the country in good stead after the Black Death.[66]

Institutions and markets

Although early modern historians are used to explaining the rapid growth in fairs after 1500 as a consequence of demographic recovery in the fifteenth century, it is clear that the phenomenon originated during the previous century of demographic contraction.[67] The fact the number of fairs continued to increase at a time of undisputed economic expansion in the sixteenth century merely corroborates the view that the proliferation of fairs in the late Middle Ages responded to the needs of a more complex and specialised economy and was not a defensive reaction to involution.[68] Had rent seeking and commercial protectionism been the fairs' main purpose, they would not have survived for long. Instead, the growth in demand for commercial services made it profitable to incur the costs involved in institutional change. Among the many challenges to the prevailing social order set off by the late medieval demographic crisis, the attack on seigniorial and urban jurisdictions over trade has gone largely unnoticed. By the early fourteenth century those jurisdictional rights had become a central feature of the system of feudal surplus extraction. They were a property right on a legal par with serfdom, but after 1300 when serfdom had either ended or was fast disappearing from large parts of western Europe – including Castile, southern France, Italy, the Low Countries, Switzerland, and parts of Germany and England – the effects of feudal jurisdiction over trade became more pervasive and more damaging to economic growth.[69] The weakening of jurisdictional bonds after the mid-fourteenth century, of which regional fairs offer a significant testimony, was an important precondition for more rapid growth through trade and specialisation.[70]

The developments I have described give some comfort to the view that

---

66　For the co-ordinating functions of the monarchy and system of county courts before 1350, see Masschaele 1997: chs.3, 5; also Hilton 1985.
67　For explanations relating to demographic recovery, see Körner 1993–4; Topolski 1985: 132; Margairaz 1988; Teisseyre-Sallmann 1990: 344–8; Baehrel 1961: 77–8; Ball 1977: 30–2; Everitt 1967: 532–43; Chartres 1996.
68　See Chapter 3, note 48.
69　See Chapter 3.
70　Chartres 1985: 439 notes that in England by 1756 'economically rich counties seem to have accumulated more fairs [than] relatively backward areas'.

institutional change is set in motion by changing relative factor prices, which in the pre-modern period were caused principally by changes in population. Although most economic historians focus on population *growth* as a source of positive economic change, it is clear that during the late medieval crisis rapid and sustained demographic *decline* caused equally beneficial shocks to the prevailing institutional framework. However, the development of fairs also shows how the effects of population change were mediated by the prevailing distribution of power. New fairs developed only where coalitions supporting institutional innovation could overcome opposition by the more powerful cities and by lesser feudal lords. The critical factor driving institutional change was the capacity of territorial states to co-ordinate between commercial rivals and to overcome jurisdictional fragmentation. The positive externalities of fair networks previously described could only arise if urban opposition to the new fairs could be quashed; thus, the high rate of growth of markets and fairs in England before the Black Death was determined by the unusually centralised character of the English state, which also set clear parameters to late medieval developments.

5   Cities and the rise of Italian territorial states

Urbanisation *c.*1300

The economic consequences of the late medieval crisis were not felt everywhere to the same extent, and its effects within individual regions were to a certain extent contradictory. On the one hand, the crisis set in motion a process of economic convergence between relatively backward countries like England and economically more advanced regions such as Flanders and Italy. Stronger competition between towns gave rise to more sharply defined urban hierarchies, and a town's size and rank were increasingly defined by its economic and administrative functions within its own – and increasingly also neighbouring – regions. Perhaps the most striking effect of state formation on urban structures was the invention during the later Middle Ages of the capital city as the political and administrative heart of the state. On the other hand, state formation also intensified regional differences. Differences in the balance of power between sovereign bodies, subject urban elites, feudal lords and rural communities created different incentives and constraints for investment, specialisation, and trade which set their economies on different developmental paths.

In this chapter I move the analysis closer to the ground and examine processes of regional convergence and divergence in post-Black Death Italy. Italy presents an interesting test bed for the arguments developed here because of its considerable institutional diversity and economic sophistication as reflected in the most dense network of towns in Europe.[1] Although the country stayed politically fragmented compared with the rest of Europe, military and economic pressures caused the consolidation by the mid-fifteenth century of six major regional states: two republican – Venice and Florence – and four monarchical or quasi-monarchical – the Duchy of Milan, the Papal States in central Italy, and the Kingdoms of

---

1 For institutional differences, see Chittolini 1994; Varanini 1992, 1994 and 1997; Fasano
   Guarini 1994; Ginatempo 1996. For a comparative study of late medieval urbanisation,
   see Ginatempo 1997.

Naples and Sicily; further political consolidation led to Lombardy, Naples and Sicily becoming attached to the Spanish composite monarchy by the early sixteenth century.

At the height of demographic expansion in the early fourteenth century, the Italian peninsula had the highest rate of urbanisation of any major European country. This is true even if the urban threshold is fixed at 5,000 inhabitants, rather than the more usual 2,000–3,000.[2] Italy had about 130 centres with a population of 5,000–10,000, about seventy cities between 10,000 and 40,000, and a dozen metropolises with more than 40,000 inhabitants. Three cities – Venice, Milan and Florence – had over 80,000 inhabitants, a size that elsewhere was matched or exceeded only by Paris (Table 5.1).[3] By comparison, early fourteenth-century Europe excluding Italy numbered approximately ninety-five cities above 10,000, only eight of which had a population larger than 40,000.[4]

Urbanisation was high across the whole Italian peninsula. Although the kingdom of Naples lacked a strong regional leader – the largest city, Naples, had just 30,000 inhabitants – the average urban percentage before the Black Death was, at nearly 30 per cent, extraordinarily high by European standards.[5] The ten largest cities alone – the smallest of these had 12,000–15,000 inhabitants – had nearly 12 per cent of the southern Italian population, placing the kingdom of Naples among the most urbanised regions of Europe. Urbanisation was nonetheless substantially lower than in the conurbations headed by Milan, Venice and Florence and, perhaps more surprisingly, in Sicily where more than 40 per cent of the population lived in the largest ten cities (Table 5.2).[6]

Several regional types can be distinguished within this extraordinary urban efflorescence. First, three regions had both very high urban ratios (possibly greater than 30 per cent) and strong regional leaders. They included a macro-region centering on the Po plain, with apexes in Venice, Milan and Genoa surrounded by a galaxy of cities over 40,000; a central Italian region centred on Tuscany, with apexes in Florence, Pisa and Siena; and in the South, Sicily with urban leaders Palermo and Messina. Second, areas with 20–30 per cent urbanisation had weaker or more contested regional leaderships. They included Piedmont, with competing regional centres in Alessandria, Asti and Chieri; the central Italian regions of

2 Ginatempo 1997.
3 The small differences in estimates between Malanima 1998 and Epstein 1998c are due to the considerable uncertainties about late medieval demography, particularly regarding southern Italy.
4 Russell 1972.
5 Epstein 1998c.
6 The question whether Sicilian towns performed fully urban functions or were mere 'agro-towns' inhabited by peasants has still to be satisfactorily answered. See Epstein 1992: ch.2; Malanima 1998.

Table 5.1 Urban population in Italy, by size, *c*.1300–1550

	1300				1400				1500			
	(1)		(2)		(1)		(2)		(1)		(2)	
	%		%		%		%		%		%	
80,000+	4	1.8	3	1.4	2	2.1	2	2.0	3	1.9	3	2.0
40–79,000	8	3.7	9	4.2	1	1.1	1	1.0	7	4.5	10	6.6
20–39,000	14	6.5	12	5.6	12	12.6	11	11.2	8	5.1	8	5.3
10–19,000	52	24.0	62	28.8	11	11.6	10	10.2	33	21.2	29	19.2
5–9,000	139	64.1	129	60.0	69	72.6	74	75.5	105	67.3	101	66.9
Total	217	100.0	215	100.0	95	100.0	98	100.0	156	100.0	151	100.0
Population/town	11,849–11,958				11,377–11,737				8,583–8,867			

Sources: (1) Malanima 1998; (2) Epstein 1998c

Romagna, Marche, Umbria, and Lazio, with regional centres in Bologna, Ancona, Perugia and Rome; and the kingdom of Naples, with regional hegemons in Naples, Salerno and Aversa on the western coast, Melfi and Lucera in the interior, and Taranto, Brindisi, Monopoli, Barletta, Bari, Bitonto and Trani on the eastern seaboard. Third, geographically peripheral regions like Friuli, Trentino, and Sardinia had both low urbanisation and poorly developed urban networks.

One of the more significant features of these patterns is the absence even in the more heavily urbanised areas of clearly defined hierarchies among towns. Few Italian regions before the Black Death had a single unchallenged urban leader; for the most part the role was still being contested by a large number of middle ranking towns with 10,000–20,000 inhabitants (Table 5.1). The high proportion of medium-ranked cities seems in retrospect to be one of the most distinctive features of Italian urbanism before the plague. With their regional ambitions stunted by intense political competition and high barriers to trade between independent city-states,

Table 5.2 Urban indices in Italy, *c*.1300–1550

	1300	1400	1500	1550
Veneto	23.4?	n/a	n/a	29.0
Lombardy	19.3?	n/a	n/a	23.1
Tuscany	32.0	27.0	n/a	24.0
Naples	11.7	13.6	16.3	22.3
Sicily	47.8	29.8	34.1	30.4

Sources: Russell 1972: 235 (Veneto and Lombardy); Beltrami 1961 (Veneto); Beloch 1937–61: vol.3, 169; Malanima 1998 (Tuscany); Sakellariou 1996: ch.2 (Naples); Epstein 1992: ch.2 (Sicily). The urban index measures the proportion of residents in the 10 largest cities out of the total population.

these towns seem to have functioned mainly as marketing and administrative centres for their immediate hinterland. By contrast, the main
distinguishing feature of the dozen or so Italian metropolises above 20,000
inhabitants was their role in international trade and banking, where paradoxically – because of the intense political and commercial competition
between towns on *domestic* markets – transaction costs may have been lower
and 'first mover' advantages correspondingly greater. In the highly fragmented political conditions prevailing in Italy before the Black Death,
metropolitan growth depended more on establishing a position as a
commercial gateway or node in *international* trade and finance than on
dominating a successful *regional* economy.[7]

Urbanisation *c.*1350–1550

Italy lost between 40 and 60 per cent of its population in the century after
the Black Death.[8] Population loss and displacement, warfare and
commercial disruption hit towns especially hard. By the early fifteenth
century the number of settlements with over 5,000 inhabitants was less than
half what it had been before 1350 (Table 5.1), while the proportion of urban
dwellers had fallen from 20 to 14 per cent of the whole population.[9] These
setbacks were quickly reversed once the population began to recover during
the 1440s and 1450s, and by the early sixteenth century the proportion of
townspeople had returned to its pre-Black Death level. However, urbanisation in Italy made no further gains before the second half of the
eighteenth century.[10] Elsewhere in Europe, by contrast, most regions
managed to breach the plateau achieved by 1300. Even though the total
population was substantially smaller in 1500 than 1300, the proportion living
in European towns above 10,000 was on average 15 per cent higher, and
gains by individual regions were frequently far more substantial.[11]

Beneath Italy's apparent stability, major changes were also taking place.

---

7 See Hohenberg and Lees 1985 for the relation between hierarchical (central place) and
   nodal functions of towns.
8 Del Panta *et al.* 1996.
9 Malanima 1998: 98. Direct evidence of urban contraction is available for Sicily (Epstein
   1992: chs.2–3), the kingdom of Naples (Sakellariou 1996: ch.2) and Tuscany (Epstein
   1991). The collapse of the Visconti regime and civil war in the early fifteenth century
   probably damaged Lombard cities; for Como's problems in the early fifteenth century,
   see Mira 1939.
10 Malanima 1998: 109 estimates that Italian urbanisation declined from 20.6 per cent in
   1300 to 17.9 per cent in 1500.
11 For the general estimate see de Vries 1984: 41–3, drawing on early fourteenth-century
   data from Russell 1972 and Génicot 1973 who may have underestimated urban populations before the Black Death. For evidence of rising urbanisation after 1350 in individual
   regions, see Stabel 1997; Hoppenbrouwers 2000; Sanchez León 2000; Scott and Scribner
   1996; Palliser 2000: 130.

Population losses caused the number of towns above 5,000 to fall from 215–17 before the Black Death to 151–6 in 1500 (minus 27 per cent), but losses among cities over 10,000 were much greater (minus 42 per cent) (Table 5.1). Proportionally more people lived in the largest and the smallest towns in 1500 than 1300, while the share of the middle-ranking centres with 10,000–40,000 inhabitants dropped from 32 to 25 per cent of the total urban population. The overall result was the creation of increasingly polarized and hierarchical regional conurbations.

The handful of 'super-giants' at the very top of the new urban hierarchies still included Milan and Venice. Florence and Genoa, which had been demoted as a result of the 'crisis', were replaced first by Naples, whose fivefold growth from 30,000 inhabitants in the 1450s to 150,000 in 1500 propelled a second-ranking provincial centre onto Europe's centre stage, and a few decades later by Rome, re-established by the Reformation as the capital of European Catholicism. Thus, during the fifteenth and early sixteenth centuries the continued fragmentation of domestic markets, and new opportunities to head international commercial (Venice, Milan), political (Naples) and religious (Rome) systems, permanently entrenched Italy's multipolar structure and the presence of several competing macro-regions, which has remained a defining feature of the country's political and economic history ever since. The most important change was the substitution of the structure dominated by north Italian commercial emporia (Venice, Milan, Florence and Genoa) that existed before the Black Death, with a geographically and functionally more balanced network covering the entire peninsula.[12]

By 1500 the proportion of cities with 40,000–80,000 inhabitants had also increased, although by then towns which by contemporary European measures were still metropolises had become little more than provincial leaders by Italian standards, playing out their political (Ferrara, Bologna, Palermo and initially Rome) or industrial and commercial (Brescia, Cremona, Verona, Genoa and Messina) functions in a regional arena; others like Genoa and Messina acted as commercial 'gateways' between their regions and more distant markets. What distinguished these centres from Venice, Milan, Naples and Rome, however, was that they did not combine *both* functions, which would have required privileged access to a large domestic market for food and raw materials and to international networks at the same time. For by contrast with the great metropolises before the 'crisis', which based their success on their activities as mediators in international East-West trade, at the dawn of the sixteenth century

---

12 See de Vries 1984: 109–12, who in addition to Venice, Rome and Naples mentions Genoa as another early modern leader of an urban system situated largely outside Italy; I suggest substituting Genoa with Milan. See also Malanima 1998; Ginatempo and Sandri 1990.

Venice, Milan, Rome and Naples projected their influence as much *inwards* towards their agrarian and urban hinterlands as outwards onto the international arena. A distinctive feature of metropolitan growth in Italy before the Black Death had been the disconnection between political power and economic rank. The main source of Genoa's, Florence's, Milan's and Venice's primacy before the plague was not the political and economic exploitation of a subject *contado*, a practice they shared with most central and northern Italian towns, but their *de facto* control of international trading networks. By 1500, power and rank were combining together. Metropolitan leadership now also required economic hegemony over a large and vibrant domestic hinterland; the failures of Genoa and Florence must be ascribed to the former's lack of a significant territorial state and to the latter's counterproductive exploitation of the territory it had.

Below the supra-regional and regional leaders the rise of territorial states affected urban size and rank in two ways. First, political frontiers began to be defined more strictly as a means to establish political sovereignty and to tax cross-border trade. Second, domestic trade tariffs were reduced, by integrating formerly independent feudal and urban territories, by repealing feudal and urban rights to tax trade, or by supporting new markets and fairs in the countryside.[13] More sharply defined external boundaries and lower domestic transaction costs diverted trade from external to domestic markets and intensified urban competition within territorial states. Market-driven redistribution was accompanied by fiscal redistribution, as middle-ranking cities lost their political and economic independence, and occasionally became the object of punitive taxation by the new regional elites. Smaller towns on the other hand mostly benefited from territorial integration, which gave them new administrative and political duties and provided them with a better hearing from the central authority in their legal, fiscal and commercial conflicts with the larger cities.[14]

Heightened political and economic pressures forced towns to specialise and created more sharply defined urban hierarchies. However, the 'crisis' affected regions very differently; at least three patterns can be discerned. Regions with stagnant or declining urban ratios clearly outnumbered those experiencing urban growth, suggesting as stated previously that Italian urbanisation as a whole declined. Urban stagnation or decline was most noticeable in central Italy (Emilia-Romagna, Tuscany, Umbria, Marche) and in several of the more land-locked southern regions (Abruzzo Citra, Basilicata, Calabria Citra, Capitanata, and Principato Ultra).[15] Towns in many of the more urbanised Italian regions before the

13 See Chapters 3, 4, and 7 in this book; also Sakellariou 1996: chs.4–5.
14 Chittolini 1987 and 1995; Epstein 1991; below, Chapter 6.
15 Ginatempo 1993; Sakellariou 1996: ch.2.

plague, including Lombardy, the Veneto, Sicily and southern Calabria (under Messina's influence), recovered their losses but grew proportionally no further: in other words, stagnated by comparison with the early fourteenth century. Only in a handful of regions, including Piedmont – which benefited from the rise of Turin as the new regional capital and of the 'protoindustrial' towns of Casale Monferrato and Mondovì – Lazio (Rome), Terra di Lavoro (Naples), and Abruzzo Ultra – where the industrial and commercial town of L'Aquila grew strongly – did the urban sector show serious evidence of growth.

The urban sector grew where it could benefit from the rise of new capital or 'imperial' cities like Rome and Naples (where the quintupling of Naples' population between 1450 and 1500 propelled urbanisation in its region, Terra di Lavoro, close to 60 per cent) or because of the rise of new industrial centres in northern Abruzzi and Piedmont. In both cases cities expanded because they had access to supra-regional sources of income, be it as administrative and fiscal centres or as industrial exporters, and because they lacked serious neighboring competition: urbanisation in these regions was largely 'new' growth. Urban decline, by contrast, was usually a consequence of institutional factors already in place before the Black Death. One type of decline occurred when the leading city in a highly urbanised region lost some of its earlier functions, as in Tuscany, where Florence lost its earlier dominance over long-distance trade in southern Italy and was driven to over-exploit its small regional state, or in Emilia-Romagna, where Bologna's pre-Black Death hegemony was challenged by new territorial principalities headed by Ferrara, Parma and Piacenza. Elsewhere after the Black Death, a balance of power between rival towns and the absence of a clear regional leader which could solve conflicts and enforce agreements made it easier for vested interests to maintain protectionist legislation and trade barriers. Such conditions applied to Umbria and the Marche, which were nominally under papal sovereignty but where a weak papacy was led to pander to urban claims to jurisdictional 'independence'.[16] The third type of urban failure arose in areas of the South whose towns were politically and jurisdictionally weak and lacked a strong centralising power, and which reacted to the 'crisis' by converting the economy to extensive agriculture and pastoralism.[17]

In sum, urban growth occurred where towns were politically weak and territorial states were strong, while towns declined in size and vitality where they were powerful and central political coordination was weak. Where the state and cities achieved some kind of political equilibrium or stalemate,

---

16 Ginatempo 1993 and 1996. The consequences of prisoner's dilemmas for pre-modern growth are outlined in Chapter 1 of this book.

17 Sakellariou 1996: ch.2.

the urban sector recovered its pre-Black Death size but expanded no further. Urban economies grew where territorial states were not hijacked by urban vested interests which stood to lose from lower tariffs and weaker controls over industry and trade, and where a clear regional leader – most often the political and administrative capital – emerged to coordinate the distribution of resources in a region.

Political integration

To understand how political and market institutions related in practice, I compare state-driven integration in three Italian states of roughly comparable size – Sicily (25,000 km^2), Tuscany (12,000 km^2) and Lombardy (27,000 km^2 at its fullest extent, but only about half that by the 1550s) – between the early fourteenth and the mid-sixteenth centuries. Although the fourteenth-century epidemics subjected the three regions to shocks of similar intensity, with Tuscany and Sicily losing two thirds of their population and Lombardy not much less, their political institutions evolved quite differently. In 1300 the main institutional demarcation ran between Tuscany and Lombardy, which were controlled by independent city-states with strong rural jurisdictions, and Sicily, which had been ruled by a feudal monarchy since the eleventh century and where urban juris-diction over the countryside was consequently very weak. Over the following two centuries, political structures in the two northern regions diverged while those in Lombardy and Sicily became increasingly similar. Tuscany turned into an urban territorial state under Florentine rule, whereas Lombardy and Sicily were subsumed within the Spanish composite monarchy.

Sicilian towns lacked the political and jurisdictional trappings of city-states and were unusually unstable in terms of size and ranking because of a large population of highly mobile and landless individuals which reacted by migrating to volatile food prices and changes in local economic circum-stances.[18] During the latter half of the thirteenth century, Palermo and Messina had three to four times the population of the third largest Sicilian town and dominated the western and eastern halves of the island respec-tively (Table 5.3). They were, in practice, distinct, non-competing regional metropolises with important political and administrative functions extending to the southern Italian mainland. Regional integration at this time was therefore weak.

The War of the Vespers (1282–1372) and the civil war (1348–62) changed the urban hierarchy significantly. First, trade relations with the mainland disintegrated, followed after the Black Death by Sicily's domestic market. Palermo and Messina lost their administrative and

18 The following section summarizes Epstein 1991: 22–6; Epstein 1992: chs. 2–3.

Table 5.3 Urban rank–size distribution in Sicily, 1300–1550 (population in 1,000s)

Rank	1300	1400	1500	1548
1	88	14	30	80
2	53.2	12	28	50
3	27.2	12	25.2	19.6
4	26.4	8	14	14.4
5	17.6	6.4	13.2	13.6
6	16	6	12.4	12.8
7	15.6	5.6	12.4	11.6
8	12	5.6	11.4	10.8
9	10.52	4.8	10.8	9.6
10	10	4.4	10.8	9.6
Total	276.52	78.8	168.2	232
Primacy	0.318	0.178	0.178	0.345

Source: Epstein 1992.

political functions on the southern mainland, while retaining some within Sicily itself, but Palermo's primacy – its share of the total urban population – collapsed (Table 5.3). The reinstatement of the Catalan-Aragonese monarchy began to reverse this pattern during the early fifteenth century. Messina and Palermo recovered some earlier functions but also took up more complementary roles. Messina reinforced its traditional position as the main commercial gateway linking Sicily, the southern mainland and the eastern Mediterranean, while Palermo drew increasing administrative, commercial and financial benefits from being the official capital of the region.[19] Palermo however never achieved the ascendancy claimed by other early modern capitals like Naples, Paris or London, or indeed like Florence or Milan. Palermo's share of the population of the ten largest Sicilian cities, which had been 32 per cent in 1277 and had dropped to 17 per cent in 1464, was still no more than 32 per cent in 1548.[20]

By 1500 Sicily had attained a high degree of market integration and territorial specialization. One reason for this was the absence of strong urban jurisdictional rights over the countryside, which intensified competition between towns and between town and country. A policy of granting toll reductions and market franchises to towns in the royal demesne (as opposed to towns under feudal control), which was intensified by the newly restored Iberian monarchs in the 1390s in order to curry favour with demesne towns against the feudal aristocracy, turned the demesne into a

19 Conditions in late medieval Sicily are reminiscent of late sixteenth-century Brabant, with Palermo like Antwerp acting as the political capital and Messina resembling Bruges as the main centre of trade (Hohenberg and Lees 1989).
20 For Sicilian population figures see Beloch 1937: 96–161; Epstein 1992: ch. 2.

quasi customs-free zone. Since the Crown demesne included half or more of the Sicilian population and all the largest cities, the existence of a free trade regime there also benefited the rest of the economy.

The towns of late medieval Tuscany were far more stable in terms of relative size and rank than those in Sicily. Between 1350 and 1550 the ten largest cities stayed the same and changes in urban rank declined. By contrast with Palermo, Florence increased its lead over its peers, taking its share of the urban population from 48 per cent before the Black Death to 56–57 per cent after the early fifteenth century (Table 5.4).[21] Although Tuscany lost more than 60 per cent of its population during the Black Death and its aftermath, the muted effects of the crisis on the *relative* size of towns suggest that the growth of the Florentine territorial state did not fundamentally change how resources were allocated by political and market processes.[22] The most significant result of state formation was to redirect an increased share of the region's resources to the capital itself.[23]

There are two possible explanations for why Florence increased its lead within Tuscany after the Black Death. Leadership of an urban hierarchy – known as urban primacy – is the result of economic and political forces which play to a city's advantages in terms of size and power. *Economic* sources of primacy are economies of scale at the firm and industry level, demand and cost linkages and technological spillovers arising from the proximity of other firms, lower transport and transaction costs, and ease of access to credit markets. The existence of these forces mean that simple market pressures will make the rich cities richer and the large cities larger.[24] *Political* sources of primacy are economic protectionism and political authoritarianism and insta-bility, which redistribute resources towards the institutionally defined leader.[25] Political leadership may in principle therefore subvert economic pressures towards urban concentration, but in the Florentine case clearly it did not. Economically, Florence after the Black Death benefited from its industrial, commercial and banking dominance and from lower transaction costs which reduced the 'natural' protection afforded by tariff barriers to weaker regional competitors.[26] However, a comparison with Milan makes clear that Florence's growing regional dominance was not simply the result of comparative advantage and economies of agglomeration. Although before the Black Death Florence and Milan had similar advantages in terms of size over other towns in their region and Lombard commercial integration after 1350 progressed just as fast, Milan never achieved anything like Florence's

21 For the decline in Tuscany's population, see Ginatempo and Sandri 1990: 258–63.
22 This was one of the highest rates of loss in Italy (Pinto 1982: 68, 77).
23 See Chapters 6–7 of this book.
24 Glaeser, Kallal *et al.* 1992; Krugman and Venables 1996.
25 Ades and Glaeser 1995.
26 Malanima 1983; Tangheroni 1988.

Table 5.4 Urban rank–size distribution in Tuscany, 1300–1550 (population in
1,000s)

Rank	1300	1300[a]	1400	1400[a]	1540–52	1540–52[a]
1	110	110	37	37	59	59
2	50	30	14	7	20	9.9
3	30	18	8	4	19	7.75
4	25	13	7	4	9.9	6.85
5	18	12	4	3	7.75	6
6	13	12	4	3	6.85	5.2
7	12	11	3	2	6	3.75
8	12	9	3	1.8	5.2	3.2
9	11	8	2	1.7	3.75	2.5
10	9	6	1.8	1.5	3.2	2
Total	290	229	83.8	65	140.65	106.15
Primacy	0.379	0.480	0.442	0.569	0.419	0.556

[a] Without Siena and Lucca.
Sources: Ginatempo and Sandri 1990; Malanima 1998.

position. What Milan lacked, and Florence had, was the political clout to
discriminate politically and fiscally against smaller towns and the countryside
within the territorial state.[27]

Florence expanded territorially without integrating the new lands in a
regional administration and economy.[28] Administrative consolidation
during the late fourteenth and early fifteenth centuries left existing jurisdictional imbalances between towns and their territories in place,
including the many barriers to trade between different *contadi*.[29] Urban
monopolies, for example in the important textile sector, were challenged
only if they damaged the Florentines' own economic interests, and fiscal
policy was used to punish rebel cities like Pisa and to effect a huge transfer
of wealth from countryside to town. With the exception of the grain trade,
the Florentine oligarchy pursued regional integration in an *ad hoc* and
instrumental fashion without significantly transforming the cluster of
largely self-contained urban markets that existed before annexation. The
lack of competitive integration is reflected in the increasingly 'flat' dispo-
sition of the urban hierarchy, that is, in the lack of specialisation and
differentiation between subject towns, and in the unusually slow pace of
the demographic and economic recovery from the late medieval crisis.[30]

27 For the Florentine economic strategy after the Black Death, see Epstein 1991 and 1996a;
    Franceschi 1994; Chapters 6–7 of this book.
28 Chittolini 1979: 293.
29 Chittolini 1979: 292–5; Fasano Guarini 1976: 16; Fasano Guarini 1991; Guidi 1981:
    vol.III; Zorzi 1990; Diaz 1989.
30 For the lack of differentiation between subject towns, see Chapters 6 and 7 of this book.
    Hohenberg and Lees 1989: 455 identify a similar pattern in seventeenth-century Castile.

Both total population and the rate of urbanisation took several centuries to get back to pre-Black Death levels, regional cloth industries contracted, and average living standards declined.[31]

Patterns of urbanisation in late medieval Lombardy were half-way between those in Sicily and Tuscany. Lombard towns felt the industrial and commercial upheavals brought about by the 'crisis' far more severely than in Tuscany, as changes in their relative standing reveal. The most significant changes saw the decline of Cremona from second to fourth position behind Milan, Brescia and Piacenza, possibly because of problems in the local fustian industry, and the rise of Vigevano and Alessandria; Vigevano went on to be one of the few north Italian towns that were formally chartered as a new city (*civitas*) after 1500.[32] Recovery was also faster in Lombardy, however, where Lodi, Piacenza, Vigevano and Alessandria outgrew their previous peak size by the late fifteenth century, and most cities were back to their pre-Black Death sizes by the early sixteenth century.[33] In Tuscany cities were still considerably smaller in 1500 than in the 1330s.

Milan's economic and demographic pre-eminence in central and western Lombardy (then including Brescia and Bergamo, which fell under Venetian rule in the 1420s) before 1348 was similar to that of Florence in Tuscany (Table 5.5). However, territorial integration did not increase the city's primacy. In fact, Milanese primacy actually fell from 40 per cent in the early fourteenth century to 27 per cent by 1550: a rate that was substantially below Florence's and even Palermo's in the same period. Milan's relative decline might seem to be a consequence of the unfortunate combination of civil war, foreign invasion and the duchy of Lombardy's loss of Bergamo, Brescia and Crema in the 1420s and Parma and Piacenza in the 1530s. However, the new political divisions in central Lombardy do not seem to have caused commercial disintegration, while urbanisation in Lombardy at this time was either stable or rising.[34] As an established economic leader, Milan should in any case have withstood instability better than smaller urban centres. In sum, Milan's share of the domestic economy was falling at a time of rising economic integration and competition. The most plausible explanation is that political integration and

---

31 For a slow recovery after the Black Death see Ginatempo and Sandri 1990: 109–15. For industrial contraction, see Chapter 6 of this book.

32 For the fustian industry, see this book, Chapter 6. Vigevano became a chartered city in 1530 (Chittolini 1996: 100; Chittolini 1992).

33 Ginatempo and Sandri 1990: 73–9, 250–1.

34 Despite the political divisions, the cities mentioned continued to gravitate economically on Milan. In 1470 it was decided to continue to exempt trade between the provinces of Cremona, Brescia, Bergamo and Crema from taxation (*Provigioni de dacii di Cremona*, Cremona 1590: 14). See Roveda 1988; Rossini and Zalin 1985; Ventura 1964: 382; Moioli 1986: 174–6. For the level of urbanisation, see de Vries 1984: 160–2.

Table 5.5 Urban rank–size distribution in Lombardy, 1300–1550 (population in 1,000s)

Rank	1300	1400	1500	1500[a]	1542–8	1542–8[b]
1	150	100	100	100	80	80
2	45	30	48	40	44	40
3	45	30	40	25	40	16
4	30	20	28	18	30	10
5	25	20	25	16	27	7.5
6	23	15	18	10	19.5	6.5
7	20	10	16	10	17	6
8	16	10	15	8	16	5
9	12	7	10	7	11	4.5
10	12	7	10	6	10	4
Total	378	249	310	240	294.5	179.5
Primacy	0.397	0.402	0.323	0.417	0.272	0.446

[a] Without Bergamo, Brescia, Mantova and Crema.
[b] Without Bergamo, Brescia, Mantova, Parma, Piacenza and Crema.

Sources: Ginatempo and Sandri 1990; Malanima 1998.

competition by other towns was undermining some of Milan's earlier rent-seeking activities.

The territorial state which emerged during the fifteenth century from a century and a half of dynastic state building by the Visconti and Sforza was based upon a polycentric and politically pluralistic urban system.[35] Two aspects of their policies were significant from a politico-economic perspective. First, they did not align themselves with the interests of a single class – urban, feudal or peasant – in the same manner as the Florentine elites. Acting more as political brokers and mediators than as territorial monarchs, they gave rise to a degree of institutional pluralism and to a constitutional distinction between political, judicial, and economic powers which were lacking in city-state regimes like Florence. The Lombard rulers' greater detachment from vested interests also ensured greater political stability.[36]

Second, Lombard rulers from the early fourteenth century promoted cross-regional trade through a variety of means, including commercial agreements with neighbouring states, the standardisation of customs and tariffs duties, and the extension of the region's network of navigable channels.[37] By the early decades of the fifteenth century the Visconti had full authority to establish new markets and fairs and to set road tolls; the

35 Ginatempo and Sandri 1990: 198–9, 214–15.
36 This book, Chapters 2, 7.
37 Noto 1950; Ugolini 1985: 201–8.

Sforza followed similar policies after 1450.[38] Such policies responded paradoxically to the still considerable political, jurisdictional and fiscal independence of the Lombard communes. Because the Visconti and Sforza found it hard to tax the cities directly, they turned to regional and inter-regional trade where they could help coordinate and enforce inter-urban and international agreements.[39] The Visconti and Sforza also tried to weaken urban vested interests by supporting alternative centres of privilege. Increasingly during the fifteenth century, they supported lesser feudal lords, rewarded loyal mercenary leaders (*condottieri*) with feudal tenure and lordship, and granted fiscal and jurisdictional 'liberties' to rural communities and small towns situated at the strategic periphery of the state.[40] They took care nonetheless to exclude commercial, market and excise rights from such concessions, with the result that the devolution of urban power tended to lower institutional barriers to domestic trade.[41]

Both the political and the fiscal aspects of ducal policy intensified market competition and weakened the cities' jurisdictional and economic rights over their hinterland. The dukes' support for rural fairs has been mentioned in a previous chapter; their actions to stimulate competition in the Lombard cloth industry and to establish an integrated grain market are discussed in Chapters 6 and 7.[42] Ducal policy explains why Milan did not extend its primacy over the region in the way that Florence did. Milan attempted to consolidate the advantages derived from its position at the crossroads of transalpine trade with Germany, Switzerland and France and from its *de facto* capital status by extending its *contado* privileges to the whole duchy, but was met by victorious resistance from the other cities.[43] Monopolistic attempts were undermined further by competition from centres of the calibre of Venice, Genoa, Brescia, Bergamo, Piacenza and Parma, with which Milan maintained strong commercial relations but over which it had no authority.[44]

While Florence extended its regional primacy through institutional privileges which stunted the Tuscan economy, Milanese primacy was first and foremost economic. The point is underlined by the absence of significant

38 Mira 1955 and 1958; Annoni 1970; Kellenbenz 1982.
39 Bueno de Mesquita 1988; Black 1988; Massetto 1990; Storti Storchi 1984, 1988 and 1990; Varanini 1976: 703–6.
40 Bueno de Mesquita 1960; Chittolini 1979: 36–100; Chittolini 1982; Chittolini 1996: chs.4, 6.
41 Bognetti 1927: 267-8; Mira 1955: 114; Chittolini 1979: 45–51, 65–9. See below, Chapter 7.
42 A further example of resistance to special pleading is a ducal project of the 1460s to build a channel for transporting timber to Pavia and Milan from the territory of Piacenza, which was developed against Piacenza's objections (Roveda 1989: 1028–9).
43 Chapter 6 of this book.
44 Note 34 of this chapter.

anti-Milanese animosity among Lombard cities, which must be compared to the intense hatred of Florentine rule exemplified by the diaspora of the commercial elite of Pisa after Florentine conquest in 1406, by Volterra's revolts in 1429, 1471 and 1501, by Pisa's rebellion of 1494-1509, by Arezzo's uprising of 1502, and by a string of lesser examples of sullen hostility.[45] Political centralization in Tuscany came at the cost of political and economic polarization which ultimately lost Florence its state.[46] Lombardy's greater political pluralism sustained more balanced relations between town, country and the central state and consequently a better integrated and more dynamic economy.

Jurisdictional integration and the state

Late medieval economies were defined as much by institutional constraints on trade as by geography and natural endowments, and those constraints played a critical part in the growth of urban hierarchies after the Black Death. The more integrated urban hierarchies of early sixteenth-century Europe identified by de Vries did not emerge spontaneously from the late medieval social and economic crisis.[47] They were shaped by changes brought about by state formation in the political relations between town and country, between towns and the state, and between the towns themselves.

Social and political conflict had important dynamic effects on market structures and economic trajectories. Emerging territorial states redefined relations of authority between town and countryside and between the towns themselves. In Sicily, the Catalan-Aragonese political restoration of the 1390s nipped exclusive urban territorial jurisdictions in the bud and promoted trade by granting new markets and fairs, and by reducing internal tolls. In Lombardy, the Visconti and Sforza backed requests by lesser communities to loosen urban jurisdictions, while taking care to extend and enforce their jurisdiction over tax and regional trade. Although political integration increased governmental, administrative and fiscal centralisation in the *de jure* or *de facto* capitals of Sicily and Lombardy, the centrifugal force of market competition pressed in the opposite direction. Florence, by contrast, used its increased territorial powers to tighten its grip on the Tuscan economy and to strengthen the political

45 Political instability in late medieval Lombardy stemmed from the difficulty of binding together subject cities and formerly autonomous territories (Chittolini 1990), rather than from the oppression by one city of many (see e.g. Fossati 1914b for Vigevano's rebellion of 1499). For the aftermath of the conquest of Pisa, see Petralia 1987. For Volterra's revolts, see Brucker 1977: 494–5, 505; Fiumi 1977; Fubini 1977: 363–6, 547–53. For Arezzo, see Luzzati 1973; Pezzati 1842.
46 See Chapter 2.
47 de Vries 1984: 253–7.

foundations of its primacy. As the Florentine chancellor, Leonardo Bruni, stated proudly in the early fifteenth century, 'the city itself stands in the center, like a guardian and lord, while the towns surround Florence on the periphery, each in its own place'.[48] As a result, it took five centuries for Tuscany to recover from its demographic and economic collapse after the Black Death.

The analysis in this and previous chapters also suggests that the more powerful town elites took a largely reactive and obstructive stance in the late medieval crisis, attempting either to resist, obstruct and divert attempts to extend state jurisdiction, or to harness state powers in order to capture new political rents. Cities did not resist state formation because centralising states were fiscally exploitative and undermined trade, as Tilly and Blockmans have suggested.[49] On the contrary, central-ising states could offer cities something the cities themselves seldom provided, namely an external source of territorial security, of dispute settlement, and of the rule of law that overcame the economic and political rivalries and hence the coordination failures which dogged one-to-one relations between towns. Central states could also offer towns the commercial privileges which were a fundamental source of profit in pre-modern trade.[50] But these were offers which at times could be refused.

Italian history proves that commercial success was not antithetical with political and institutional power. Urban economic, jurisdictional and territorial aggrandizement went hand in hand. North-central Italian cities were not anomalous because they had 'coercive' aspirations over their surrounding territory – these were a basic feature of all pre-modern towns – but because the lack of strong territorial competitors allowed them to formulate those aspirations more effectively than anywhere else in Europe.[51] The substantial differences in the extent of urban privileges across pre-modern Europe arose from differences in political circum-stances rather than from alternative economic strategies by towns.[52]

Whether a town supported or opposed jurisdictional centralization therefore depended on the urban elite's assessment of alternative costs and benefits rather than on *a priori* hostility to state sovereignty. Towns resisted state encroachment if the loss of jurisdictional rights and prerogatives

---

48 Bruni 1978: 144 (*c*. 1403–4).
49 See Chapter 2.
50 See Lane 1958 and 1975.
51 Chittolini 1989. Such unusually favorable opportunities for 'coercive' urban growth meant that north-central Italian political powers 'did not experiment at all successfully with forms of economic organization that were distinct from political forms. Their means of pursuing commercial objectives, food supply, or the control of production were oriented chiefly to political conquest and subjugation of the territory' (ibid.: 695).
52 See Hibbert 1963; Miller 1963; van Werveke 1963; Cipolla 1963a; Nicholas 1971; Kiessling 1996; Chevalier 1982; Nader 1990; Chapter 2.

outweighed the expected gains. Cities under royal control in fifteenth-century Sicily allied themselves with the monarchy against the feudal aristocracy and underwrote the growth of state finance and bureaucracy, because they had experienced the alternative, namely seigneurial particularism, and it was worse.[53] In Tuscany, subject cities were given no choice. Florentine rule was coextensive with economic power, and Florence saw no need to compromise or grant its subjects more rights.[54] In Lombardy, city-states had found it harder than in Tuscany to subdue rural communities and federations and feudal lordships in the period of communal expansion before the Black Death; after 1350, the Visconti and Sforza used those competing centres of power to circumvent or pry open urban prerogatives.

Thus the constitutional powers of towns contributed to, but did not determine, late medieval state formation and regional integration. The stronger jurisdictional rights held by north Italian cities were not the root cause of enduring economic differences between North and South: macro-economic performance for two centuries after 1450 tended on the whole to converge. The differences between Italy and the rest of pre-modern Europe were on the whole greater than those within the peninsula itself. The most distinctive features of pre-modern Italy and the main causes of the country's regional diversity were its enduring political divisions and its position at the commercial, political and religious crossroads of Europe, Africa and the Middle East.

53 Epstein 1992: ch. 7.
54 Chittolini 1979: 292–352; Fasano Guarini 1976; Berengo 1974: 691; Epstein 1991: 31 and 1996a.

6 The origins of protoindustry, c.1300–c.1550

Late medieval 'protoindustry'

The growth of rural and small town textile manufactures for regional and supra-regional markets was among the most significant features of the late medieval economy. However, opinion about its causes is sharply divided.[1]

---

1 See Kellenbenz 1963; Carrère 1976; Bridbury 1982; Kowaleski 1995: 13–40; Bolton 1980: 267–73; Holbach 1994: 47–208; Dini 1990a. Work in progress by John Langdon suggests that the proportion of fulling mills in the total number of English mills grew from 6–7.5 per cent in 1300–48 to 12.2 per cent *circa* 1400 to 15.9 per cent *circa* 1500-10, despite a small decline in the total number of mills over the same period. Munro 1997 has recently extrapolated from the collapse in the 1320s and 1330s of Flemish and northern French production of 'cheap, light cloths' (*draperies légères, says*) to propose a broader interpretation of late medieval industrial developments. He suggests that the growing incidence of warfare, which raised transaction costs in long-distance trade, led Flemish, Catalan and Italian cloth industries to convert from 'cheap' to higher-quality cloth production. The trend intensified after the Black Death, when increased income disparities stimulated conspicuous consumption among the wealthy but reduced living standards and demand for cheap cloth among the lower classes. The view that the production of cheaper cloth for low-income strata increased after the Black Death is dismissed as 'naïve' (Munro 1997: 65, 71–3, 113 note 141). Munro's argument however draws on a limited review of the evidence, particularly for Italy which was the largest cloth producer in Europe outside the Franco-Flemish conurbation. In Italy, contrary to Munro's extrapolation from developments in Florence (where a shift to higher quality cloth did occur), production of cheaper woollen cloth increased considerably in the early fourteenth century and even more significantly after the Black Death (below, Table 6.1 and Figure 6.1; Dini 1990a; see also Hoshino 1983: 185). These industries produced both for the middle and upper classes which had previously bought Flemish *sayetteries* and for low income strata, for whom even the most modest Flemish light cloth was quite inaccessible. (On the last point, suffice it to say that the price of one *canna* (2.3m.) of the least valuable *say* from Ghistelles (Munro 1997: 55 Table 5) in Florence in 1318–23 was equivalent to two years' worth of a building labourer's budget for clothing, or a year's savings by a master; one *canna* of the most expensive 'light cloth' from Hondschoote would have cost a labourer five years' savings and a master two. A simple cape required two *canne* of cloth, while a complete vest and tunic used three or four times as much. For Florentine wages and estimated budgets, see *de la* Roncière 1976: vol.1, 295 Table 54bis, 345 Table 58, 413 Table 70. Gowns distributed to the poor by the hospital of

One view, associated with theories of early modern protoindustriali-sation, is that late medieval urban merchants shifted production from town to country in response to the inflexibility of the craft guilds and to market restrictions which raised manufacturing wages in the towns, and to demand for supplementary income by increasingly impoverished peasants in overpopulated or economically peripheral parts of the coun-tryside.[2] An alternative view agrees that the main advantage of rural over urban industry was the lower cost of labour, but also states that late medieval protoindustries arose in response to growing popular, including peasant, living standards.[3] In one version of this second theory, the prosperity of rural protoindustry depended in a quasi-Malthusian fashion on the changing size of the population. At times of population growth, real rents increased, real wages declined and the elites' demand for higher quality urban products expanded; by contrast, mass demand for cheap consumer goods made in the countryside fell. Demographic growth therefore benefited urban industries and harmed protoindus-tries. Falling population on the other hand raised real wages and pushed land rents lower. Thus during the late Middle Ages peasants and labourers had more disposable income to spend on protoindustrial goods, while elite customers had less to spend on luxury urban manu-factures. The theory explains industrial growth in terms of price and income effects and views it as a zero-sum game, with rural and urban industry growing at each other's cost.[4]

Neither of these explanations is particularly compelling. Neo-Malthusian immiseration seems an unlikely condition in the depopulated later Middle Ages, and most late medieval 'protoindustries' seem in any case to have been established with no urban input or even despite urban craft and merchant hostility.[5] The demand-side model is empirically more satisfying, noting correctly that popular demand for low-cost consumer goods rose after the Black Death, but it leaves too many questions unanswered. The

Orsanmichele in the 1340s measured two *canne* (see Henderson 1994: 339 note 117.) Finally, Munro's claim that the Black Death had no significant impact on wage-earnings and therefore did not cause demand for low-quality cloth to increase is based on Flemish data, which are not representative of developments elsewhere. Flemish wages did not rise significantly after the Black Death because population losses were much lower than in the rest of Europe (Thoen 1988: 941–62; see also van Zanden 2000 for a similar argu-ment about post-Black Death Holland).

2 van Zanden 2000. For a recent overview of the protoindustrial literature with extensive bibliography, see Ogilvie and Cerman 1996. For the analogy between late medieval and seventeenth-century protoindustrialisation, see Kellenbenz 1963; Thomson 1983; Epstein 1998b.

3 Małowist 1972.

4 Hohenberg and Lees 1985: 113–20.

5 See Scott 1996: 13 for the region of Lake Constance; Scott 1997: 104–21 for the Upper Rhine region.

characterisation of urban and rural industries as organisationally and commercially antithetical raises two objections. In the first place, most late medieval 'protoindustry' was based in small and middle-sized villages and towns rather than in dispersed farms and homesteads, and its success over the longer term seems to have depended on the adoption of many of the organisational trappings of 'traditional' urban crafts. It was thus more 'semi-urban' than rural in both location and structure. Second, the gains made by semi-urban producers after the Black Death seldom led straightforwardly to a loss for urban industries. Rather than destroying the 'traditional', regulated manufacture in the towns, semi-urban competition forced craft-based industries to convert to higher-quality products where they could exploit their labourers' better technical skills. Although urban industries were not all equally successful in managing industrial conversion, the existence of a general crisis of craft-based manufacture has never been proven, and indeed the increase in Europe's urban population between 1300 and 1500 discussed in Chapter 5 indicates the opposite.[6]

The late medieval textile industry in both its urban and non-urban forms was in fact far more complex than the theories previously discussed imply. In the countryside, supply was basically unrestricted – capital requirements were low, many peasants had basic spinning and weaving skills, cheap wool, flax and water to power fulling mills were easily accessible, and lower demographic pressure after 1350 released agricultural labour – while the elasticity of demand for clothing was high.[7] In theory, therefore, late medieval protoindustries should have developed freely wherever favourable supply factors prevailed, and as simple extensions of peasant household production, they should have produced basic, homogenous goods. In practice, protoindustry was both geographically highly concentrated and technologically very diversified, indicating that more complex locational and industrial forces were at play.

The rise of rural and small town cloth industries in the fourteenth and fifteenth centuries was an important aspect of the process of creative destruction described in previous chapters, which prepared the ground for the growth during the seventeenth century of the larger and more specialised protoindustries that have concerned most economic historians. Although the original claim by Mendels and others that seventeenth-century protoindustrialisation was the 'first phase of the industrialisation process' has, after two decades of international research, been comprehensively refuted, there is little doubt that protoindustry had an important role in increasing labour

---

6 See Holbach 1994: 47–208 for an overview of western European developments with the exclusion of Iberia and Italy. The argument that English urban cloth industries did not decline in aggregate after the Black Death is put forcefully by Bridbury 1982: ch.6.

7 As the proliferation of sumptuary laws against upwardly mobile consumers after the Black Death shows (Owen Hughes 1983; Bulst 1988).

productivity by employing excess agricultural labour. Late medieval protoindustrialisation must be seen in this light like its early modern counterpart as a manifestation of pre-modern Smithian growth.

Late medieval protoindustrialisation was nonetheless in many ways unprecedented, for three sets of reasons. In the first place, the rise of new textile industries stimulated a rapid realignment in the division of labour between 'town' and 'country', where 'country' refers primarily to small towns and large or growing villages rather than to dispersed peasants. Urban producers responded to competition in the lower-value segments of the market by raising barriers to entry. Their standard initial reaction was to outlaw competitors by legally monopolising production in the urban hinterland. Such measures could sometimes stop non-urban production in its tracks, but guild controls and repression were often simply circumvented. The craft guilds' next and more effective response was to exploit their better skills base by diversifying into new fabrics, fashions, and industries like silk or high quality linen, and by offering technically sophisticated finishing services to the semi-urban industries themselves.[8]

Second, late medieval protoindustries tended to cluster in compact areas or fledgling 'industrial districts' with shared topographical, commercial and institutional characteristics. Some of these were 'marginal' upland or coastal areas unsuited to cereal production which in the depopulated conditions prevailing after the Black Death specialised in livestock and cheap manufactures, but manufacturing clusters also developed in the cereal-growing plains nearer the large cities, while in some regions like Castile the new industries arose within the cities themselves. However, the tendency to view urban and semi-urban industries as radically antithetical misses the most significant aspect of industrial growth after the Black Death. The most successful industrial clusters developed where a strong tradition of guild-based urban industry already existed, because semi-urban industries benefited from the technical and knowledge spillovers and the more intense contacts with buyers and suppliers – the technological, organisational and commercial externalities – available in densely urbanised areas. Industrial clustering lowered the costs of information, monitoring, enforcement and transport, created a larger, more homogeneous and skilled pool of labour, and increased the returns to, and the speed of, technical innovation. Clustering, which was in

---

8   The most detailed work on urban industrial restructuring in response to the protoindustrial challenge concerns the Low Countries; see Van der Wee 1988; Boone and Prevenier 1993; Boone 1995; Stabel 1997: 138–58; Thoen and Soly 1999. The long-standing debate on urban 'crisis' in late medieval England can be recast in these terms; see Palliser 1988 and Britnell 1993: 170–1 for references. A general increase in demand for skilled labour explains why late medieval craft guilds introduced more rigorous standards of training and craftsmanship and devised ways to improve the movement of skilled labour between towns (Epstein 1998a: 692–3).

principle self-reinforcing, explains why so many late medieval industrial districts persisted for centuries, and in some cases even to the present day.[9]

The third major feature of late medieval protoindustrialisation was the growing role of the state. As a highly capitalised, labour- and skills-intensive industry that could also be easily taxed, urban cloth manufacture and the trade in raw materials had begun to attract rulers' attention from the late thirteenth century, the introduction of a wool tax by England's Edward I in 1294–7 being a classic case in point. However, the increasingly bitter conflict between urban and semi-urban producers after the Black Death stoked requests for states to arbitrate between the jurisdictional rights of the guilds and the appeals for exemption by protoindustries. Territorial rulers on their part found this an irresistible opportunity to broaden their political base and strike a blow against urban privilege, which provided a major source of resistance to their authority. State concessions of privileges and 'freedoms' against urban monopolies were frequently critical for the new industries' survival, acting as a form of 'infant-industry protection' and permanently changing a region's industrial pattern and comparative advantage. Even where the state did not actively support protoindustries, political integration helped establish more competitive markets and lowered the barriers to entry for industries in smaller towns and upstart villages.[10]

To establish how political structures shaped industrial growth we cannot examine individual manufactures in isolation, therefore, but must situate them in an economic and institutional context which was fundamentally regional. This chapter examines the rise of textile protoindustries in three Italian regions – Lombardy, Tuscany and Sicily – between 1300 and 1550 from this perspective.[11] The regions shared many important macroeconomic features, including high rates of urbanisation, well-developed infrastructure, stable property rights, similar rates of demographic loss from 1350, stable or rising real wages, and ease of supply for raw wool, flax and cotton. They also had among the highest industrial concentrations in fifteenth-century Italy (Figure 6.1).[12]

---

9   For evidence of regional clustering, see Schremmer 1972; Stromer 1986; Bridbury 1982: ch.5; Holbach 1994; Thomson 1996; Beonio Brocchieri 1995. For models of clustering and its consequences, see Krugman 1991; Becker and Murphy 1992; Zilibotti 1994; Ciccone and Matsuyama 1996.

10 See van Werveke 1963: 354–6; Nicholas 1971: 203–21; Boone 1997; Noordegraaf 1992; Scott 1996: 16; Miller and Hatcher 1995: 321–2. On the importance of legal privilege in the development of protoindustry, see Pollard 1997: ch.4.

11 For recent work on late medieval Italian 'protoindustry' from this perspective see Comba 1988a: 125–61; Comba 1988b; Albini 1993; Beonio Brocchieri 1993; Grillo 1993.

12 For post-Black Death Italian clothmaking, see Borlandi 1953; Heers 1961: 227–9; Romano 1974: 1849–53, 1855–6; Jones 1978: 181–3 and note 14; Grohmann 1969: 85, 87, 137, 173, 211, 297, 414, 427; Leone 1983; Comba 1988a: 125–41 and 1988b; Dini 1990a.

However, as discussed in Chapter 5, their political trajectories were very different. Lombardy was a hybrid between a principality and a federation of city-states; Tuscany came under the rule of the Florentine republic; while Sicily, an independent monarchy between 1282 and 1416, later became part of the Iberian-Neapolitan composite state. The three regions therefore offer the closest approximation to a controlled historical experiment on the influence of economic and institutional forces on late medieval industrial growth.

Sources

In their early years, before they became fully institutionalised, semi-urban industries left few written records. They lacked craft guilds and their attendant legal and administrative trappings, they generally relied on external commercial expertise to market their wares, and they were anxious to avoid scrutiny by neighbouring towns. They were most frequently mentioned in urban records as objects of repression and, more incidentally, in state and urban legislation, in customs lists and tax returns, and in dowries and probate inventories describing changing patterns of consumption. The quality and quantity of such records differs markedly in the three regions. Due to the stunted growth of guilds in Sicily, official craft records survive only for Lombardy and Tuscany, and records of craft activities survive only for Florence. Admission lists of rural cloth workers who fell under an urban craft's jurisdiction exist for the wool guild of Milan and the wool and linen guilds of Florence, but only the latter seem to have enforced their rural prerogatives strictly; on the other hand, the activities of the more successful rival industries fell outside the urban guilds' jurisdiction.[13]

The best evidence of textile manufacture in Lombardy comes from the statutes of local communities, which were drawn up in their hundreds at the height of the communal movement in the thirteenth and fourteenth centuries and were further encouraged by territorial rulers in the fifteenth. The approximately 240 statutes of 128 Lombard communities which survive for the three centuries before 1550 (with twenty nine of them drafted before 1350) include a large number of economic by-laws, many of which regulated activities relating to textiles.[14] Although statutes, like all legal sources, must be used with caution and checked against independent

---

13 The Milanese registers record 77 rural matriculations between 1393 and 1480, 37 of which occurred after 1470 (Santoro 1940). The Florentine lists are discussed below.

14 Microfilmed copies of all statutes are stored in the Istituto di Storia del Diritto italiano at the University of Milan. I am grateful to Prof. Antonio Padoa Schioppa and Prof. Claudia Storti Storchi for granting me unrestricted access to the material. The comparison has been broadened by taking Lombardy to include the State of Milan as it stood at Charles V's accession in 1535, the Valtellina and the territory of Piacenza

Figure 6.1 Woollen manufacture in fifteenth-century Italy

Key to Figure 6.1

1.	Como	2.	Torno	3.	Lecco
4.	See Figure 6.2a, nn.36, 39–44	5.	Bergamo	6	Monza
7.	Milan	8.	Pinerolo	9.	Genoa

14 (continued)

(which was lost to Milan only a few years before), and the territories of Brescia and Bergamo, which came under Venetian control in 1426–28 but maintained strong economic ties with the lands to their west. See Roveda 1988; Rossini and Zalin 1985; Moioli 1986; Corritore 1993 and 1995; *Provigioni* 1590: 14 (1477), for a decision to continue not raising customs dues on trade between the territories and cities of Cremona, Mantova, Brescia, Bergamo and Crema.

sources, the latter confirm that community statutes accurately portray semi-urban industry in the region.[15]

Community statutes are far less useful for late medieval Tuscany, where the Florentine *signoria* used them to extend its provincial jurisdiction and undermine that of subject cities by striking out all the clauses – including any norms on cloth production – that contravened the city's laws and the jurisdiction of its guilds.[16] Florence forced local practices into its own legal straitjacket and gave its guilds the means to monitor manufacturing in the state; not surprisingly, Tuscan rural statutes are singularly unhelpful about industrial activities – but as we shall see, this actually reflects the weakness of Tuscan protoindustries.

Tuscany has two sets of records that are not available for Lombardy and Sicily. Membership lists survive unbroken for Florence's wool and linen guilds from the fourteenth century through to their abolition in the eighteenth. Both guilds began to record the presence of artisans in the Florentine *contado* from 1382, indicating increased concern about the competitive threat of rural manufacture and growing jurisdictional powers. Rural registrations, which begin to be less reliable from the 1490s but continued into the sixteenth century, can be used to chart the number and location of *contado* weavers and entrepreneurs for the best part of two hundred years.[17] They can be integrated with data from the so-called *Catasto* or tax assessment of 1427–30, which reports the professional activities of taxpaying heads of household and offers a more detailed snapshot of the textile activities in the whole region. Although a significant proportion of taxpayers, including more than 40 per cent in Florence and Pisa, did not declare their occupation, those who did provide a reasonably accurate cross-section of the whole population.[18]

Nothing along the lines of the Lombard or Tuscan documentation exists for Sicily, because Sicilian craft guilds were first being established in the fifteenth century when rural industries were also emerging, and guild jurisdiction was in any case weak. Community by-laws were standardised to

15   A full list of statutes is published in Epstein 1993; see also Toubert 1976. For the institutional aspects of statutory legislation, see Chittolini and Willoweit 1991; Chittolini 1996: 105–26; Storti Storchi 1988, 1990, 1992; Cortesi 1984; Tiraboschi 1880; Gualazzini 1950–1: 109–67; Solazzi 1952–3. The distribution of late sixteenth-century protoindustry north of Milan largely coincides with the patterns described on the basis of local statutes (Beonio Brocchieri 1995).

16   Fasano Guarini 1991.

17   The decision to register *contado* craftsmen (no women were recorded), which was explicitly linked to the change in political regime in January 1382 (ASFi, AL 46, f.134rv), may have been a sop to the Florentine wool guild by the new aristocratic rulers whose actions provoked the flight of hundreds of skilled craftsmen from the city. See note 90, this chapter.

18   Herlihy and Klapisch Zuber 1985: 124.

those of Messina, Palermo, Catania and Trapani and have few original features. Evidence of cloth manufacture is therefore largely circumstantial and comes from local tariff lists, private inventories and dowry lists, notarial contracts, and references to local raw materials, fulling mills, and dyeing facilities.[19]

Lombardy

Raw materials

The statutes, which regulated flax production because of the noxious smells caused by retting, indicate that flax was grown most intensively across central Lombardy in the provinces of Novara, Alessandria, Tortona, Bergamo, Brescia, Cremona, Crema and Lodi. Flax was less common in central Lombardy around Milan and Pavia and around Piacenza, and it was even rarer in the province of Como.[20] The sixteenth-century statutes of the Valtellina to the north do not refer to flax at all.[21] Local differences in quality and production gave rise to a regional trade in linen thread in the fifteenth century, with major markets at Treviglio in the district of Bergamo and Orzinuovi (Brescia), which served the eastern provinces of the Venetian Terraferma and the districts of Cremona and Milan, in Sondrio in the north-east, and in the main provincial capitals.[22]

The statutes have little to say about wool supplies, since the poor quality of Lombard wool (*lana nostrale*) forced urban manufactures and the more ambitious semi-urban industries to import their wool from Abruzzo, Puglia, Sicily and Sardinia in central and southern Italy and from southern France, Spain, Burgundy and England.[23] The same applies to the cotton thread used in the production of fustian, which came from southern Italy and especially from the Levant by way of Venice and Genoa.[24] The statutes' silence about woad, which was Europe's main source of blue dye until the late seventeenth century and which post-Black Death Lombardy produced and exported in large quantity, is more surprising.

---

19 For dowries and inventories in Lombardy and Tuscany, see Mazzi and Raveggi 1983; Caso 1981; Roveda 1948.
20 Cenedella 1990: 234, dates the introduction of flax to the dry uplands to the north of Milan to the late fifteenth century. See also Crotti Pasi 1984: 28. Flax was widespread in the Lomellina to the north of Pavia (Chiappa Mauri 1997: 10–12). Racine 1977: 289 mentions contracts for growing flax south of Piacenza in the mid-thirteenth century.
21 Chiappa Mauri 1986: 139.
22 See notes 31–37, this chapter.
23 Several mountain communities regulated sheep husbandry (Toubert 1976: 475–83).
24 Fennell Mazzaoui 1981: ch.7.

Woad, which needs rich and well-manured soil and has a high bulk-to cost-ratio (its pigment is extracted from the dried leaf), was grown in the vicinity of towns where it could be fertilised with night-soil and industrial residues. While woad is a less effective blue pigment than madder, which was also grown in Lombardy, it had several advantages from the growers' point of view, including the fact that it could be cropped up to five times a year compared with madder's single crop every two years, that it could be sown and cropped between the summer harvest and the sowing of winter grains, and that the industrial residues could also be used as animal fodder and fertiliser. It was particularly useful as a means for peasants to smooth income from more volatile cereal harvests.

For much of the thirteenth century north Italian industries had been supplied with woad from the neighbourhood of Bologna and of Arezzo, Borgo San Sepolcro and Città di Castello in south-eastern Tuscany. Increasingly unstable conditions along the roads between Tuscany and northern Italy during the late thirteenth century led to the crop being introduced to western Lombardy, and after the Black Death cultivation rapidly increased. The price of one *soma* (approximately 100–120kg) of woad in Lombardy, which had already fallen from 6.78 florins in 1278 to 3.12 florins in the 1350s, dropped by a further two-thirds to 1 florin by 1470, for a total nominal decline of 85 per cent.[25] By the fifteenth century Lombard woad had become a major export to Catalonia and northern Europe (including England) and was an important source of tax revenue for the duke.[26]

Linen

The sources distinguish three kinds of linen manufacture by technical complexity (Figure 6.2). The simplest kind was domestic production for home and local consumption, which community statutes ignored but which is normally found in probate inventories. Slightly more specialised, small-scale and lightly regulated production for provincial markets was widespread in the upland provinces of Novara, Bergamo and Brescia but was less common elsewhere in the region.[27] More specialised industries,

25 Production of woad increased after 1350 also in Languedoc, Normandy, Artois, Picardy and Gascogne, in southern Flanders, and in the central and lower Rhineland.
26 Borlandi 1949. The price of Lombard madder also collapsed from 8.14 florins/*soma* in 1280 to 3.91 florins/*soma* in the mid-fourteenth century. Borlandi explains this in terms of a slump in demand, but a trade agreement of 1335 between Como and the Mesolcina valley refers to madder exports (ASCo, Archivio Storico Comunale, Dazi 13/1, ff.46-8). For the *soma*, see Frangioni 1992: ch.10; for fourteenth-century exports to Catalonia, see Mainoni 1982: 23.
27 BA, ms. S.C.T. VII, p.54 rubr.205 (Cannobio, 1357); Odorici 1876: col.1584 notes 108–9, 139 (1248), 244 (1292); Noto 1950: 112–13 note 222 (1354).

which required detailed regulations on cloth size, density of warp and other technical features, existed in most provincial capitals. The most sophisticated manufactures were situated in Novara, Alessandria, Tortona and Pavia, followed by Milan, Lodi, Cremona, Piacenza and the territory of Bormio in the Valtellina. Como displayed little interest in linen, Brescia apparently developed a local industry only in the sixteenth century, while in Cremona the linen and fustian industries joined up during the fourteenth century and are no longer mentioned separately.[28] Outside the large cities, specialised producers were most numerous in the provinces of Novara (at Biandrate (1395), Ornavasso (1404) and possibly Arona (1318–19)) and Pavia (at Romagnese (1412), Vigevano (1418) and Voghera (1389)), although higher quality linen industries were scattered across most of the region, in Borgo San Martino (1380–90) near Alessandria and at Bellano (1370?) near Como, possibly at Romano di Lombardia (1368) in the district of Bergamo, at Palazzolo (1425) and perhaps Riviera di Salò (1425) near Brescia, and at Crema (late fourteenth century) and Monza; only the district of Piacenza seems to have had none at all.

Statutes and tariff lists show that the Lombard industry expanded and became more specialised after the Black Death. While Vigevano's late fourteenth-century statute had merely listed tolls on linseed and linen cloth, its statute of 1418 fixed the length (thirteen *braccia*) and weft (1,400 threads for fine cloth, 1,300 for lesser quality cloth) of local linen in a bid for more valuable markets.[29] A comparison between two Milanese customs lists dating from 1330-50 and from the latter half of the fifteenth century indicates a sharp increase in the variety of linen cloth sold on the urban market.[30] The correspondents of the 'merchant of Prato', Francesco di Marco Datini, complained in the 1390s about the poor quality of 'Lombard' linen sold to the papal court at Avignon, but they were actually referring to the linens of Milan which were far from the best the region could offer.[31]

Access to cheap raw materials and labour did not, however, determine industrial location. Abundant flax and 'marginal' upland populations in the Novara, Bergamo and Brescia regions were associated with low-quality craftsmanship; the countryside of Alessandria developed both specialised flax production and high-level industry; and only the urban industries of Tortona, Cremona and Crema seem to have benefited from good supplies of flax in their regions. Specialised industries grew in Romagnese,

---

28 For linen weaving in the sixteenth and seventeenth centuries, see Larsimont Pergameni 1948–9: 182; Sella 1978; Beonio Brocchieri 1993; Beonio Brocchieri 1995 (for fustian).

29 Colombo 1933: 346–7, 486 (1371–92, 1418).

30 *Statuta* 1480: 192v (1396); Noto 1950: 17.

31 Milanese linen at Avignon was worth just over half that of Crema (Frangioni 1986a: 63–4); see also Frangioni 1983: 67–72. Early fifteenth-century Florentines seems to have considered the best Lombard linen to be from Lodi (ASFi, ARSL 8, ff.4v, 15v).

Voghera, Vigevano and Pavia despite the lack of good local supplies of flax, but failed to emerge in the *contadi* of Milan and Piacenza where market conditions were similar.

Fustian

One element that *could* help determine the linen industry's location was the presence of a strong fustian industry, which competed for labour and raw materials (fustian was made with a combination of linen and cotton). The Lombard fustian industry was not only more capital intensive and better established than linen manufacture, having produced for international markets since the thirteenth century, but could also count on stronger political support. Most fustian industries had been granted a quasi-monopoly over supplies of linen warp long before the rise of independent linen industries. Brescia forbade the export of linen thread from its *contado* and *distretto* as early as 1248.[32] Piacenza also began to regulate the trade in spun flax in the thirteenth century, and banned exports of cotton and linen thread from the *contado* in 1346.[33] Cremona set a ban on the export of thread in 1318 and again in 1430; its fustian industry tried to restrict the wholesale trade in thread to four markets in Cremona's district.[34] Pavia banned all thread exports in 1368.[35] Milan passed a law exempting linen thread from gate tolls in 1338 and followed this up by banning thread exports from its *contado* and *distretto* with an oft-repeated law of 1354.[36] The city responded to the development of an integrated regional market in warp thread by extending their ban to the entire duchy with the support of Cremona's fustian makers.[37]

Thus, in cities with strong traditions in fustian production like Milan, Cremona, Piacenza, Brescia (which also produced *mezzelane*, a mixture of linen and wool) and even Bergamo (where fustian emerged in the fifteenth century), linen industries were simply crowded out.[38] Only Alessandria and Vigevano managed to produce high-quality linen and

---

32   Odorici 1876: col.1584 note 139.

33   Castignoli and Racine 1967: rr. 100–4, 373–4, 432, 588; Pancotti 1925–30: vol.3, 325.

34   Meroni 1957: 112; Sabbioneta Almansi 1970: 127–9, 132–3, 143, 159; Mainoni 1994a: 103. See also Sabbioneta Almansi 1970: 186, 188 (1410–30).

35   Paganini 1971–3: 487 note 24. For flax production in Pavia's hinterland see Chiappa Mauri 1997: 69–91.

36   Noto 1950: 106 note 201, 112 note 221 (the ban was repeated in 1414, 1425, 1444, 1448 and 1452).

37   Barbieri 1938: 65–6; Fennell Mazzaoui 1981: 85, 147, 148, 197 note 43, 220 note 52; this chapter, note 34. In 1444 duke Filippo Maria Visconti banned exports from the territories of Cremona, Novara, Saronno and Gallarate not directed towards Milan. In 1448 the Milanese fustian makers claimed that thread was being smuggled to Cremona and Florence (Natale 1987: 72-4; Fennell Mazzaoui 1981: 85, 148).

38   For mezzelane, see *Statuta* 1480: 191v; Noto 1950: 17. For fustian, see *Volumen* 1686: 32

fustian concurrently from the early 1400s, while the linen manufacture in Pavia was successful only because its fustian industry was in terminal decline.[39] The market for linen thread was also facing demand from several new fustian manufactures that sprang up in the small towns of Lecco (in the late fourteenth century), Vigevano (1392), Melegnano (1425), Busto Arsizio (*c.*1407–18) and the Riviera di Salò (1425).[40] Most were situated in the districts of Pavia and Milan, where the linen industry was poorly developed; the hinterland of the largest fustian manufacturer in Lombardy, Cremona, had none (Figure 6.2).[41]

Although most of the new fustian industries produced cheaper cloth for the regional market, some competed at the lower end of the international market dominated by Milan and Cremona. At first the latter probably underestimated the scale of the threat, in part because small town competitors often began as subcontractors to the big cities, like the weavers in Melegnano who in the early fifteenth century made rough cloths for dyeing and finishing in Milan. By the 1470s they had also taken over the dyeing, causing the Milanese to protest at the poor quality of their black.[42] But the Milanese also had to compete with central European products since 1370–80, and from the mid-fifteenth century faced growing competition by cheap cloth from Piedmont, Liguria, Piacenza and Pavia.[43] After battling for decades, both Milan and Cremona decided to avoid a price war they could only lose and diversified into higher quality production. In the case of Milan, this also meant converting to the technologically more advanced and more profitable silk industry.[44]

(1457). Cremona's linen craft was incorporated into the fustian guild between 1313 and 1388; see Sabbioneta Almansi 1970: 22. At Piacenza the last reference to linen weaving in the statutes appears to date from 1396, and appears in the statute of the wool guild (Pallastrelli 1869: 29 rubr.71). The linen weavers of Milan, who were already organised as a group in 1385 (Martini 1980: 233), were granted guild statutes only in 1460.

39 For fustian production in Pavia see Fennell Mazzaoui 1981: 85, 197 note 38, 224 notes 4–5, 229. Fustian joined linen weaving in Alessandria during the fifteenth century (Comba 1988a: 138), but relations between the two industries are unknown.

40 Dates refer to the first statute references. Minor fustian industries existed in Tortona in 1327–29 and possibly in Monza in 1331. Gallarate, Abbiategrasso and Bormio to the north of Milan set up manufactures in the sixteenth century (Beonio Brocchieri 1995: 158–67).

41 If Cremona was able to keep tighter control over rural manufactures than Milan, this would help explain why its fustian industry weathered the late medieval crisis more successfully. In 1391, the city took steps against illegal competitors in both town and country who were making 'infinite numbers of *pignolati* (a type of fustian) with insufficient quantities of cotton' (*Statuti* 1580?: 35).

42 Noto 1950: 122 note 5; Fennell Mazzaoui 1981: 158 (1478).

43 For competition from central Europe, see Fennell Mazzaoui 1972: 283–86; Fennell Mazzaoui 1981: 139, 144, 145; Frangioni 1986a: 64, 67; Frangioni 1986b: 89–91. For competition from Italian towns, see Heers 1961: 229; Comba 1988a; Fennell Mazzaoui 1981: 85 and 196 note 29.

44 For diversification see Mainoni 1983: 577; Fennell Mazzaoui 1981: 146, 150. For the woollen industry see Mainoni 1984: 22, 40–2. By 1500 silk had become the main textile industry in Milan (Mainoni 1994b; Grillo 1994).

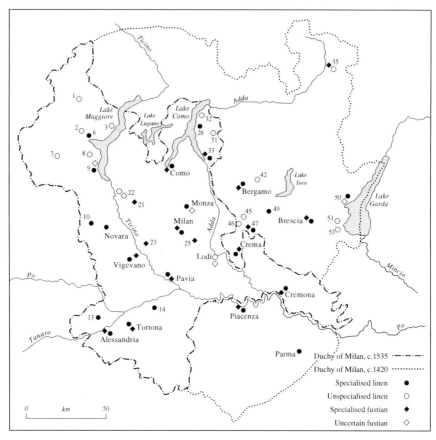

Figure 6.2 The Lombard linen and fustian industries, *c.*1350–1550

Key to Figure 6.2 and Figure 6.3

1. Val Vigezzo (NO)	2. Premosello (NO)	3. Cannobio (NO)
4. Intra, Pallanza, Vallintrasca (NO)	5. Vogogna (NO)	6. Ornavasso (NO)
7. Varallo Sesia (NO)	8. Graglia Piana (NO)	9. Arona (NO)
10. Biandrate (NO)	11. Borgosesia (NO)	12. Crevola Sesia (NO)
13. Borgo San Martino (AL)	14. Voghera (PV)	15. Romagnese (PV)
16. Valtravaglia (MI)	17. Lugano (MI)	18. Desio (MI)
19. Cuvio (MI)	20. Varese (MI)	21. Busto Arsizio (MI)
22. Gallarate (MI)	23. Abbiategrasso (MI)	24. Corbetta (MI)
25. Melegnano (MI)	26. Bellano (CO)	27. Cernobbio (CO)
28. Torno (CO)	29. Canzo (CO)	30. Cantú (CO)
31. Valsassina (CO)	32. Dervio, Corenno (CO)	33. Lecco (CO)
34. Valmadrera (CO)	35. Bormio (SO)	36. Valle Seriana (BG)
37. Val di Scalve (BG)	38. Val Brembana (BG)	39. Vertova (BG)
40. Gandino, Val Gandino (BG)	41. Albino	42. Alzano

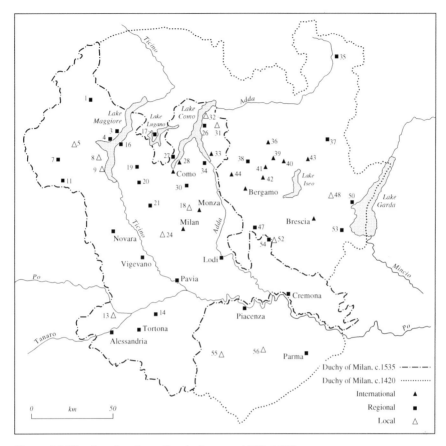

Figure 6.3 The Lombard woollen industry, *c*.1350–1550

Key to Figure 6.2 and Figure 6.3 (continued)

43. Lovere (BG)	44. Almenno, Valle Imagna (BG)	45. Martinengo (BG)
46. Treviglio (BG)	47. Romano di Lombardia (BG)	48. Val di Sabbia (BS)
49. Palazzolo (BS)	50. Riviera di Saló (BS)	51. Val Tenesi (BS)
52. Orzinuovi (BS)	53. Lonato (BS)	54. Soncino (CR)
55. Bobbio (PC)	56. Castell'Arquato (PC)	

Provinces

AL	= Alessandria	MI	= Milan
BG	= Bergamo	NO	= Novara
BS	= Brescia	PC	= Piacenza
CO	= Como	PV	= Pavia
CR	= Cremona	SO	= Sondrio

Wool cloth

Like linen manufacture, the Lombard wool industry included three or four levels of specialisation. Strong demand for heavy clothing because of the region's harsh winter climate and wool's greater technical versatility explain why new wool manufactures considerably outnumber new linen and fustian industries (Figure 6.3). Since the more specialised semi-urban industries utilised imported wool, access to local raw materials was irrelevant for industrial location. Regarding location, more specialised wool manufactures were more likely to develop in the absence of a specialised linen industry, although both industries were practically absent from the districts of Milan, Cremona and Piacenza.[45]

The determining factor for industrial location was the power of urban guilds. Most urban wool producers in Lombardy used cheaper labour from the countryside and the smaller towns for spinning and lower quality weaving, but maintained strict control over the more profitable finishing stages. Urban crafts were therefore not in principle averse to cloth production in the countryside as long as they could enforce a clear division of labour, which they tried to achieve in two ways.[46] First, they required the more skilled non-urban workers to submit to their rule, a rule that industries in the smaller towns frequently sought to mimic.[47] Second, they

45 Specialised wool manufactures included Bormio (Valtellina), Cannobio, Val Vigezzo and Varallo Sesia (Novara), Borgo San Martino (Alessandria), Voghera and Vigevano (Pavia), Bellano, Valsassina and Lecco (Como), Romano di Lombardia (Bergamo), and Lonato and Riviera di Salò (Brescia).

46 In 1377 Bergamo ordered the destruction of all dyeing, stretching and fulling plant in its northern district and a ban on woad exports to the 'Valle Imania alta, Lovieri superiori et inferiori, Brembille, Vallis Seriane superioris et inferioris', the Riviera of Lake Garda, and the *Scavalie* and *Callopii* valleys, but the attempt appears to have failed, since these areas were still making cloth in the fifteenth century. See *Contractus* 1575: f.27; BCBg, Sala I.D.7.28(9), *Statuta datiorum* 1453: rr.49-50; Mainoni 1994a: 103, 105.

47 For requirements on non-urban workers, see Magnani 1963; Finazzi 1876: col.2011 rr.36–38; Storti Storchi 1986: 157 r.69; *Volumen* 1686: rr. 65-66, 80, 83 (1457); ASCBs, Queriniana (A.M.M.) 1056, f.138v r.57 (1457). See ASCBs, Queriniana (A.M.M.) 1056, f. 171 (1479) on fraudulent woollen shearers and beaters to be expelled from the guild and banned from the city and district. In 1518 Brescia's cap makers restricted their craft to the city (ibid.: f.192). In 1392 the wool weavers of Milan and its *contado*, which had previously been separately regulated, were joined together, but the agreement collapsed after the death of duke Gian Galeazzo Visconti in 1403 (Mainoni 1994a: 214). The Milanese guild however also claimed that its statutes applied to the whole district, including the city of Como, in 1385, 1396, 1403 and 1471 (Mira 1937: 355-6; Barbieri 1938: 40–1). Cremona did the same; see *Statuti* 1580? (1388) and Vianello 1951–2: 205–6 (1504). Although the statutes of Piacenza's wool guild of 1336 did not mention non-urban production, in 1386 the guild adopted the more restrictive Milanese statute which compelled everyone within the city's jurisdiction to join the corporation; see Pallastrelli 1869: rr.22, 53–4, 59). In the same years Gian Galeazzo Visconti offered a ten-year tax exemption to immigrants to Piacenza and its district who worked in the woollen industry (Bonora 1860: 335–6). For similar controls over rural labour by the

restricted trade in raw materials and finished cloth in the city's hinterland, and controlled access to the foreign wool and dyes needed for the better quality cloth.[48] Both strategies required strong jurisdictional powers over the city's *contado* and *distretto*. Alternatively, if they had the requisite technical competence, they could follow the pattern previously described for the fustian industry and choose to compete on quality rather than cost by diversification.[49]

New industries needed time to develop the requisite technical and commercial skills to challenge the established urban producers; only a few of them, including Torno near Como and Monza near Milan, already had something of a head start in the mid-fourteenth century.[50] Most other semi-urban industries started off after the Black Death by making crude woollens known as *orbace* and semi-fraudulent imitations of the cheapest urban cloths.[51] Some never developed beyond this stage, but others – like Lecco, Cannobio and Varese that made simple *orbace* in the fourteenth century, or Canzo, Val Madrera and Cantù which are completely unknown as manufacturing centres in the fourteenth century – by the early fifteenth century were making the equivalent of Bergamo's *panno basso* ('low cloth' with reference to width), a medium quality cloth sold on regional and international markets.[52] In the early 1400s the valleys to the north of

linen guild in Pavia, see Crotti Pasi 1984: 37. For smaller towns, see Mira 1937: 366–7 (fourteenth-century Lecco); *Statuti* 1891: 169–72 (Monza, 1382).

48 In 1292 Brescia banned exports (Odorici 1876: col.1584 note 244). Como imposed tariffs on carded wool and cloth made in its district (von Liebenau 1885–6: 218–19). In 1445 the neighbouring town of Torno asked duke Filippo Maria Visconti to be allowed to sell its products throughout the Duchy notwithstanding Como's restrictions (Cristini 1987: 73–4). For restrictions by Milan see Noto 1950: 99 note 181 (1346). Piacenza tried repeatedly to ban imports of *panni alti e bassi* and ready-made clothing from the districts of Bergamo and Mantua in the fifteenth century (ASPc, Stat. Com. Corp. cat., 42 (reg. provv. 7); Pallastrelli 1869: xiii–xiv, 55–8 (1472); Bersani 1992). For Mantua's wool industry, see Coniglio 1958: vol.1, 390 note 223, 429–32, 461, 481 notes 5–7; vol.2, 430. For controls on wood, see von Liebenau 1885–6: 214–15. See also Clerici 1982–3 for Como's role in redistributing German wool to neighbouring industries, particularly Torno. For Milan see Noto 1950: 99 note 181 (1346); *Statuta* 1480: 228v–9 (only the guild of wool producers could buy the best quality wool from northern Europe). Monza became increasingly dependent on wool from Milan during the fifteenth century (Mainoni 1984: 42). For dyes, see *Contractus* 1575: 25v–6; BCBg, Sala I.D.8.5, f.9 r.41. Both instances are from Bergamo.

49 Mainoni 1983: 577.

50 For Torno, see Barbieri 1938: 64; Noto 1950: 111 note 219, 123 note 7. Monza exported cloth to Venice and Florence in the fourteenth century (Zaninelli 1969: 15–16, 24).

51 Oxhair was frequently used as a fraudulent substitute for sheep's wool. See ASCBs, BS 1046, f.77 (1355); *Statuta* 1557, f. 86 (1429); *Statuta* 1508: r.215 (1471); *Statuta* 1625: 16–17 r.24 (c.1360). In 1382 the merchants of Monza reported that 'panni debiles et non bonos' were being produced in the town's hinterland (*Statuti* 1891: 169-72).

52 Among those that did not develop, Borgosesia seems to have specialised in the production of *orbace* (Mor 1932: 166–7 r.66). For *panno basso*, see Noto 1950: 89 note 133, 96 note 166 (Lecco and Cannobio, 1346), 123 note 7 (c.1425); *Statuta* 1480: f.191v (Varese, c.1330–50). For Canzo see Mainoni 1992: 215.

Bergamo produced imitations of 'low' *and* 'high' Bergamo cloth.[53] The woolmakers of Piacenza, who had long objected to semi-urban cloth-making by reason of its poor quality, were conceding by the 1430s that non-urban products were just as good as urban.[54] In the most successful case, it took just a few decades for the wool industry of Vigevano to challenge manufacturers in nearby Pavia and Milan in their domestic markets.[55]

Industrial development and the institutional framework

The secret of Lombardy's protoindustrial success was the segmentation of the region into competing urban, feudal, small town and rural jurisdictions. Every community that successfully established a new textile manufacture could claim feudal immunities, commercial franchises, and fiscal and judicial privileges – confirmed by Lombardy's territorial rulers or granted by them afresh during the late fourteenth and fifteenth centuries – which allowed it to circumvent merchant and craft monopolies.[56] This fact explains why some of the most successful woollen industries were situated at the regional periphery in provinces of Novara, Como, Bergamo and Brescia where the Milanese and Venetian states found it strategically convenient to protect the communities' rights and freedoms. Down in the plains, Melegnano claimed a right to make fustian based on its status as *terra separata* from the city of Milan, while Monza's success in the wool industry and Vigevano's in the wool, fustian and linen industries depended crucially on their jurisdictional autonomy from Milan and Pavia; but communities in the plains found it harder to break away from urban tutelage, their bargaining powers with the central authorities were weaker, and consequently they had fewer chances of industrial success.[57]

The concession of large numbers of jurisdictional freedoms should in principle have caused the regional market to fragment, but the practical effect was the opposite. By the early fifteenth century, Lombard cities

---

53 BCBg, Y.S.1 (= MMB 728), f.73 (Val Gandino, 1428); *Pacta* 1722: 22 r.55 (1498), 24 r.15 (1475) (Lonato).

54 Bersani 1992.

55 Mainoni 1992. A cloth guild was founded in 1418 (ibid.: 219–20). For restrictions on Vigevano's cloth see Magnani 1963: 58–9; Fossati 1914a: 116–17; Mainoni 1992: 234, 238; Colombo 1988: 198 note 13.

56 See, most fundamentally on the issue of jurisdictional freedoms, Chittolini 1996, including the index for references to the individual communities mentioned here.

57 For Melegnano and Milan, see Fennell Mazzaoui 1981: 158. For Monza and Vigevano, see Magnani 1963: 34 r. 70 and BCPv, ms. A.III.15, f.20v r.93 for references to evasion by Vigevano of Pavia's restrictions on trade in linen thread. Vigevano made use of its strategic location to play off Milan, Pavia and Novara against each other; see Chittolini 1992.

had lost the right to impose commercial restrictions or to raise tariffs independently. They had already conceded this right to the Visconti lords in principle in 1346 with the passing of the *Provisiones Ianue*. The latter, so-called because they aimed to improve the transit trade between Genoa, the Lombard plain and northern Europe, established a unified customs system between the cities of Milan, Como, Lodi and Cremona and the borough of Pizzighettone (to which Novara, Brescia and Bergamo were subsequently added), in exchange for which the Visconti guaranteed peaceful trading relations across the region.[58] However, the principle of a common or single market in the region took a further century to be established. The collapse of the Lombard state into anarchy and civil war after the death of the first duke, Gian Galeazzo Visconti, in 1402 proves that the latter's policies of political, fiscal and judicial centralisation had still to shake the legal and political foundations of urban power.[59]

The rise after 1350 of textile protoindustries played an important part in the integration process. By the mid-fifteenth century, cities that wished to impose protectionist legislation had to obtain the duke's assent, but laying themselves open to public scrutiny also raised the cost of gaining a favourable ruling. In one notable example of the new lobbying process, Milan successfully petitioned duke Francesco Sforza to forbid imports to the city of wool cloth made elsewhere in the Duchy and in Italy. However, three years later, in 1457, the duke revoked the measure after his council noted that Milan's request had set off a round of competitive protectionism by other Lombard cities that risked destroying regional trade and industries and causing tax revenues to collapse. Instead of banning the low-quality wool cloth made by Vigevano and other small towns, as urban producers demanded, the duke ordered the cloth to be branded so that consumers could make an informed choice: if they wished to buy lower quality but cheaper cloth, they should be able to do so. At the stroke of a pen, Francesco Sforza overcame the prisoner's dilemma arising from urban protectionism and protected the competitive rights of the new semi-urban manufactures.[60] Jurisdictional freedoms and market integration were two sides of the same coin.

A second factor that determined industrial location, in addition to jurisdictional freedoms, was access to higher quality inputs. *Linen*

---

58 For the unified customs system, see Noto 1950: 75–83. For the role of Visconti, see Bueno de Mesquita 1941: 4–5, 303, 311; Chittolini 1982: 28.

59 See Occhipinti 1992; Varanini 1994; Chittolini 1996: 85–104. On the limits to four-teenth-century jurisdictional integration, see Bueno de Mesquita 1941: 55–6, 316–17; Black 1988. For the fifteenth century, see Chittolini 1982.

60 Barbieri 1938: 130–2; BT, *Decreta ducalia pro Cremona*, ff.138v–9 (1457). In Pavia the decree of 1457 was published in 1459; see Statuta 1625: 66–7 rubr.119.

manufacture was the least constrained in this respect, because flax was ubiquitous and linen weaving was a basic peasant skill. Low barriers to entry explain why towns rarely attempted to regulate linen protoindustries directly, even though the better flax and more skilled labour were more easily found in the larger cities with an established fustian industry.[61] Protoindustrial *wool* and *fustian* manufactures were more dependent on outside supplies of raw materials which were more easily controlled by urban merchants. Protoindustries had no difficulty in finding the cheaper grades of wool from north Africa, Italy, southern France and southern Germany, but peripheral industries in the provinces of Novara, Bergamo and Brescia and producers closest to cities found it harder to avoid the urban stranglehold over the trade in cotton, foreign dyes and the better qualities of wool.[62] Although such control over the new industries' supply and distribution networks by its very nature left few traces, an attempt in 1396 to force Monza's wool industry to market its cloth in Milan, and Bergamo's decision in the same years to forbid the trade in woad and unfinished cloth with its northern industrial valleys to its north, are indicative of the subterranean conflicts taking place.[63] Only industries which had access to competing sources of supply were able to neutralise urban hostility. The small town of Lecco benefited from its position at a commercial cross-roads between Venice and Milan, while the fustian industries in Busto Arsizio, Gallarate and Abbiategrasso in central and western Lombardy and in Pinerolo and Chieri in southern Piedmont could rely on cotton supplies from Genoa and other Ligurian ports in addition to those from Venice controlled by Milan, Pavia and Cremona.[64]

Urban and protoindustrial cloth-making was not however a zero-sum game. Faced with dozens of new linen, fustian and wool industries they could no longer control, the textile industries of the Lombard cities converted and restructured. The mid-fifteenth century crisis of the

---

61   An attempt by Alessandria to control linen manufacture in the countryside seems to have been unsuccessful; see *Codex* 1547: 89.

62   Among the protoindustries, manufacturers in Como, Torno and Lecco close to the Swiss Alpine passes used mainly German and English wool (Clerici 1982–3: 85–6; Grillo 1993: 97; Grillo 1995: ch.4; Zelioli Pini 1992: 69–72). Vigevano, which lay along the main route between Milan and Genoa, increasingly bypassed the Milanese market in order to buy directly from Genoa through a local Jewish banking and commercial enterprise, the Averlino. It used wool from Provence, Languedoc, Cyprus and Spain (Mainoni 1992: 218–19, 221, 245). Producers in Lovere to the north of Bergamo used wool from Cremona, Mantua and local suppliers (Silini 1992: 230–31). Lombard industries could also take advantage of the improvement in the quality of wool from the neighbouring Veneto (Fennell Mazzaoui 1981: 135; Tagliabue 1991–2: 130–2 for the high quality of Veronese wool).

63   *Statuta* 1480: 144v; Mainoni 1993; *Contractus* 1575: ff.9, 27v.

64   For Lecco, see Zelioli Pini 1992: 26–32, 63–6, 69–72. For the other towns mentioned, see Beonio Brocchieri 1995: 58, 165.

Milanese woollen industry, Lombardy's most oft quoted example of late medieval industrial decline, owed as much to the interruption of Spanish wool supplies after mid-century as to competition from regional protoindustries, and was more than adequately compensated by the shift in the same period to the high-growth silk industry where the city could claim first-mover advantage.[65] Como's wool industry, which underwent a devastating setback during the civil wars of the early 1400s, experienced a late fifteenth-century renaissance.[66] Other cities compensated for weakness in woollen production by diversifying to linen and fustian. The statement attributed to the Venetian Doge Tommaso Mocenigo in the 1420s, that every year Lombard cities exported 48,000 wool and 40,000 fustian cloths worth more than 900,000 ducats to Venice, described a regional industrial cluster of unprecedented size and vitality, of which the new protoindustrial towns were a vital component.[67]

Tuscany

The Tuscan cloth industry developed in a broadly similar fashion to the Lombard industries after the great plague. Output of low- and middle-range wool, linen and mixed fibre cloth expanded by comparison with that of high quality woollens, the product range became broader, and a greater proportion of manufacture occurred outside the larger towns and cities. But the differences between the two regions were far more significant. Tuscan protoindustries were anaemic; they seldom sold outside the increasingly protected domestic market, where their technically unsophisticated products posed no challenge to urban manufacture; and consequently, no industrial cluster emerged of the kind apparent in Lombardy and elsewhere in late medieval and early modern Europe. Premodern protoindustry simply passed Tuscany by.[68]

Wool cloth

Even before the Black Death, evidence from commercial tariffs suggests that the urban wool industry developed later in Tuscany than in Lombardy and was generally less sophisticated. Lombard cities exported distinctive qualities of cloth by the mid-thirteenth century, whereas Tuscan cities outside Florence only began to do so several decades later (Table 6.1). Thirteenth-century Lombardy had a strong woollen industry in Brescia, Como and Monza in addition to Milan, and an internationally known

---

65   Mainoni 1984: 22, 40–2; Mainoni 1992: 226, 231, 234; Mainoni 1994b.
66   Mira 1937.
67   Luzzatto 1965: 195.
68   See Malanima 1982: ch.2 and Malanima 1990 for the early modern period.

fustian industry in Cremona. In Tuscany, Florence's only significant rival was the small quasi-satellite town of Prato a few kilometres to its north.[69] The thirteenth-century wool industry in the second-largest Tuscan city, Pisa, made low- and medium-quality cloth mostly for captive markets in its hinterland and its colony, Sardinia.[70] Manufactures in other towns (which included Arezzo, Pistoia, San Gimignano, Colle and Volterra in addition to those listed in Table 6.1) produced largely for local consumption.[71] Before

69 See Nuti 1928; Piattoli and Nuti 1947; Fennell Mazzaoui 1984: 529–30; Cassandro 1991: 401–15.
70 Silva 1910; Castagneto 1996. The types of cloth mentioned by the guild statutes are *panni albaci, tacculini, altipascinghi, sargie, carpite*, and *celoni* (Bonaini 1857: 705–8).
71 No detailed studies exist of cloth manufacture in the smaller Tuscan towns. Scattered references can be found in Fiumi 1961; Castellani 1956: 93–137; Herlihy 1967: 173–5; Fennell Mazzaoui 1984: 529–30; Biadi 1859: 41; Muzzi 1995: 236–9; Pinto 1995a; BCV, G nera 15, Statuti di Volterra, ff.112v–13 (1336), 373rv (1348); ASAr, Statuti del comune di Arezzo e riforme 3, f.22v (1348).

Table 6.1 Lombard and Tuscan woollen industries in Italian customs lists, 1200–1429

	1200–49 2[a]	1250–99 10[a]	1300–49 25[a]	1350–1429 19[a]	Total 56[a]
		Lombardy			
Bergamo	1	2	3	5	11
Brescia	1	1	6	7	15
Como	2	2	8	10	22
Lodi	—	—	1	—	1
Cremona	—	1	—	1	2
Milan	—	5	18	16	39
Monza	1	1	4	7	13
Pavia	—	1	1	—	2
Piacenza	—	1	—	—	1
'Panni lombardi'	—	3	1	8	1
Total	5	17	42	54	118
		Tuscany			
Arezzo	—	—	—	1	1
Florence	—	8	25	15	48
Pisa	—	1	2	5	8
Pistoia	—	—	2	2	4
Prato	—	—	6	2	8
Siena	—	—	4	6	10
'Panni toscani'	—	1	1	4	6
Total	0	10	40	35	85

[a] Number of cities with listed tariffs.
Source: Hoshino 1980: 50–60.

the Florentine industry converted to high quality *panno francesco* with English wool during the 1320s, it was also quite unsophisticated compared with the best of the Lombard industries.[72]

Why Tuscan wool manufacture before the Black Death should have lagged behind that of Lombardy is puzzling. Tuscany had equally good infrastructure and similar property rights, commercial opportunities and raw materials. It produced its own dyes – woad on the hills between Borgo San Sepolcro, Arezzo and Montepulciano and near Volterra; saffron again in the vicinity of Volterra, in the upper Elsa valley, and in the surroundings of Montepulciano; and madder around Cortona and Volterra by the late fourteenth century – and had local sources of vitriol, sulphur and alum which were used as colour mordants.[73] The quality of Tuscan wool was poor, but no worse than that from Lombardy, and better wool could be imported just as easily to both regions.

What may have set the two industries on different growth paths was a different approach towards technological dissemination. Since technical transfer occurred principally through artisan migration, systematic obstacles to artisan mobility devised to protect individual crafts from the loss of in-house technical 'secrets' could seriously compromise long-term industrial performance by delaying technical diffusion, restricting the pool of skilled labour, and causing average costs to rise in relation to competitors.[74] Lombard cities pursued technical cooperation, allowed their artisans to move freely and shared a technological pool that allowed contamination and cross-fertilisation between the different textile industries. The thirteenth-century penitential movement of the *Umiliati*, whose members specialised in wool weaving and travelled far and wide in northern Italy (they set up a convent in Florence in 1239) originated in Lombardy.[75] By contrast, Tuscan cities forbade the migration of skilled labour and penalised errant masters by banishing them from their homes.[76] Significantly, on the only known occasion

---

72 The change probably responded to the growing threat to Florentine cloth in southern Italy by other Italian producers and to the decline in fine cloth exports from Flanders, which opened up new commercial opportunities (Hoshino 1983).

73 BCV, G nera 17, ff.9–14v (Volterra); Perol 1994: 81, 429 (Cortona). Florence forbade the export of madder seed from Cortona's *contado* in the early fifteenth century (ibid.: 94). For the woad trade before the Black Death, see Agnoletti 1940: 72–81; Franceschi 1994: 90; Morandi 1966: 357–9; ASFi, AL 41, ff.142v–3v (1345) for the importation of 150,000 lb. of woad from Bologna. For the later Middle Ages see Fanfani 1935; Pinto 1994; Scharf 1996: 142. For saffron, see Fiumi 1961; BCV, G nera 15, f.9v (1354); BCV, G nera 38, f.49r (1514). For mordants, see Fiumi 1943 and 1948.

74 Epstein 1998a. On technological transfer in the Italian cloth industries, see Fennell Mazzaoui 1984 and 1987.

75 For the *Umiliati* in general, see Zanoni 1911. For the *Umiliati* in Florence, see Day 1999: ch.5.

76 Thirteenth-century Florentine artisans were forbidden to work in Pisan territory or to

during the thirteenth century in which Florentine artisans migrated freely to share their skills, they went to Bologna, a staunch Guelf ally in Florence's struggle against the Tuscan Ghibelline cities of Pisa, Siena, Pistoia, and Arezzo.[77] By reducing the size of the pool of skilled labour to which individual Tuscan towns could gain access, technological protectionism restricted the potential for industrial clustering and put thirteenth-century Tuscan cloth industries at a permanent disadvantage compared with Lombard manufacture.[78]

The low degree of urban specialisation in Tuscany suggests that any new industries arising after the Black Death would compete more directly with town industries than in Lombardy and would attract stronger hostility. Although the Florentine wool guild began to take official action against petty rural production soon after the Black Death, passing its first ruling on the matter in 1353 and deciding by the early 1360s to force *contado* producers to enrol, the guild's reaction bore little relation to the phenomenon's numerical and economic significance.[79] Between 1362 and 1549, the craft recorded an average of five or six rural matriculations a year (Table 6.2), which means that during the fifteenth century no more than eighty to 100 craftsmen were practising at the same time in Florence's *contado*.[80] Since a substantial proportion of

associate with its citizens (Agnoletti 1940: 115–16), and Florentine cloth shearers could not shear cloth from Prato (ibid.: 118–19). The former prohibition was repeated in 1361 (ASFi, AL 6, f.35v) and was still in force in the fifteenth century (AL 51, ff.39v–40, 1434). For an example of enforcement of the ban on migration, see ibid., ff.72v–3r, 1435; in this case, the delinquent craftsman was allowed to return home from Perugia without penalty because of the Florentine craft's need for skilled labour.

77   For the migration of Florentine woollen craftsmen to Bologna in 1231, see Fennell Mazzaoui 1967–8: 310–9. For the lack of economic cooperation between Tuscan cities due to political hostilities that continued through most of the thirteenth and early fourteenth centuries, see Day 1999: ch.6. See also Waley 1978: Fig. 6.

78   Tuscan towns were generally more protectionist than their Lombard counterparts. The earliest Florentine statutes contain an undated ban on the sale of cheaper foreign woollens; better-quality Milanese and Flemish cloth was exempted (Agnoletti 1940: 125–6). For protectionism by the Pisan *Arte della lana* directed particularly against Florence, see ASFi, Mercanzia 142, ff.21r–2r, 24r–6r (1336); Mercanzia 145, ff.54v–5r (1340). For protectionism by the Prato industry, see Piattoli and Nuti 1947: 2. For a fuller discussion of the long-term consequences of cooperation and competition between Italian city-states, see Epstein 2000b.

79   On the forced enrolment of *contado* producers in the urban wool guild, see ASFi, AL 42, f.148v; AL 43, f.24rv; AL 44, f.104v. The pre-Black Death statutes do not mention rural producers (Agnoletti 1940). A detailed record of matriculations was introduced after the counter-revolution of 1382 (ASFi, AL46, f.134rv). Between 1362 and 1382 the matriculation book lists only 43 entries for the *contado*, whereas the guild's council records mentions 92 rural craftsmen; Table 6.3 reports the latter figure.

80   This assumes a rate of matriculation of five persons per year and an average working life between 17 years (Franceschi 1993: 135–41) and 21 years, which was the time elapsed between the matriculations of fathers and sons.

registrants lived in the city's suburbs and worked for the Florentine industry, there were probably no more than fifty independent 'protoindustrial' producers at any time, a figure somewhat below the employees in Prato's industry in 1424 (Table 6.3).

More surprisingly, the number of matriculations before the mid-1490s was not appreciably affected by the continued fall in population until the 1420s or by demographic recovery after 1450 (Figure 6.4). The Black Death and its aftermath had no obvious impact on wool protoindustry in the Florentine hinterland.[81] The sharp drop in registrations from 1493 seems to have been caused by the administrative and military upheavals caused by the rebellion of Pisa (1492–1505), which made it

Table 6.2 Matriculations in the Florentine *Arte della lana* and *Arte del lino*, 1305–1549[a]

	Wool						
	Florence				*Contado*		
	Aliens[b]	*%*	*Total*		*Aliens*[b]	*%*	*Total*
1305–49	558	100.0	558				
1350–99	941	67.6	1393		145	92.4	157[c]
1400–49	477	21.7	2201		191	80.6	237
1450–99	425	18	2364		129	70.9	182
1500–49	137	12.9	1065		386	81.3	475

	Linen						
	Florence				*Contado*		
	Aliens[b]	*%*	*Total*		*Aliens*[b]	*%*	*Total*
1365–99[d]	263	100.0	263		24	96.0	25
1400–49	596	99.7	598		190	91.8	207
1450–99	513	96.6	531		185	80.1	231
1500–49	367	87.6	419		2	33.3	6

[a] Tailors and retailers from the *Arte dei rigattieri, linaioli e sarti* not included.
[b] Excluding free (*pro beneficio*) matriculation of craft members' relatives.
[c] Beginning 1362 for the *contado* (ASFi, Arte della lana 44, f.60r).
[d] Beginning 1365 for Florence, 1383 for the *contado*.

Sources: ASFi, *Arte della lana* 27, 540-1; *Arte dei rigattieri, linaioli e sarti* 10, ff. 130r-59v.

81 The number of fulling mills for wool cloth can be used as a rough proxy for industrial development. The number of fulling mills in the Florentine *contado* increased sharply between the thirteenth century, when W. R. Day 1999: ch.5 note 68 counts four, and the 1420s, when the Catasto listed sixty for a somewhat larger territory (Muendel 1981). However, the timing of expansion has yet to be ascertained, and most fulling mills in 1424-7 were situated at the *contado's* periphery, where they were not affected by competition from Florence and where they were used to make rough *panni bigelli* (ASFi, DAC 372, ff.159-63, 6 Feb. 1391; *Statuta* 1778–83: L.V, rr.26, 31). See also note 114.

Table 6.3 Tuscan cloth industries, 1424–7

No. of declaring professionals	Local/ subregional 10–49	Regional/ supraregional 50–99	International 100+
Colle Valdelsa	17W, 1L		
San Gimignano	20W, 1L		
Montepulciano	29W		
Volterra	30W, 2L		
Cortona	33W		
Pistoia	40W, 17L-S		
Prato		55W, 5L-S	
Arezzo		60W, 41L-S-C	
Pisa		80W, 48L-S, 34O	
Florence			1434W, 386L-S-C, 62O
Total	169W, 21L-S	195W, 94L-S-C, 34O	1434W, 386L-S-C, 62O

W = wool; L = linen; S = silk; C = cotton; O = other

Source: 'Census and Property Survey of Florentine Domains in the Province of Tuscany, 1427-1480', ed. D.Herlihy and C.Klapisch-Zuber, software by F. Bonomi.

harder for Florence's wool guild to monitor developments on the ground, rather than by a collapse in manufacturing activities.[82] The lull in matriculations lasted until the 1530s, when the Medici began a registration drive in order to map the region's industrial capacity, but most of the registrants were probably not new (Table 6.4).[83]

Although guild records do not survive for other Tuscan cities, there is little to suggest that strong protoindustries developed in neighbouring *contadi* either. Most evidence comes from the *contado* of Volterra, a small town to the south-east of Florence which in 1421 set up a new wool guild, possibly as protection against rural competition.[84] The nature of the response reflects Volterra's industrial weakness (the Catasto of 1424–7 listed only thirty workers (Table 6.3)) but by the same

82 An undated provision from the early 1490s exempted inhabitants of the *contado* from matriculation fees in Florentine guilds (ASFi, AL 13, ff.155r–6r).

83 An earlier attempt by the Medici to raise matriculations in 1525 collapsed with the regime's fall in 1527 (ASFi, AL 62, f.146v).

84 Volterra made the cheapest varieties of cloth known as *panno fioretto, panno fioretto berrettino, pannicello* and *orbace* with a warp of 840–1,200 threads (BCV, G nera 16b, f.24v); its artisans bought their tools in Florence (Pagliazzi 1939: 28, 33). The surviving fifteenth-century gate tolls show that the town shipped forty-two cloths between August and October 1434 and fifty-three cloths in August-September 1470, but only twenty-two in April and August 1490 and thirteen in August – September 1527. The sharp decline in output may have followed the sack of the town by Florentine troops in 1470. By October 1548, however, it was showing mild signs of recovery with twenty-five cloths shipped (BCV, A"", Giornali di gabella 1, 9).

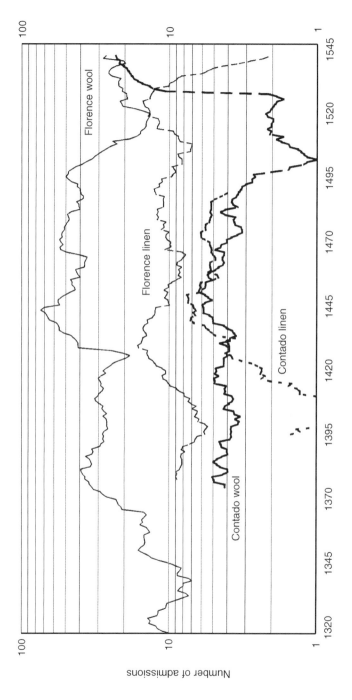

Figure 6.4 Admissions to the wool and linen crafts in Florence and its *contado*, 1320–1549 (17-year moving average)

Table 6.4 Wool and linen industries in the Florentine *contado*, 1350–1549 (by matriculation)

	1350–99ᵃ	1400–49	1450–99	1500–49	Total
Barberino	—	—	1W	30W	31W
Borgo San Lorenzo	3W, 1L	12L	14L	10W	13W, 27L
Castelfiorentino	7W, 2L	23W, 7L	1W, 7L	12W	43W, 16L
Cavallina	—	—	7W	8W	15W
Certaldo	3W	21W	5W	4W	33W
Empoli	5W, 3L	19W, 15L	14W, 18L	40W	78W, 36L
Figline	10W, 2L	4W, 7L	6W, 9L	15W	35W, 18L
Marcialla	24W	4W	11W	1W	40W
Montelupo	13W	6W	9W	17W	45W
Montevarchi	4W, 1L	5W, 9L	4W, 6L	9W	22W, 16L
Poggibonsi	15W, 1L	4W, 3L	2W, 6L	8W	29W, 10L
Ronta	4W	6W	1W	8W	19W
San Casciano	—	6W, 5L	6W, 15L	20W	32W, 20L
San Donato in Poggio	4W	1W	—	6W	11W
San Giovanni Valdarno	22W	3W, 7L	5W, 3L	6W	36W, 10L
Terranuova Bracciolini	7W	2W	—	17W	26W
Total	121W, 10L	104W, 65L	72W, 78L	211W	508W, 153L

ᵃ1362–99 for wool, 1383–99 for linen.

Sources: see Table 6.2.

token exaggerates the scale of rural competition.[85] The more robust industries of Pisa, Arezzo and Pistoia acted earlier and left no room for development in their *contado*, and even the small town of Borgo San Sepolcro which set up a new wool craft in the late fourteenth century was later careful to establish a monopoly over the surrounding district.[86]

Figure 6.5 maps urban and semi-urban woollen production after the Black Death on the basis of evidence culled mainly from the Florentine matriculations and the Catasto (Tables 6.2 and 6.3). Both sets of data must be used cautiously. Fewer than half the household heads

85 See BCV, G nera 16b, *Statuti dell'Arte della lana di Volterra* (1422), ff.1–4v for the names of rural weavers matriculated between 1425 and 1471; the largest number (eight) came from the village of Pomarance. Pomarance was explicitly mentioned in the provision authorising Volterra's wool producers to matriculate rural weavers in their guild (BCV, G nera 16c, f.30, 1 July 1425). The rural weavers' annual fee was set at 5 *soldi*, which must be compared with the 2 *lire* paid by master weavers in the contado of Florence (BCV, G nera 16b, f.27v; ASFi, AL 44, f.104v) and with the 12 to 18 *lire* that a Volterran wool cloth was worth in 1400 (BCV, G nera 17, ff.9–14v) (1 *lira* = 20 *soldi*).

86 Rural production was restricted to the kind of *panni romagnoli di lana grossa nostrale* made in the *contado* of Arezzo in the mid-fifteenth century (DAC 372, f.716, 12 Jan. 1461). For Borgo San Selopcro, see Fanfani 1933; Scharf 1996: 96; DAC 372, ff.664–5, 20 Mar. 1458. San Sepolcro sold cloth in Rome in 1451–76 (Hoshino 1980: 286).

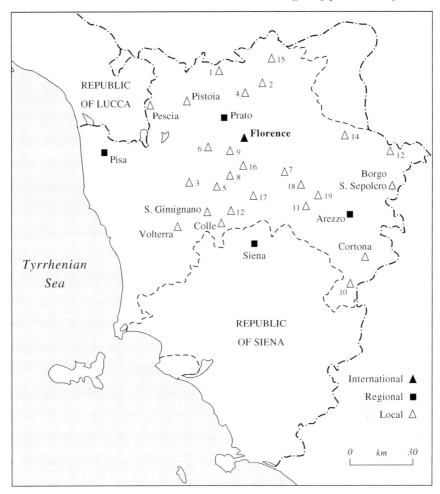

Figure 6.5 The Tuscan woollen industry, c.1350–1550

declaring for the Catasto reported their profession, meaning that the total number of textile 'professionals' in the larger urban centre could be up to double the figures reported in Table 6.3.[87] Occupational mobility and a lack of clear professional demarcations make it hard to identify practising artisans, while less than 20 per cent of *contado* residents who matriculated in the *Arte della lana* between 1417 and 1427 appear in Catasto records for their declared place of abode. Despite these caveats, the picture is unambiguous and internally consistent.

87 For the purposes of this study, no attempt has been made to distinguish these professionals by occupation.

Low- and mid-quality cloth production in late medieval Tuscany was situated overwhelmingly in the larger towns. Output in the countryside and small towns was quantitatively minuscule and technically crude and supplied only the local community and its environs (Table 6.4).[88] Despite the lack of protoindustrial competition, however, urban industry performed poorly and fell increasingly under the Florentine shadow. Of the 2,531 bales of foreign wool sold by the Florentine Cambini company between 1454 and 1480, 2,383 (94.2 per cent) went to Florence, 115 (4.5 per cent) were sold to Prato, eleven went to Pisa, and the rest was bought by producers in San Casciano, Poggibonsi, Castelfiorentino, Marcialla, Empoli and the Mugello valley.[89]

Tuscany's increasingly rigid industrial hierarchy was partly also a consequence of Florence's response to its own industrial crisis, whose origins can be traced back to the defeat in 1382 of the guild-based regime inspired by the Ciompi labourers' insurrection of 1378. Fearing reprisal, hundreds of craftsmen and workers fled for Pisa, Lucca, Perugia and Venice; although their places were taken by migrant artisans from Germany and central Europe, the subsequent industrial collapse – output fell by two-thirds between 1373 and 1437 and quality declined – indicates that the skills lost as a result of the civil war were not recovered.[90] The Florentine wool industry's difficulties made it ever more sensitive to competition, and during the troubled 1390s and early 1400s – at the height of the city's struggle against Gian Galeazzo Visconti of Milan who controlled the vital routes between Florence, Pisa, Lucca and Siena – it increasingly indulged its fears in the domestic arena.

In 1392, 1394 and again in 1396 Florence's *Arte della lana* claimed that it was losing labour, capital and raw materials to regional competitors and lobbied for protective tariffs; in 1406 it identified the manufacturers of Pistoia and Prato as a major threat. A year later it ordered that manufacturers in the *contado* use only the worst-quality, Tuscan wool or *lana nostrale*.[91] Repression was efficiently ruthless; fines of up to 500 *lire*, equivalent to two years' salary of a master builder, were especially persuasive.[92] Although outside their contado the Florentines had to

---

88 Much was made of a proposal in 1418 to make up to 50 cloths annually in San Miniato (Rondoni 1877: 217).

89 Hoshino 1980: 302.

90 For artisan migrations after 1382, see Franceschi 1989; Franceschi 1993: 119–35. The industry's problems were magnified by difficulties with the supply of English wool and by political instability in the southern Italian markets in the first quarter of the fifteenth century. See Franceschi 1993: 11–13, 18, 21–3; Hoshino 1980: 233.

91 DAC 372, ff.170r–3r (1392); ASFi, AL 47, ff.72v, 102r, 103r, 127rv, 129 (1392–6); ASFi, AL 48, ff.98r, 113v–14r (1406-7).

92 Franceschi 1988: 580–2. For fines, see ASFi, AL 6, ff.90v–1v (1407).

tread more carefully, between 1407 and 1415 they passed several regulations concerning the region's woollen industry which, in the wool guild's new statutes of 1428, turned into a full-blown industrial policy. The statutes envisaged a tripartite division of labour between the Florentine industry, which was granted a monopoly over the best north European wool and dyeing materials and the better qualities of cloth; the smaller cities, which could use the better types of wool from Spain (*lana di San Matteo*), southern France and northern Africa (*lana di Garbo*), but were restricted in the quality of their dyes; and at the bottom, producers in the *contado* and *distretto* who could only utilise the poorer qualities of central and southern Italian wool and were not allowed to dye their cloth.[93] The resulting division of labour between the export-led industries of Florence and the domesticated industries elsewhere in the state would remain in place for three hundred years.[94]

It is perhaps no coincidence that the period of sharpest Florentine repression in the early fifteenth century also witnessed a sharp crisis among other urban industries.[95] The worst hit was Pisa, whose wool industry collapsed entirely after the Florentine conquest of 1406 caused most of the city's craft and merchant communities to flee, and led to the abolition of the local wool guild.[96] The Tuscan wool industry was further penalised during the fifteenth century by protectionist legislation that barred imports of all but the most expensive foreign cloth. The Florentine government claimed to be responding to similar moves by unspecified foreign countries, but given the indiscriminate nature of the tariffs this seems implausible. In fact, tit-for-tat protectionism was particularly damaging for the less specialised Tuscan industries which competed on price rather than quality, and the tariffs' main purpose

93 ASFi, AL 7, ff.62rv, 65r–6r; Franceschi 1988: 586; Franceschi 1994: 85.
94 Late medieval excises list only urban production. The Pisan tariff of 1362 mentions cloth from Florence, Siena, Prato and Pistoia (Hoshino 1980: 57), while Arezzo's tolls of 1387 list cloth from Florence and Pisa (taxed 160 *soldi* per *soma* of 400-500lb.), San Sepolcro (s.60/*soma*), Arezzo itself (s.45), and Colle and Prato (s.30) (ASAr, SRD 4, ff.1r–17r); in 1468 the tariff on cloth from Colle was raised to s.36 (ASAr, SRD 5, ff.1–5). In 1354–71 and 1383–1402, the average annual value of Tuscan cloth shipped abroad from Pisa (excluding Florentine cloth) was as follows: Lucca and Pistoia jointly, 5,003 florins; Siena, fl.3,557; Prato, fl.3,456; Arezzo, fl.507; Volterra, fl.66 (Melis 1989: 123). Early sixteenth-century Florentine tariffs listed Prato and Pistoia as making the best second-grade cloth, followed by Montopoli (which made *panni di Perpignano*, introduced to Florence in the early fifteenth century (ASFi, AL 49, ff.87rv (1420), 106r (1424), 127rv (1427); AL 51, f.142rv (1437); AL 52, f.15rv (1440)) and San Gimignano, Volterra and Colle (ASFi, DAC 431, ff.2r, 48v–9r). Arezzo and Pisa had dropped out of the list. For production in late seventeenth- and eighteenth-century Tuscany, see Malanima 1990: 191–6.
95 For the decline of Prato, see Cassandro 1991: 437–8. For Pisa and Volterra, see notes 84 and 96. For Pistoia, see Melis 1989: 166–8. For Arezzo, see ASAr, Camerlengo generale, Saldi di entrata e uscita, 1–140 passim (data on trade flows).
96 Banti 1971: 88, 140; Silva 1910; Petralia 1987; Bratchel 1995: 143–4, 151–7; Berti 1980.

seems to have been to strengthen the Florentine industry's grip over the domestic market.[97] In the same years that the Florentine wool industry was trying to shield the Tuscan market from foreign competition, it was shifting production from the high-quality *panni franceschi* on which its had built its medieval reputation to the more down-market *panni di Garbo* for the Levantine market. The conversion in effect cannibalised the medium quality production which Florence had assigned to its subjects.[98] The inward-looking, autarchic (authoritarian) and autarkic (self-sufficient) system established by Florence in the fifteenth century was partly mitigated by Alessandro de' Medici after 1533, but restrictions on quality and trade remained in place and the industrial system's low-level equilibrium founded on the Florentine monopoly was not broken.[99] Although Florence's wool industry recovered during the late fifteenth and sixteenth century, output at its height in the late sixteenth century was no more than it was immediately following the Black Death.

Fustian, cotton and linen

About the other textile sectors excluding the silk industry (which was largely concentrated in Florence) we may be brief. Although flax cultivation was ubiquitous in the Tuscan countryside and the linen industry in particular grew rapidly after the mid-fourteenth century (Tables 6.2 and 6.3), neither it nor the fustian industry have attracted much attention.[100] Linen and fustian production was even more centralised

97 The first general tariffs were raised in 1392 (DAC 372, ff.170–3) and were repeated in 1451 (DAC 372, ff.578–80) and 1535 (ASFi, AL 13, ff.210v–12). In 1439 a general ban was passed on cloth from countries that imposed similar restrictions on Florence (ASFi, AL 13, f.113r). See also Franceschi 1994: 109–12; Epstein 1992: 283–4. In 1478 it was decided to abolish export tariffs on domestically-produced cloth experimentally for five years (ASFi, DAC 372, ff.1013r–15r). More selective bans were passed in later years (ASFi, AL 13, ff.152v–3r).

98 Franceschi 1993: 31. In 1461 Pisa and Livorno were allowed to import cheaper cloth valued at less than 20 *soldi* per *braccio* that was not made locally (ASFi, AL 13, f.19rv). In 1489 weavers of the *contado* were allowed to make *panni alla soventona* and *rascie*, worth 15 *soldi* per *braccio*, which the Florentine industry had begun making a few years before (AL 54, f.119r; AL 62, f.17v).

99 Reform laws of 1535 aimed to establish a self-sufficient market; only some unspecified kinds of rough cloth 'for the poor' could be imported. Like his counterparts in fifteenth-century Lombardy, Alessandro decided to allow production of lower quality 'imitations' as long as their place of origin was clearly marked. However, the measure's potential benefits were neutralised by restricting trade in lower quality cloth to the districts where it was produced. The trade in woad was similarly restricted (some years earlier Arezzo had successfully petitioned to export woad from the region similarly to Cortona and Castiglione Fiorentino; see ASFi, AL 55, f.74v, 1510). See AL 13, ff.210v–12r for the reform; AL 15, ff.30v–1v, 39v–41r, 45v–8, 49r, 52r, 54r–6r, 64r–9v, 77rv, for local trade markings.

100 Flax cultivation expanded in the neighboring territories of Siena and Lucca (Cherubini

than wool; fustian was manufactured only in Florence, Arezzo and Pisa.[101] However, Florence did not dominate these industries as fully as it did wool manufacture, in part because barriers to entry were lower and the city's technological superiority less pronounced – in the 1430s Florentine artisans had to travel to Lombardy to learn the secrets of the fustian trade – but also because its merchants found it more profitable to exploit the city's comparative advantage in woollens.[102] Florence's support for its own linen and cotton industries was only half hearted, and an attempt to stop linen workers from being poached by competitors was the closest the city officials got to manipulating regional market structures.[103]

Florentine neglect reduced the opportunity costs for Arezzo and Pisa of shifting away from wool.[104] Arezzo was part of a network of central Italian towns which included Siena, Perugia, Città di Castello, and Foligno and which specialised after the Black Death in linen and cotton.[105] Pisa had also been steadily improving the quality of production. Before 1350 Pisan fustian, linen and possibly cotton were shipped to Sardinia, though product quality was probably low; by the

---

1981: 384 note 3; Hicks 1986). A document of 1418 mentions different qualities of flax from Pistoia, Pisa, Cortona, Prato and Campiglia (ASFi, AL 5, ff.115v–16r). Flax processing is frequently mentioned in local statutes (ASFi, Statuti delle comunità autonome e soggette 18 (Albiano), f.17rv; BCV, G nera 12 (Monteverdi), f.32v; Calamari 1927: 107; Camerani Marri 1963: 96; Casini 1968: 101, 167–8, 171–2; Roncière 1976: vol.3, 800, 909 and vol.4, 307 note 159; Berti and Guerrini 1980: 165; Berti and Mantovani 1985: 19). For rural linen weaving for home consumption, see Mazzi and Raveggi 1983: 184–5.

101 San Miniato imported raw cotton from Pisa before 1370, probably for padding quilts and mattresses (ASFi, DAC 372, ff.60r–2r, 28 Mar. 1371; see ASFi, ARLS 14, f.41 (1471) for padding)).

102 For the fustian trade, see ASFi, ARLS 5, ff.133v–4r, 2 Jan. 1435.

103 Jurisdiction over linen weaving in the Florentine *contado* was in the hands of the *Ufficiali del biado* who were in charge of the city's cereal supplies, presumably because flax seed was also eaten and pressed for oil (Masi 1934: 135). The provision against poaching was passed in 1437 (ASFi, Ufficiali della Grascia 156, filza 1). Protectionism was less intense than in the wool industry. In 1426, 1432 and 1473 Florence forbade imports of cotton *pignolati* and *guarnelli* for finishing or sale, but it rescinded the ban in 1474 (ASFi, DAC 372, ff.469r, 1009r); in 1429 it briefly commuted the ban into a punitive tariff (ASFi, Consoli del Mare 3, ff.20v–2v). In 1426 it had also raised tariffs on imported *guarnelli* (ASFi, DAC 373, ff.142r–3r). In 1472 it authorised production in the *contado* of *guarnelli vergati* and cotton candlewicks (ASFi, DAC 373, f.12r). In 1454 and 1475 it forbade imports to Tuscany of cotton veils (ASFi, DAC 372, ff.966r–7r; DAC 373, ff.146r–8r, 148r–50r).

104 The cheapest variety of Tuscan cloth sold in Rome in 1451–76 came from Arezzo and Pisa (Hoshino 1980: 286).

105 For Arezzo's industries see Dini 1984; Dini 1990b: 101–3. For linen processing, see ASAr, SRD 4, f.27. For imports of unprocessed cotton (*bambagia soda*), see ASAr, Camerlengo generale, Saldi di entrata e uscita, 82, ff.2r–14r.

early 1360s list Pisans were already importing better qualities of flax.[106] Despite Florentine repression, by the mid-fifteenth century they were able to establish a new guild of linen weavers.[107]

In the first half of the fifteenth century linen weaving in the Florentine *contado* may have grown more quickly than wool (Figure 6.6), but by contrast with Lombardy local statutes are completely silent on matters of technical proficiency and quality.[108] However, the frequent presence of linen weaving in the same centres that made low-quality wool cloth, and the lack of centres specialising solely in linen weaving (with the exception for a time of Borgo San Lorenzo) suggests that production was relatively crude. As previously mentioned, fustian was only made in the larger cities.

Industrial development and the institutional framework

Between 1350 and 1500, urban industry in Tuscany contracted and rural and small town industry failed to take off. The consequences were far-reaching. Tuscany lost its medieval splendour; its urban population stagnated; the economy became more agrarian; living standards declined.[109] How can this process of involution be explained?

Melis argued that the urban manufacturing crisis was caused by Tuscany's demographic collapse, but this can be dismissed on the grounds that similar demographic losses in Lombardy produced very different outcomes.[110] Malanima has suggested instead that the peculiarly Tuscan form of mixed crop sharecropping (*mezzadria poderale*) inhibited the rise of a rural woollen industry because sharecroppers had no spare time available to work a loom.[111] *Mezzadria poderale* had yet to be fully established in the period under discussion, however, and in any case it did not exclude protoindustrial activities on the side: Tuscan sharecroppers

---

106 Tangheroni 1973: 120. Cotton *barracani* were woven in the *contado* (Brugaro 1912: 390–1).

107 ASPi, Comune di Pisa A, 240, ff.1–16r (1360); Comune di Pisa B, 8, *Arte dei tessitori di pannilini* 1452–55. The guild of doublet-makers and retailers (*farsettai*) was established in 1493 (ASPi, Comune B, 11). For a price list of linen cloths with various degrees of fineness, see ASPi, Comune C, 4, ff.5, 7rv (1495). The first Florentine statutes of linen makers and retailers were drawn up in 1296 (Sartini 1940).

108 Very few statutes mention the density of the warp, which is the clearest indication of a degree of technical specialisation. See Roncière 1976: vol.3, 800; Camerani Marri 1963: 157.

109 See this book, p. 10.

110 Melis 1989: 208–9. Population losses were in any case not wholly due to independent factors; depopulation was hastened by Florence's tax and industrial policies (Epstein 1996b).

111 Silk production, by contrast, could thrive because sharecroppers could easily integrate growing mulberry trees into their seasonal work (Malanima 1982).

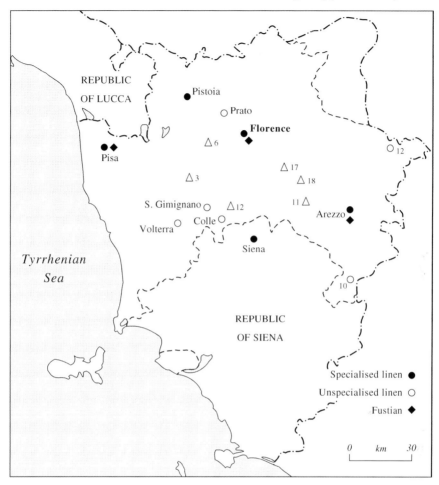

Figure 6.6 The Tuscan linen and fustian industries, *c.*1350–1550

found time to spin and reel wool, linen and silk for urban merchants and to weave linen cloth for the home, and in the countryside of Siena, landlords provided female sharecroppers with wool and shared the output equally.[112]

Herlihy's suggestion that rural impoverishment, largely brought about by Florentine fiscal policy, held back "the development of a strong local market for inexpensive manufactures" may be somewhat closer to the mark, but institutional restrictions on supply appear nonetheless to

112 See Brown 1982 for silk; Piccinni 1985 for wool and linen. For Sienese sharecropper arrangements, see Piccinni 1982: 117–20.

have been pre-eminent.[113] Among the most distinctive features of the Renaissance Tuscan state was the absence of pockets of institutionalised, chartered 'freedoms' outside the towns' and especially Florence's control. State formation under the Florentine republic followed two overlapping routes. First, Florence confirmed subject cities' jurisdiction over their *contado*, but punished any attempted urban rebellions by 'detaching' the rebels' *contadi* and integrating them jurisdictionally into its own. Second, Florence granted extensive privileges to individual communities and entire valleys in the still partly feudalised Apennines to its north. Although the charters were similar in appearance to those that freed non-urban communities in Lombardy from urban juris-diction, Florentine concessions had to be renegotiated every five or ten years and so were effectively in the city's gift. The limited practical utility of Tuscan privileges was also a consequence of the fact that Florence's ruling classes controlled its major craft and merchant guilds, which gave the latter an unusual degree of control over industrial activities in the state.[114]

The poor performance of Tuscan linen and fustian industries was an unintended consequence of the city's policy towards the woollen industry. The Lombard case shows that successful protoindustrialisation required, in addition to corporate freedom, a large and mobile pool of skilled labour, which in turn needed a vibrant and competitive system of craft guilds to be appropriately trained.[115] In Lombardy, where no city monopolised the industry and no single guild monopolised the skilled labour force, competitive cooperation between towns nourished the rise of rural and small town industries. In Tuscany, monopolistic compe-tition between towns slowed technical diffusion in the thirteenth century, forced Florence to resort to foreign technicians after the mass exodus of skilled labour in 1382, and checked growth in 'old' industries like wool and 'new' ones like fustian and linen.[116]

113 Herlihy 1978: 155. On poverty in rural Tuscany see Herlihy 1968; Mazzi and Raveggi 1983; Epstein 1991 and 1996b.
114 The charters are published in Guasti 1866 and Gherardi 1893. Only the charters of Palazzo Fiorentino in the Casentino (1402) and Sarzana near Lucca (1468) among the hundreds that survive mention the production of wool cloth; those of the Montagna fiorentina (1349, 1369) refer to fulling mills. All three were peripheral communities which never established significant protoindustries; for production in the Casentino valley, see Della Bordella 1984 and Benadusi 1996: ch.4.
115 See Epstein 1998a for a theory of craft guilds as purveyors of technical skills through apprenticeship.
116 It is assumed here that the skills associated with textile production could be easily trans-ferred from one sector of the cloth industry to another. The demands of the growing Florentine silk industry will have placed an additional burden on available trained labourers. Dini 1993 provides an overview of the Italian and Florentine industries in the late Middle Ages. For the sixteenth and seventeenth centuries, see Malanima 1982.

Sicily

Sicily before the Black Death had no specialised cloth manufacture to speak of, so the growth in late medieval Sicily of new wool, cotton, fustian and linen cloth industries is all the more significant. By the fifteenth century there were at least a dozen distinctive cotton manufacturers, and a well-established fustian industry was exporting its products abroad; linen and hemp cloth weaving was less developed although it was also becoming more specialised. Low- and medium-quality wool cloth was also made, but several attempts to establish high-quality woolen industries were unsuccessful (Figure 6.7).[117]

Although Sicily's textile industries are not very well documented, three general features stand out. First, Sicilian craft guilds had been held in check during the high Middle Ages by a strong centralised monarchy which feared the subversive role they had played in the rise of the north Italian communes. Sicilian craft guilds first emerged after central power collapsed during the 1340s and 1350s, and spread more widely during the 1430s when king Alfonso of Castile needed their political and financial support; but relations with local and central government remained strained and Sicilian guilds lacked institutional influence throughout the early modern period.[118]

Second, Sicilian towns had weak jurisdictional powers over the countryside, so rural cloth manufacture did not require freedoms or charters to protect itself from craft and merchant encroachment, and could be located where production costs were lowest rather than where communities happened to have received protective franchises.

Third, although Sicily's natural freedoms gave rise to more intensive protoindustrial activities than in Tuscany, Sicily's textile industries remained even more domestically focused. Although they were quite capable of satisfying most domestic demand – higher quality cloth imports accounted for only 5 per cent of local consumption – they were generally too unsophisticated for export markets. The reason was not, however, industrial protectionism as in Tuscany, for Sicily was an entirely open market, but instead the lack of an adequately trained labour force: Sicily's industrial weakness stemmed from the absence of a strong craft tradition which could develop and transmit artisan skills. Although it had a high rate of urbanisation and an institutionally competitive domestic market, pre-modern Sicily was therefore unable to create vibrant industrial clusters like Lombardy and remained an industrial backwater.

---

117 For a more detailed discussion and references, see Epstein 1989; Epstein 1992: 182-200.
118 See Savagnone 1892; Leone 1956; Mineo 1997: 137–39. For the sixteenth and seventeenth centuries, see Lombardo 2000. For apprenticeship in Palermo, see Corrao 1980.

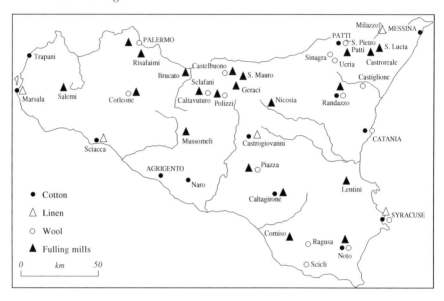

Figure 6.7 The Sicilian cloth industry, *c.*1350–1550

Conclusion

The rise of semi-urban textile industries after the Black Death displayed marked regional diversity, as a map of the fifteenth-century Italian wool industry illustrates (Figure 6.1). The map portrays a country of strong, but highly polarized manufacture divided into three distinct zones: a densely industrialised and export-oriented macro-region stretching from Piedmont to the east through Lombardy deep into the Venetian Terraferma, a dense but less specialised and diversified industrial agglomeration which included Tuscany and Umbria and extended down to L'Aquila south of Rome, and in the South, two smaller southern clusters around Naples and in eastern Sicily that produced primarily for domestic, regional markets. Regional differences in cotton, fustian and linen production were probably even starker (see Figs. 6.2, 6.6 and 6.7). Although regional differences had existed to some extent before 1350, the Black Death and its aftermath accentuated the strengths and weaknesses of different industrial and institutional models and entrenched them until the Industrial Revolution.

Our comparison of three regional clusters casts doubt on several assumptions of the protoindustrial model, and in particular on the linkage between population, property rights to land, peasant 'immiseration' and protoindustrial by-employment. In the original model, the quantity and availability of rural labour were a joint function of the rate of disguised unemployment (caused by rural overpopulation) and of land fragmentation (caused by systems of partible inheritance), which forced peasant households to integrate a dwindling income from the land with non-agri-cultural activities. Protoindustry should therefore have been situated mainly in marginal zones poor in natural resources and beyond the control of urban guilds. In fact, late medieval protoindustry expanded at a time of rising living standards in the countryside and achieved the greatest concentrations in highly urbanised regions including Lombardy, the Low Countries and the zone between Lake Constance and Swabia.

The picture of protoindustry as a response to the technological conser-vatism, rent-seeking habits and high-cost base of urban crafts is even more problematic.[119] Cities and craft guilds were in fact indispensable for the development of protoindustrial clusters after the Black Death. First, cities offered specialised commercial skills and services which helped connect dispersed and small-scale non-urban industry to regional and international markets. Second, successful protoindustries required corporate privileges or freedoms which acted as a form of 'infant-industry protection' and which were urban in all but name. In terms of size, economic ambitions, and capacity for direct negotiation with the territorial ruler, many of Lombardy's new industrial communities were *de facto* or 'quasi' cities.[120] Protoindustries elsewhere in Europe were also frequently situated in communities which aspired to urban status.[121] Third and most importantly, successful proto- or semi-urban textile industries depended on a steady supply of skilled labour from the more technically advanced industries of the towns.

Protoindustries after the Black Death faced two obstacles to growth. The first obstacle was the lack of a skilled workforce. Although many urban cloth manufacturers had employed non-urban labour since the thirteenth century, they had restricted rural and semi-urban tasks to simple opera-tions like carding, combing and spinning which did not require much training.[122] The lack of a trained workforce was, for different reasons, the main constraint in Tuscany and Sicily. The second obstacle was the urban guilds' opposition to the manufacture of higher-quality cloth outside the cities. A semi-urban manufacture had to obtain jurisdictional freedoms that allowed it to bypass craft privileges, gain access to regional distribution networks, and attract trained labour from the towns; a successful protoin-dustry would usually also set up its own craft guilds to enforce training and production standards.[123] Successful textile protoindustries needed the

---

119 See Ogilvie 1997 for this scheme. For more moderate views of the town–country dichotomy, see Berg, Hudson and Sonenscher 1983b; Allegra 1987; Jeannin 1987.

120 Chittolini 1996: 85–104 (*'quasi-città'*).

121 See Thoen and Soly 1999 (Flanders and Brabant); Britnell 1993: 170 and Miller and Hatcher 1995: 321–2 (England); Thomson 1996 (Spain).

122 Holbach 1993: 235–6.

123 See Ogilvie 1997, who however interprets the frequent 'corporatisation' of pre-modern protoindustry as simple rent-seeking.

combination of a strong urban network, a developed system of craft-based production, and a competitive institutional and commercial setting in which urban craft and commercial monopolies could not be enforced.

Two institutional variables appear therefore to have determined the fortunes of protoindustry after 1350: the nature of political relations between cities and the territorial state, and the extent of jurisdictional fragmentation across territorial states. States had to be strong enough to challenge guild monopolies, but not strong enough to abolish craft guilds as an economic institution. By challenging the guilds' right to protect their consumer markets from 'unfair' competition from protoindustries, states solved the prisoner's dilemma of monopolistic competition between industrial towns and benefited consumers; by granting industrial franchises to non-urban competitors and challenging the guilds' monopoly over industrial employment, states increased competition and indirectly supplied more trained labour. The equivalent of 'infant-industry protection' was required to achieve the returns to scale which came from 'spillovers' in technical knowledge concentrated in the cities.

Jurisdictionally powerful cities – whether coextensive with the territorial state, as in the Florentine case, or because they faced a weak territorial state and little inter-urban competition, as in Umbria and Marche in central Italy – were therefore generally detrimental to protoindustrialisation.[124] Jurisdictionally weak towns were in principle more advantageous, but in practice much depended on other circumstantial factors. The optimal circumstances, which existed in Lombardy, the Low Countries and central and southern Germany, combined weak territorial states and jurisdictional fragmentation, which allowed protoindustries to spring up in the interstices of urban power, with strong urban networks and inter-urban competition.[125] A somewhat less positive outcome, which arose in late medieval Sicily and, for example, England (which was less urbanised but had more developed guild structures than the Italian region), occurred where powerful territorial states did not allow strong urban rights and specialised crafts to develop.[126]

---

124 For the weakness of the late medieval wool industry in central Italy, see Figure 6.1. In late medieval Castile, however, towns monopolised cloth production not because they had powerful guilds – guilds were established *after* the rise of a local textile industry – but because the towns offered obvious technical advantages over the countryside in what for the region was a wholly *new* industrial sector (Thomson 1996).

125 Developments in late medieval Lombardy were thus not an 'exception to the rule' of a general economic crisis, as claimed by Miani 1964 and Dowd 1961.

126 Modern studies specifically devoted to the rural cloth industry in late medieval England are lacking. See Hare 1999 and Swanson 1999: 57–8 for references.

7 Markets and states, *c*.1300–*c*.1550

Introduction

We discussed in Chapter 3 how growing political centralisation and the consolidation of state sovereignty during the later Middle Ages lowered tariffs and gave institutional backing for more efficient and integrated trading networks. Centralisation however threatened traditional privileges and freedoms and therefore faced strong feudal and urban resistance, which tended to channel state reforms within existing regional rather than towards as yet notional national frameworks.[1] Even where political centralisation occurred in territories with 'national' dimensions like France, Spain and the Burgundian empire, most of the jurisdictional and fiscal barriers between constituent 'regions' remained in place and exerted similar effects to the frontiers separating smaller independent territorial states.

The argument that institutional and economic boundaries tended to coincide has been criticised for confusing the concept of the economic-functional 'region' as defined by economic geographers, with that of the institutional 'region' as defined by political and legal historians. According to the critics, an 'economic region' is shaped by purely commercial forces, among which transaction costs rank highest, whereas the frontiers of an 'institutional region' are the result of largely random historical and political events; the boundaries between the two will therefore only coincide by chance.[2] It is none the less clear that frontiers are economically significant inasmuch as the bundle of laws and tariffs that underpin transactions vary between states. In this chapter I address the question of how significant for market integration institutional structures actually were, focusing on the development of direct and indirect taxes on trade, including food provisioning systems, and on the market power of special interest groups in Florentine Tuscany and the duchy of Lombardy after the Black Death.

---

1 Proto-national markets first emerged only after the 'seventeenth-century crisis'. See Chapter 2, note 59.
2 See Malanima 1996.

Customs and tolls

Before the War of the Eight Saints and Arezzo's submission in 1384, the Florentine government followed the two-pronged economic strategy typical of most contemporary city-states: in the *contado*, it encouraged the development of an efficient road system, controlled the number and functions of marketplaces, strove to enforce the use of the city's own weights and measures, and extended its control over rural surpluses at times of dearth; further afield, it agreed reciprocal tariff reductions and exemptions with neighbouring communes to ensure regular food supplies and sustain its commercial interests.[3] After 1384, having embarked irreversibly upon territorial expansion, Florence tried to extend the arrangements devised for its *contado* to its newly acquired *distretto* (the territory outside its direct jurisdiction) with a particular focus on restricting the subjects' independent rights to raise tolls and excises.[4] The Florentine fisc, the *Camera*, became directly responsible for the gabelles of Arezzo, Cortona and Pisa, and only Pistoia, whose fiscal independence had been established in some early fourteenth-century tariff agreements with Florence, managed to evade the latter's control.[5]

For several decades after 1384 Florentine rulers seemed to view commercial sovereignty mainly as a means to maximise tax revenues.[6] By the early 1420s, however, a commission for the newly appointed Consuls of the Sea to enquire about the state of Tuscan trade and manufacture indicates a new and more sophisticated understanding of the territorial economy.[7] Although the Florentine elites continued to view the territorial state, including the inhabitants of the subject cities, as a glorified *contado* to be fiscally and economically exploited, they also began to make more allowance for local differences and to view the region as a more integrated whole.

Between the 1420s and 1460s Florence embarked on a series of reforms

---

3　Roncière 1976: vol.3, pp.871–906. For weights and measures, see ibid., vol.3, pp.951–64, 995, 1003–6; vol.4, pp.337 notes 41–2; Guidi 1981: vol.3, pp. 161 note 16. I have found only one provision in the Republican period whose purpose was to unify regional measures along Florentine lines (ASFi, PR 119, ff.278v–9, 27 Nov.1428). A law of 1407 which standardised all Pisan measures to those of Florence was only fully applied by the 1520s (Luzzati 1962–3). For tariff reductions, see Roncière 1976: vol.3, pp.887–90.

4　PR 75, ff.28v–9, 17 Apr. 1386: the *Signoria* and the *Regolatori delle entrate* assert full jurisdiction over 'quibuscumque gabellis et pedagiis civitatis comitatus Aretii tam ordinariis quam extraordinariis et tam usitatis quam non usitatis', with the right to modify existing gabelles and to introduce new ones.

5　For the Florentine fisc, see PR 110, ff.96–7, 30 Sept. 1420 for various changes to the gabelles of Cortona, including a 25 per cent increase in the main gate tolls. For Pistoia, see Herlihy 1967b: 160; Connell 1991: 529; ASFi, DAC 373, ff.276–8, 1401; ASFi, PR 91, ff.21v–2v, 1402.

6　The only available studies of indirect taxation refer to the period before 1380 (Roncière 1968; Herlihy 1964).

7　ASFi, PR 112, ff.245v–6v.

to its domestic tariff system aimed at increasing revenue collection. During the late 1420s the share of the main transit toll (*gabella dei passeggeri*) in the *distretto* rose from 5–10 percent to 13–15 per cent of Florence's total receipts, indicating a redistribution of the tax burden away from the dominant city and its *contado*.[8] Fiscal efficiency was improved more slowly and haphazardly. For example, it took the Florentines the better part of a century to determine the final location of their customs houses, with the slow pace of reform resulting both from the need to respect subjects' juris-dictional privileges and from Florence's own anxiety over evasion.[9] The presence of at least nine customs houses on the road from Florence to Pisa suggests that the Florentine customs office was more concerned with taxing internal than external trade. The sense of fiscal insecurity becomes quite palpable by comparison with the Duchy of Milan, which had propor-tionally far fewer customs posts and relied far more extensively on tax-farming even though it was surrounded by more easily accessible foreign markets and was therefore more susceptible to smuggling.[10]

Territorial expansion also changed Florence's commercial policies. Fifteenth-century policy combined the authoritarian and short-term controls typical of the late thirteenth and fourteenth centuries with attempts to stimulate the transit trade through lower tariffs.[11] Although Florentine gate tolls increased between 1350 and 1400, and continued to rise more modestly over the following century, the effects of the nominal increases were mitigated by inflation and were not matched elsewhere in the state; in subject communes, gate tolls seem to have declined in real terms.[12] Several tariffs between Florence and subject communities were reduced in nominal terms or abolished altogether, for example in the

8   See ASFi, CCPM 1–45, 48. However, the burden may have shifted again after 1450 when Florence repeatedly increased its own gate tolls (Molho 1987: 205).

9   Major customs reforms are recorded in DAC 372, f.494, 1438–9; PR 147, ff.101v–3v and DAC 372, f.635, 1456; DAC 375, passim, 1474; DAC 375, c.230rv, 1503. In July 1490 the *Balia* of the Seventeen Reformers proposed to review the entire system of tolls, ports and customs (Brown 1992: 108, 111, 115–16), but the measure was not recorded in the reg-isters of the *Dogana* which list all subsequent reforms.

10   In addition to its own paid officials, the Florentine customs resorted to the state's net-work of castellans, captains and podestà; see DAC 319, ff.67, 109, 110. For tax-farming and smuggling in Lombardy, see Saba 1986; Romani 1986; Belfanti 1986.

11   Short-term controls included a one-off tax on the pilgrims to Rome; see PR 119, ff.90–1, 223v–5, 21 June 1428, revoked 15 October 1428, and PR 161, ff.107–8, 1470.

12   For Florentine gate tolls, 1350–1400, see note 6 to this chapter. Average receipts fell about 12 per cent between 1342–57 and 1390–99 (figures from Roncière 1968: Table I and ASFi, CCPM 6–15). The decline may have occurred as a consequence of the loss of fiscal autonomy previously referred to, which allowed Florence to increase direct taxa-tion. After 1402 Florence forbade Pistoia from increasing the salt tax and the gate tolls to the detriment of the *contado* (Herlihy 1967: 159 note 22). Machiavelli 1960: ch.3 was probably reflecting on a Tuscan practice when he stated, regarding the acquisition of 'new' states by old, that one should not 'alter either their laws or their trade dues (*dazi*)'.

former feudal jurisdictions of the Casentino valley; although most reductions applied to trade flowing towards the ruling city, at least in the case of Pistoia the reductions were bilateral.[13]

Florence responded to occasional shortages in food staples like wine, olive oil and meat with temporary export bans and import bounties, but pursued fiscal moderation with regard to international trade, for example in locally scarce commodities like iron or in sheep and cattle transhumance.[14] Whereas foreign trade in the communal era had been treated as dependent on Florence's industrial and commercial requirements, from the early fifteenth century onwards it began to be promoted independently as a source of tax revenue. The conquest of Arezzo (1384) and Borgo San Sepolcro (1441) to the south-west, and the acquisition of Porto Pisano and Livorno (1421) and of the territories bordering Lucca to the east and north-east (in the 1430s), but especially the conquest of Pisa of 1406, which gave Florence control over an important maritime trade route between the western Mediterranean and north Italy through which it could channel foreign supplies of grain, made the Florentine elites more aware of their region's strategic position at the cross-roads between south-central Italy, the western Mediterranean, and the Lombard and north European plains. The city thereafter relied less on the tried and tested policy of bilateral trade agreements, and reduced customs dues unilaterally if it feared that trade might be diverted away from the region and in order to promote trade between the western Mediterranean and northern Europe.[15] Although territorial expansion and military competition increased the Florentine state's financial requirements, the threat

13 For tariffs between Florence and subject communities, see PR 64, ff.283v–4v, 1377. For tariffs on inward trade flows, see Epstein 1996b: p.881. A further case of discrimination occurred in 1465 when Florence raised the duty on livestock moving from its *contado* to the district. Arezzo and Cortona complained that this would damage their fairs and asked to exempt the livestock sold there (PR 157, ff.246–7v and DAC 373, ff.555–7, 1467). Subsequently the *Signoria* decided to reduce the tariff on plough oxen (but not cattle 'for trade', *per mercatantia*) from 2 florins to 12 *soldi* in the *distretto* (PR 166, ff.64v–5, 1475). For Pistoia, see Connell 1991: 529.

14 For wine, see PR 129, ff. 246–7, 1439; PR 157, f.147rv, 1466; PR 201, ff.48v–9v, 1511. For olive oil, see PR 118, ff.49v–51v, 1427; PR 127, f.296rv, 1437; PR 133, ff.118v–19v and 183rv, 1442; PR 137, ff.129v–30, 1446; PR 205, f.59, 1522. The reduced pressure on food supplies caused by declining population is examined by Pinto 1987. For tariff reductions on iron see PR 122, f.284rv, 1431; PR 123, f.135v–6, 1432; PR 132, ff.211-12, 1441; PR 136, ff.38v–9, 1445 (the latter includes changes to tolls levied in Cortona, Arezzo and Montecchio to increase iron imports from Perugia, the Marche and Abruzzo). Volterra's rebellion in 1472 was followed by an increase in its gate tolls in 1475; see PR 166, ff. 65–6. After the reorganization of the *Dogana del bestiame* in 1428 (PR 119, c.91rv), the *Signoria* set out to attract transhumant flocks to the Florentine Maremma (PR 122, ff.207v–8, 1431; PR 123, ff.240v–1, 1432; PR 126, ff.241v–2, 1435; PR 144, ff.82v–3, 1454; PR 1465, ff.11-12, 1465).

15 Bilateral trade agreements, which had been typical of the communal age, were however

of fiscal competition by neighbouring states explains Florence's unusual moderation in the use of the trade boycotts, reprisals and punitive tariffs that had been its stock-in-trade as an independent city-state.[16] In this, however, fifteenth-century Florence was doing no more than adopting a policy of fiscal coordination and standardisation that the Lombard Visconti had already established with the *Provisiones Ianue* of 1346.[17]

Economic franchises and freedoms

Territorial expansion was also associated with policies which would appear at first glance to undermine political integration. During the late fourteenth and fifteenth centuries, the Florentine Signoria granted subject communities jurisdictional privileges whose main economic purpose was to exonerate the recipients from control by some Florentine guilds, to reduce or abolish entirely most tariffs on trade, and to authorise trade in otherwise restricted goods. The apparent result of this was to increase jurisdictional fragmentation and to undermine both the letter and the spirit of political integration. To what extent did the policy of jurisdictional devolution neutralise the economic benefits of political integration?

Whereas the political and constitutional implications of pre-modern privileges and freedoms are a well-studied feature of the Ancien Regime, their economic implications have been either ignored or consigned to the historical rubbish heap of the 'dead-weight costs' engendered by premodern states. This oversight is based on the view that pre-modern freedoms were an anachronism which delayed the course of political and

---

never wholly abandoned. See PR 79, ff.95v–8v, 31 May 1390 for an agreement with the lord of Ravenna; PR 157, ff.103v–4, 27 June 1466 for renewal of a commercial treaty of 1370 with Bologna. For fears that trade might be diverted, see PR 119, ff.187–8, 1428; PR 170, f.15rv, 1479; PR 180, ff.95–6, 1489; PR 200, f.129rv, 1510. For the Mediterranean and northern Europe, see PR 120, ff.17v–18, 1429 (trade with England and Flanders); PR 128, f.3rv, 1437 (Lombardy, Venice); PR 131, cc.167v–8, 1440 (Lombardy); PR 171, f.18rv, 1480 (Lombardy, for four years). Florence was far less concerned about trade relations with central Italy; an example in PR 179, cc.87–8, 1489 (trade with Siena, Città di Castello, Faenza and Bologna). In 1529 it decided to confirm a 33 per cent reduction of customs dues in Pisa and Livorno in view of the rise in the tax returns that the reduction had caused (PR 207, f.74rv). See Pistarino 1986 on trade between Tuscany and Milan.

16 See Conti 1981: 134, 2 May 1401 (right of reprisal granted to merchants of Volterra and Pistoia against other Pistoians); PR 99, f.82rv, 1410 (punitive tariffs of 50 per cent *ad valorem* on Genoese and Savonan merchandise); PR 127, ff.281v–2, 1436 (trade ban with lands under the control of the duke of Milan). In 1504 Lucca suffered Florentine reprisals, possibly because it had given aid to the Pisan rebels (PR 195, cc.1–2). In 1428 Florence came to a tariff agreement with Siena, making it easier for the Sienese to trade in, and bring livestock into, Florentine territory (PR 119, ff.223v–5). For the use of commercial reprisals by fourteenth-century Florence see Astorri 1993: 70–2; Bowsky 1981: ch.5; Epstein 1992: 284–7.

17 See Chapter 6, note 58.

economic progress, and reflects a fundamental misunderstanding of pre-modern markets. In fact, as previous chapters have shown, jurisdictionally 'free' enclaves in premodern Europe were a fundamental source of economic competition against the commercial and manufacturing monopolies of powerful towns. In the manufacturing sector, jurisdictional autonomy underpinned the rise of rural and small town protoindustries against opposition by urban crafts.[18] In the trading sector, temporary or permanent tariff reductions and the right to trade freely in restricted commodities stimulated growth and specialisation. Paradoxically, then, so long as market power was directly exercised through jurisdictional power – that is, so long as markets were not 'free' in the nineteenth-century liberal sense – concessions of jurisdictional autonomy could be economically beneficial.[19]

The reasons why Renaissance states made these concessions were none the less not fundamentally economic. Although concessions of 'freedoms' could in theory undermine or fragment state power, in practice they strengthened the state's legitimacy and extended its sovereignty over competing feudal and urban rights. Jurisdictional privileges were thus a powerful tool of political centralisation. In institutional terms, late medieval states employed fiscal concessions to claim sovereignty over taxation and commerce. In economic terms, jurisdictional freedoms enabled recipients to challenge the monopolies of the towns. If nothing else, a tariff exemption or reduction improved the living standards of the recipients, but economic privileges could also act as *de facto* institutional barriers against encroaching urban guilds. Ancien Regime 'freedoms' were the institutional equivalent of modern 'special economic zones'.

The ambiguity of jurisdictional freedoms is apparent also in Florentine practices. Economic franchises, particularly tariff reductions, were used systematically during the period of territorial expansion between the 1370s and the 1440s.[20] Concessions, made when a community formally capitulated, granted exemption from most forms of indirect taxation and a reduction of the compulsory salt tax; only Florence's gate tolls were never reduced. Exemptions, which generally lasted five or ten years and could be renegotiated, might also be rescinded as political and financial circumstances changed.[21] The best terms were invariably granted to strategically placed frontier communities like the Casentino, the Alpi fiorentine and the Valdinievole, whose commercial privileges went back as far as the 1350s and which became zones of permanent fiscal and corporate exemption;

18 See Chapter 6.
19 However, the benefits of jurisdictional exemptions only applied if the beneficiaries were not granted rights to tax trade in their own stead, as occurred for example in sixteenth and early seventeenth-century Castile (Nader 1990; Sanchez Léon 2000).
20 See Fasano Guarini 1976: 17–18.
21 In a few cases in the later fifteenth century concessions on gate tolls were extended for

smaller and less well organised communities closer to Florence found it nearly impossible to renew their fiscal concessions.[22]

The manner by which central power was built upon the devolution of power was illustrated in a previous chapter on the rise of periodic fairs after the Black Death.[23] New fairs responded to real needs for more complex marketing systems, but they were strongly resisted by trading centres that feared greater competition and the loss of revenue from tolls and therefore required special jurisdictional dispensations. Most states were willing to support new fairs because such concessions challenged the jurisdictional claims of towns and extended the state's territorial remit. Developments in Tuscany fit this general mould well. Between 1350 and 1560 no less than thirty-eight seasonal fairs were established or given a new lease on life. At least seventeen fairs were exempted from all major tolls. Fifteen offered participants temporary immunity (*securitas*) from arrest for debt, including tax arrears owed to Florence, a not insignificant concession, given the ubiquity of tax debts and the fact that fairs were patrolled by state officials. The fairs specialised mainly in livestock and to a lesser extent in cereals, and were held in larger towns like Florence, Arezzo, San Gimignano, Prato and Pistoia, in smaller semi-autonomous boroughs such as Monte San Savino, Anghiari, Borgo San Sepolcro, Poppi, Pieve Santo Stefano, Pontassieve, Borgo San Lorenzo, Firenzuola and Pescia, and in centres located at the strategic northern and southern frontiers of the state such as Villamagna, Greve, Montevarchi, Bibbiena and Pratovecchio.

A similar pattern applied to weekly markets, no less than thirty-four of which were newly established between the mid-fourteenth century and the advent of duke Cosimo. Twelve of these (and twenty-six others whose origins are unknown) obtained *securitas*; at least twelve markets were exempted from major tolls. Most of these new events, which were distributed quite regularly across the Florentine *contado* and the northern valleys of the Casentino, the Mugello and the Valdinievole, survived well into the early modern period.[24]

The initiative for a new market or fair came invariably from the communities themselves; Florence took the initiative only for the fortified town of Firenzuola, which it had established to monitor the Apennine pass leading to Imola and the Romagna. Florence however had the power to reject a community's request, and decisions were invariably shaped by the opportunity to stimulate cross-border trade with its regional neighbours. The main purpose of the string of fairs created along the southern borders with

periods up to twenty-five years; see PR 159, ff.194v–5v, 1468 (Poppi and Fronzoli). A six-teenth-century survey revealed that most of the previous tariff exemptions were no longer in use (DAC 838, *passim*).

22 See Guasti 1866: 75–6 (Valdinievole), 89–90 (Alpi fiorentine).
23 See Chapter 4.
24 See Pult Quaglia 1990: 261–4; DAC 373, ff.236–57 and *passim*; DAC 838, ff.141–55.

Siena and the smaller communes of the Marche and Umbria was to attract the supplies of grain and livestock which the Florentines believed they were unable to produce themselves (Figure 7.1).[25] Florentine policy therefore contrasted with strategy in the duchy of Lombardy. Although the dukes, like the Florentine oligarchy, aimed to achieve regional self-sufficiency in food, the duchy produced grain and livestock surpluses for export and therefore the government's attitude towards fairs was much

25 The purpose of these trading points was explicitly stated in a request of 1441 for immunity at the ancient market of Greve on the frontier with Siena (PR 132, ff.290–1). For similar concerns during the communal era see Roncière 1976: vol.3, pp.957, 995 and Pinto 1978: 107–8. For Florentine beliefs about the 'sterility' of their lands see Epstein 1996b: 888.

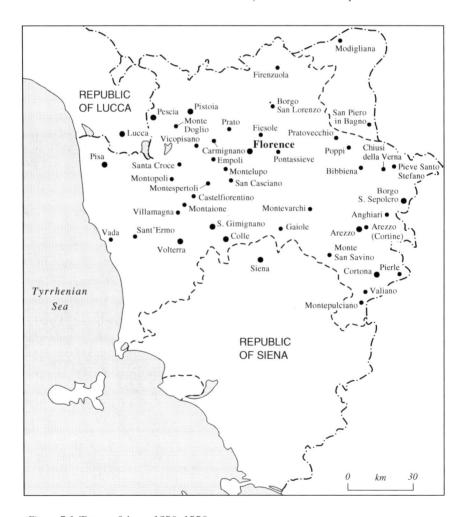

Figure 7.1 Tuscan fairs, *c.*1350–1550

more restrictive. Rather than a means to attract imports, fairs and markets were seen as a way by which precious resources were transferred outside the region, and consequently only a small number of fairs was established outside the cities, and markets within 5 kilometres of the state's frontiers were forbidden (Figure 7.2).[26]

Florentine strategy was also affected by political concerns.[27] It was on political rather than economic grounds that the city refused to confirm a new market in Colle because the inhabitants had created it without seeking Florentine consent, the *Colligiani* going so far as to exempt the fair unilaterally from all tolls;[28] it was for political reasons that Florence abolished at a stroke all concessions of immunities from debt and forced the recipients to buy the privileges back;[29] and it was for political reasons that the ruling city occasionally upheld *pro legibus suis* the claims of rural communities in the *distretto*, which formally fell under the control of subject towns and which wished to set up a market against the neighbouring town's hostility.[30] Yet Florence had also to come to terms with the subject towns' political sensitivities. Although few jurisdictional conflicts on marketing rights are recorded, the fact that the *contadi* of Pistoia, Volterra, Arezzo and Pisa were virtually free from rival markets and fairs and that new non-urban fairs were set up only in chartered communities indicates that urban opposition to them was generally successful.[31]

Grain markets

Most historians view the regulated systems of urban grain supply which were established through much of Europe between the thirteenth and the sixteenth centuries as a rational response to fundamental and unavoidable economic constraints. A perverse combination of agricultural, technological and organisational backwardness provoked wild and unpredictable fluctuations in price, causing sharp swings in consumption which threatened the health and stability of urban society.[32] Since grain imports

26 Mira 1955 and 1958; Greci 1983; Belfanti 1986.
27 Roncière 1976: vol.3, pp.1015–19.
28 Archivio di Stato di Siena, Comune di Colle, Deliberazioni 140, ff.137v–40v, no.7, 22 June 1410 (reference provided by Oretta Muzzi).
29 PR 126, f.359rv, 1435, which refers to a general revocation in 1427.
30 See Martines 1968: 225 for Pistoia.
31 The best documented of the conflicts on marketing rights is that which opposed Arezzo to its banlieu, known as the Cortine, over the latter's insistence on establishing a fair; the most plausible reason why the evidence for this has survived is that Arezzo, unusually, lost its case. See Black 1993: 24–8; Black 1996: 228; PR 182, ff.85v–6v, 24 Feb. 1492; PR 187, ff.131v–2v, 19 Feb. 1497. For examples of trade monopolies, see Gherardi 1893: 432–3 (1385), 470–1 (1395).
32 There is a vast, albeit mostly descriptive, literature on pre-modern grain markets. For overviews of conditions in pre-modern Italy, with references to the broader European

Figure 7.2 Lombard fairs, *c.*1350–1550

could not easily mitigate local scarcity because of high transport costs, urban authorities introduced a complex array of price controls and barriers to domestic and international trade to dampen price volatility. Free trade was only introduced once agricultural improvements and falling transport costs made protectionism unnecessary.[33]

This explanation of pre-modern market regulation, which assumes that European towns followed roughly similar policies across space and time, confuses two different kinds of urban regulation. The first type was found

literature, see Cipolla 1963a: 399–407; Pinto 1985; Palermo 1990: ch.1; Fazio 1990. The welfare effects of early modern grain markets are discussed in Walter and Schofield 1989b, Weir 1989, and Persson 1999, with reference to Sen 1981, Ravallion 1987, and Ravallion 1997.

33 For a clear exposition of this model see Persson 1999; for a somewhat different argument, see Fogel 1992.

in slightly different guises in most pre-modern European towns. It included a variety of public storage systems, price controls and subsidies to the price of bread, and was a form of welfare support that aimed to keep prices stable and reduce price volatility for the urban consumer. Eighteenth-century polemicists however were mainly concerned with the second, macroeconomic form of regulation, which aimed to stabilise aggregate grain supplies and maintain low average prices through a combination of export bans and import bounties. Macro-economic regulation displayed greater geographical variation, however, for although the prevailing attitude among states towards the grain trade was defensive and protectionist, some countries followed a more liberal course. The best-known example of a liberal trade regime was enacted in post-Revolutionary England, but a less well-known instance of free domestic trade and liberal foreign trade which predated England by nearly three centuries and stayed in place for the entire early modern period, was established by the small kingdom of Sicily in the 1390s.[34]

The examples of Sicily and England challenge the claim that free-trade policies were introduced only once higher agricultural productivity and falling transport costs made protectionism outdated. Trade liberalisation in the two countries preceded both any appreciable change in domestic transport costs and strong rises in agricultural productivity and grain exports. In fact, in both instances liberalisation occurred at times of major institutional upheaval, in Sicily during the 1390s when a new Iberian monarchy was establishing itself, in England soon after the Restoration with the Grain Acts of 1663. On the other hand, many countries applied trade restrictions even though they produced regular food surpluses. One such was ducal and Spanish Lombardy, which had one of the most productive agricultural systems in Europe supported by an efficient distribution network; another was Florence, which maintained autarchic policies for the entire fifteenth century even though it faced no major subsistence crisis before the 1490s.[35] In none of these cases was the availability of food supplies the main factor determining grain policy.

The choice of trade regime seems to have been dictated by political circumstances rather than agricultural and commercial technology, with urban control over the grain trade being the most important discriminating element. By the fifteenth century at the latest, most European towns could

---

34 For England see Appleby 1978; Outhwaite 1981. For Sicily see Epstein 1992: 136–48; Fazio 1993.

35 Thus the list in Pinto 1985:633–4 of Italian regions which exported grain and of the city-states 'that under normal circumstances were self-sufficient and in good years were in a position to export part of the harvest' includes both areas which practised restrictive trade policies and areas with a more liberal approach. Munro 1984:57 also notes that grain price fluctuations in the Low Countries bear no apparent relationship to depopulation.

claim privileges that allowed them to control the grain trade in their hinterland when supplies were deficient. Trade controls were meant both to ensure adequate supplies on the town's own market and to trump similar measures by neighbouring towns, for non-interventionism in a world of protectionist legislation was a self-defeating strategy: as long as a town expected its neighbours to restrict trade, it had every incentive to do so too. The result, however, was a system of reciprocal trade vetoes whose consequences were the opposite of the towns' intentions. As the eighteenth-century *philosophes* argued, the tariff and non-tariff barriers to trade that were erected to defend urban supplies also raised the average cost of grain for urban consumers and created disincentives for farmers to increase output.[36] Protectionism may have also increased price volatility because it made imports from outside the territory more unpredictable. Any delay in foreign grain shipments due to protectionism would force the administrators in the food-deficient town to build up reserves, putting increased pressure on local prices until imports brought prices lower and forced excess urban stocks to be sold below cost.[37]

Although the lack of cooperation between towns increased instability on the grain market, individual towns had no incentive to abolish trade controls unilaterally, since they had no means of ensuring that their counterparts would do the same.[38] This prisoner's dilemma could only be broken by an outside authority like a monarch or an autocratic parliament that could credibly commit towns to a policy of free trade by punishing uncooperative agents. Given the inherent instability of an uncoordinated system of grain supply, it should in principle have been in the interest both of territorial rulers and urban consumers to force towns to cooperate more closely; but a successful transition from regulated to unregulated markets had to happen quickly and be rigorously enforced, for a partial liberalisation would benefit non-compliants disproportionately if the penalty for delay was lower than the expected gains. In other words, the likelihood of trade liberalisation was inversely proportional to the costs of legal enforcement, and the latter were directly proportional to the extent of jurisdictional fragmentation. The

---

36 See Persson 1999: ch.2, for a demonstration that controls over the grain trade reduced average output and farmer profits.

37 See Persson 1996: 699–701 for statistical evidence that the towns of Pisa, Siena and Cologne regularly built up excess stocks between August and December. As has been suggested, this build-up would occur because of poor information about urban competition for supplies and about the level of foreign stocks.

38 Game theory predicts that cooperation will arise spontaneously in the presence of repeated games (regular commercial interaction) between towns. Such an outcome would however occur only if supply networks were stable and impervious to exogenous shocks, an unlikely condition in most pre-modern political and commercial circumstances.

more state jurisdiction was contestable, the less likely it was that the state could enforce a single, coordinated grain policy. Thus, for example, the French reforms of 1763–4 failed because many provincial and urban administrations could refuse to liberalise the grain trade with virtual impunity.[39] Similarly, the Sicilian and English monarchies' success in liberalising the grain trade within their own countries was a direct consequence of their strong political credit and of weak resistance at a time of institutional and political upheaval.

The main implication of the previous argument is that jurisdictional fragmentation was the main cause of price volatility in grain, and that political centralisation which reduced coordination failures between markets increased market integration. The collapse across much of late medieval Europe in the price volatility of grain by 50 per cent or more offers prima facie support for this hypothesis (Figure 7.3). The dimensions and positive consequences for consumer welfare of the gains in market integration, were permanent and occurred at a time when the interregional grain trade probably contracted. They were similar to the collapse in real interest rates that occurred in the same period and must have been largely caused by the increased political stability and lower transactions costs within territorial states.[40] Here, the hypothesis is tested in more detail with respect to Lombardy and Tuscany, on the basis of standard measures of price volatility, price correlation, and price convergence; attempts have also been made to estimate the impact of structural breaks in integration caused by legislative and political changes.[41]

All measures of market integration tell a similar story. Price synchronisation in both regions increased sharply during the fifteenth century, and although synchronisation fell repeatedly as a result of military invasions in the sixteenth and seventeenth centuries – indicating that warfare and more generally political instability, which easily destructured 'thin' pre-modern markets, was the most important source of economic regression in the period – each crisis was followed by intensified integration (Figure 7.4).[42] Price volatility on the other hand followed a nearly constant declining trend (Figure 7.5). Regional prices also converged as political integration reduced tariffs and improved opportunities for arbitrage between markets, with the greater gains made in towns situated at a greater distance from the regional leaders,

---

39 Miller 1999: 43–49.
40 See Chapter 3, Figure 3.1.
41 The latter were estimated using the STAMP 5.0 (Structural Time Series Analyser, Modeller and Predictor) program developed by S. J. Koopman, A. C. Harvey, J. A. Doornik and N. Shephard.
42 The impact of war on market integration is discussed by Gutmann 1980; Hoffman 1996. See the Appendix to this chapter for price sources.

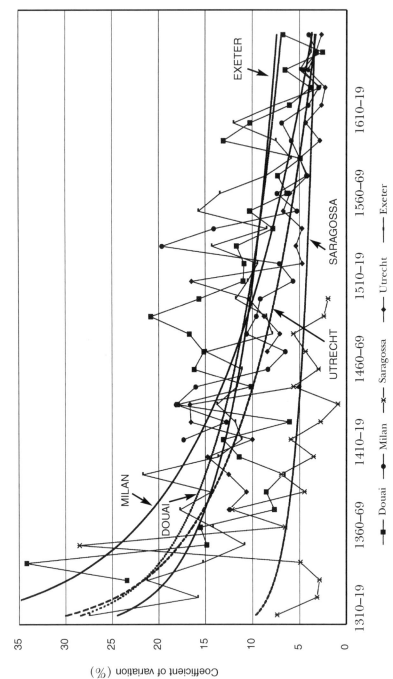

Figure 7.3 Price volatility of wheat in Europe, 1310–1649

Coefficient of variation (%)

—■— Douai   —●— Milan   —✕— Saragossa   —◆— Utrecht   —— Exeter

Florence and Milan. Price convergence in Tuscany (Figure 7.6) seems to have been less significant than in Lombardy, where the data however are less robust, with average prices rising by 11 per cent in Cremona and falling by 60 per cent in Como compared to Milan's (Figure 7.7). Some of the gains were simply a consequence of the return to commercial stability in the 1450s after decades of civil war, but Lombardy's higher levels of integration and lower volatility in peacetime compared with Tuscany in the period to the 1620s may also have been caused by differences in trade policy.

Tuscan policy was directed by Florence, which by and large chose institutional inertia over structural reform. Up to the 1450s Florentine policy towards the *contado* combined paternalistic and authoritarian norms established in the early fourteenth century, including rural export bans and forcible supplies at fixed prices to the city, the forced distribution of grain imports and excess stocks among the peasantry, and loans to stimulate agricultural recovery.[43] After annexing Arezzo in 1384, Florence abolished the protectionist legislation in subject cities which had caused some of the worst Florentine subsistence crises before the Black Death, and modified Pisa's tariffs in order to make it cheaper to export grain to Florence than to supply Pisa itself.[44] Despite providing short-term crisis aid to smaller towns such as Volterra, Cortona and Castiglion Fiorentino, Florence also had no hesitation in imposing forcible distraints and

---

43 For the early fourteenth century, see Roncière 1976: vol.2, 551–61. For Florentine policy before the Black Death see Pinto 1978: Introduction. For forcible supplies, see PR 40, ff.73–5, 1353; PR 77, ff.150v–1, 1388. For forced distribution among the peasantry, see PR 41, f.134v and PR 42, ff.51v–2, 1355 (to Florentines); PR 72, f.172rv, 1383 (to rural communities). For loans to stimulate agriculture, see PR 74, ff.100v–1v, 1385 (3,000 florins to Arezzo); PR 92, ff.228–9, 1403 (400 florins to Civitella in 1397).

44 For the effects of early trade bans on Florentine supplies see Pinto 1978: 84–5, 350–4; PR 40, f.149, 18 Sept. 1353 refers to a consignment of foreign grain to Florence via Arezzo which the latter requisitioned. For later developments see Herlihy 1967: 160; Fiumi 1956: 49 and note 104, 50 note 106; see also *Statuta* 1778–83: 279. Significantly, the main provider of public assistance and food relief in Arezzo, the Fraternita dei Laici, began to record its grain sales on the town market soon after the city's submission in 1385, presumably so as to provide Florence with information about local food stocks. Nonetheless, before the 1460s larger towns like Arezzo and Pistoia stayed outside Florence's main supply orbit, while smaller communities like Pescia and Volterra bore the brunt of Florentine pressure. For requisitions of grain in Pescia see Brown 1982: 139; for Volterra see Fiumi 1956: 49 and note 104. In 1414 Florence granted itself preemptive rights over food exports from Pisa's hinterland (PR 113, ff.280v–1); in 1418 it abolished tolls on victuals (*grascie*) transported to Florence from the *dominium* (PR 108, c.158rv); in 1456 it removed its gate tolls on cereals for a year (PR 147, ff.165v–6v). Thanks to its early pacts with Florence, Pistoia probably had the most favourable trading arrangements of all subject towns (Herlihy 1967: 158–60). Relations with Pisa were always more ambiguous. See Epstein 1996b: 881 note 45 for a discussion of the discriminatory tariffs applied to Pisa in 1408. These were partly mitigated in 1418, by which time the Pisan economy had virtually collapsed (PR 108, ff.156v–8); but only in 1440 was Pisa allowed to import grain toll-free from its hinterland (PR 131, ff.100rv, 184).

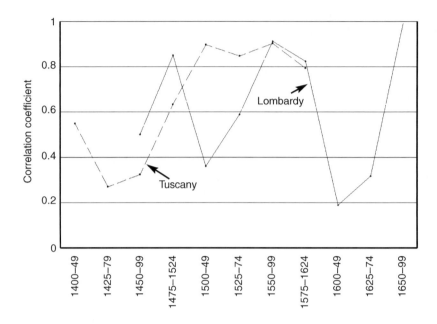

Figure 7.4 Price synchronisation in Lombardy and Tuscany

compulsory pricing across the state.[45] Fifteenth-century Florentines perceived their territorial *dominium* in terms of a subject *contado*, and they acted simply to mitigate the worst consequences for their own city of urban protectionism without addressing the underlying causes. Neither the institution in 1413 of a system of export rights (*tratte*) from Pisa's former *contado*, nor the creation in 1448 of the new *Dogana dei traffichi* to oversee the customs system, had any discernible effect on the pattern of grain prices in the region.[46]

Concern for Arezzo was even less evident. In 1461 Florence specified that the toll franchise granted to Arezzo's new fair did not apply to victuals brought in from the countryside (PR 151, ff.380v–1); and it took until 1465 to modify the town's gabelles on grain, which were three times as high on imports as on exports (PR 156, ff.85v–6v).

45 For aid to smaller towns, see PR 164, f.113rv, 1473 (Volterra); PR 126, ff.230v–1v, 1435 (Cortona); PR 138, c.25rv, 1447 and PR 153, c.194rv, 1462 (Castiglion Fiorentino). For forcible distraints, see PR 126, ff.424v–5, 1436; it is unclear whether this provision was ever enacted. See also PR 144, ff.58–9, 1454 for a forced distribution of Florentine grain in its *contado*, in Pisa and in the Pisan *contado*. Black 1996: 231 refers to an order for Arezzo to send grain in aid of San Sepolcro in 1477. For compulsory pricing, see PR 155, ff.224v–5v, 1465.

46 For the *tratte*, see PR 102, ff.113v–14v. The authority of the Florentine *Abbondanza* over exports from Pisa was confirmed in 1442 (PR 133, cc.23v–6v). During the fifteenth century

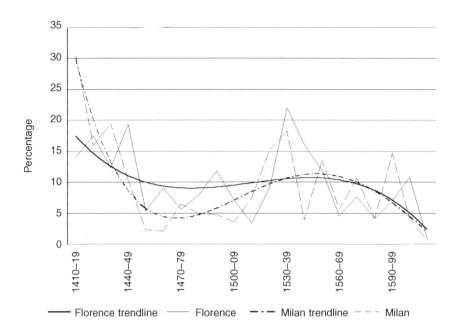

Figure 7.5 Price volatility in Florence and Milan, 1410–1619

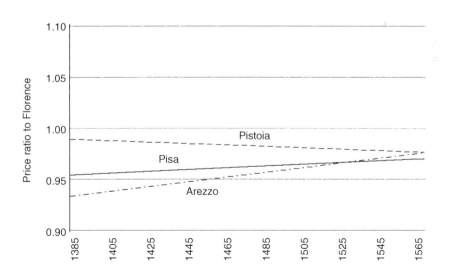

Figure 7.6 Price convergence in Tuscany, 1372–1619 (relative to Florence)

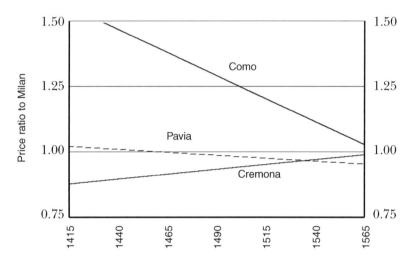

Figure 7.7 Price convergence in Lombardy, 1415–1619 (relative to Milan)

A series of customs laws passed in 1461 known as the *Legge dei passeggeri*, specifying which roads and passes domestic and foreign traders had to use, was more significant. The statutes, which were intended to bolster Florence's commercial leadership in the region and to make it easier to tax trade, also focused road investments on Tuscany's main commercial arteries, which were close to collapse after a century of demographic and economic decline.[47] The reorganisation and improvement of the road system caused regional price integration to surge in the space of a few years from 50–70 to 85–95 per cent (Figure 7.4).[48] On the other hand, regional grain policies were unaffected, the provisioning offices of Tuscan communes continued to act independently and in uncoordinated fashion until the early 1560s, and price volatility consequently did not fall (Figure 7.5).[49]

The Lombard grain market was similar in many ways to Tuscany's;

the Florentine *Signoria* authorized export licences in 1422–4, 1427–8, 1442, 1444, 1447, 1465, 1471, 1475, and 1493; further grain exports from Pisa are recorded for 1473, 1478, 1481–2, 1491 and 1495. Florence banned exports in 1412, 1435, 1441, 1464, 1466, and 1468; it authorised overseas grain imports on twenty-three occasions, and elected officials to the *Abbondanza* in thirty-one years. For the *Dogana dei traffichi*, see Dini 1984: 23-6. Florentine attitudes were formulated with characteristic starkness by Machiavelli, who argued that Arezzo's rebellion of 1502 should have been punished by razing the city to the ground; this would have enhanced Florence's political and military security and reputation and provided it with adequate food supplies (Machiavelli 1960: Discorsi, bk.II, ch.23).

47   For a discussion of the *Legge* (see DAC 373, ff.34–8), see Dini 1984: 24–6; Dini 1986: 289.
48   See also Epstein 2000c: 115 Figs. 5.5a–b.
49   For policies up to the 1560s, see Pult Quaglia 1990: 70.

there were extensive controls over rural supplies, urban stocks and prices, and both towns and the state kept a vigilant eye on the export trade. But regarding grain supplies the regional leader, Milan, was *primus inter pares* rather than hegemon. Although Milan shared with Pavia the right to obtain grain supplies anywhere in the state without restrictions, neither city benefited from lower tariffs like Florence. Perhaps more fundamentally, Lombardy instituted much before Tuscany a central office to monitor and license the domestic and foreign grain trade. The Lombard arrangement, which was set up in the 1450s, had two major advantages over Tuscany's system of competitive urban monopolies. First, it aligned the interests of the grain merchants who wished to bypass urban trade controls with the fiscal interests of the state. This made it easier to maintain trading relations and patterns of specialisation even after the political unity of the duchy was broken, so that the regional patterns of trade and division of labour apparent in the 1450s (Figure 7.8) would remain in place until at least the seventeenth century.[50] Second, it offered a cheap means to collect, collate and coordinate information about grain flows in 'thin' markets in which information costs were high, thereby reducing the price volatility caused by information failures in more fragmented markets.

In Tuscany, the Florentine elites were too heavily implicated in existing arrangements to introduce a reform which could be credibly arbitrated and enforced. A credible reform required the political will to cut through vested interests and, perhaps more importantly, the authority derived from the subjects' perception that the reformers themselves did not stand to gain from change. The Florentines faced a credibility gap because they were inevitably suspected of acting out of self-interest. This made it more costly to modify inefficient institutions like the individual urban food agencies (*Abbondanze*) because the latter appeared to protect their subjects from Florentine pressure.[51] Whatever its motives, it was therefore unlikely that the Florentine republic could solve the political stalemate, offering a clear demonstration of how inefficient institutions could 'lock-in' because of the coordination problems faced by institutional reform. Not suprisingly, the opportunity for reform first arose under a triumphant territorial prince rather than under the urban republic, when Duke Cosimo I de' Medici, flush from his victory in the early 1560s over Florence's great rival Siena, created a permanent

---

50 See Corritore 1995 for regional agricultural specialisation *c*.1650, which matches the pattern outlined in Figure 7.8.

51 Subject cities were responding to the perception, articulated by Hume, that 'the conquerors, in such a [Republican] government, are all legislators, and will be sure to contrive matters, by restrictions on trade, and by taxes, so as to draw some private, as well as public advantage from their conquests' (Hume 1993c: 17). See also, Chapter 2, p. 33.

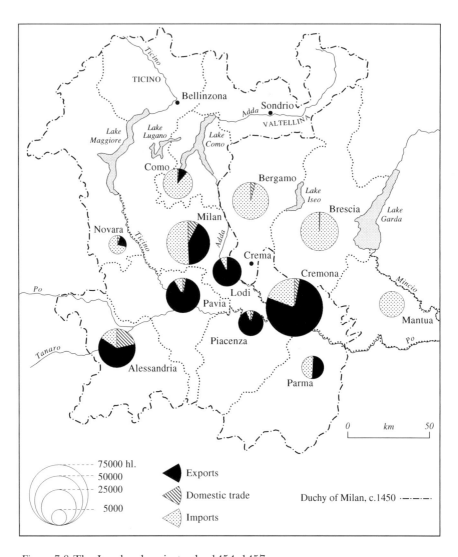

Figure 7.8 The Lombard grain trade, 1454–1457

regional supply office (*Abbondanza*) to coordinate the importation and distribution of grain supplies in the territorial state.[52] The measure abolished traditional urban vetoes over local grain supplies and caused an immediate fall in price volatility (Figure 7.5). Market liberalisation required an authoritarian ruler to cut the Gordian knot of competing

52   Pult Quaglia 1990: 47–62.

interests;[53] but the economic costs of delay contributed to Tuscan economic stagnation.[54]

Political and market integration

The evidence we have surveyed indicates that political integration rather than technical change was the principal driver of market integration after the Black Death. Political integration increased domestic stability, which was the main precondition for trade; it established a quasi-customs union between formerly 'foreign' markets and reduced the incidence of local tariffs; it enabled weaker rural communities to establish markets and fairs against urban opposition; it stimulated the rationalisation of road networks; and it improved market coordination. Each one of these developments was a result of political bargains, and political structures were therefore decisive for the speed and character of integration.

Market integration depended directly on jurisdictional integration, for three reasons. First, jurisdictional integration was necessary to achieve the separation of economic and political powers which were organically unified under feudalism. Market fragmentation under feudalism was caused by the fact that feudal lords and towns derived income from political and legal coercion. The centralisation of sovereignty deprived feudal lords and towns of jurisdictional powers and displaced rent-seeking from the local to the territorial and national arena; rent-seeking became more transparent and costly and forced feudal and urban lordships to compete by economic instead of political means. Second, jurisdictional integration solved the market failures in the industrial, agricultural and commercial sectors that we have discussed in this book. Third, jurisdictional integration helped overcome the huge legal and informational costs caused by the myriad overlapping and competing feudal sovereignties. Pre-modern Smithian growth, which was a function of market integration, therefore depended ultimately on the progress of state sovereignty.

---

53 A point made by Persson 1999 for the eighteenth century.
54 See Chapter 1, for estimates that Tuscan GNP per caput contracted from the fifteenth century onwards, and Chapter 6 for a discussion of the region's poor industrial performance during the same period.

Appendix: manuscript and published sources for the price of wheat

For archival references, see Abbreviations.

Arezzo: AFL 1204, 1522, 1618–1769, 2243–4, 2529–31, 3353, 3411, 3532–3; ASAr, Squarci dei prezzi del grano 4.

Bergamo: BCBg, Archivio della Misericordia Maggiore 4, 7, 76, 128, 130, 132, 152, 633, 725, 728, 756–7, 812, 1543, 1551, 1725, 1868, 3067, 3409, 3568.

Bibbiena: ASFi, CRS 30, nn.12, 27–8.

Borgo S.Sepolcro: Fanfani 1940: 79–112.

Brescia: ASCBs, Archivio Martinengo dalle Palle 69, 70, 74, 78, 84, 88, 90.

Como: ASCo, Ospedale di S.Anna 1–2; Monastero di S.Carpoforo 35–6; Calmieri dei grani 371–3; Mira 1941.

Cortona: ASFi, CRS 59.

Cremona: ASCr, Istituto generale elemosiniere, Corpi soppressi 379–81, 389; Jacopetti 1965; Meroni 1957.

Douai: Mestayer 1963.

Exeter: Beveridge 1929.

Florence: Roncière 1976: IV, pp.457–8; Pinto 1981; Goldthwaite 1975; Florence, Bibliotea Riccardiana 23412, fos.234–5 (data kindly provided by Richard Goldthwaite); ASFi, Compagnia poi Magistrato del Bigallo 651; ASFi, CRS 79 n.20; 88 nn.23–4; 89 n.10; 98 n.25; 108 nn.10–11; 113 n.86; 119 nn.683, 687–8, 691; 140 n.39; Monastero del Paradiso 148-9; Ospedale S.Matteo 250–1, 326–9; S.Maria Nuova 4403, 4411, 4413, 4415, 4419–20,4422-3, 4429

Milan: ECA, Fondo Divinità, Mastri 1–2; ECA, Fondo Quattro Marie, Libri mastri 1–14, 49–64, 75–77; ECA, Carità in Porta, Libri mastri 9-10; ECA, Misericordia 62; ASMi, Trivulzio, Registri 82-4; ASMi, Trivulzio, Ospedale della pietà, Libri mastri 85, 92; di Raimondo 1975–6; Biasibetti 1976–7; de Maddalena 1950: 157-9.

Parma: Romani 1975.

Pavia: Zanetti 1964: 155–9.

Pisa: ASPi, Opera del Duomo 91, 120–1, 442–8, 1084–90, 1164–5; Corporazioni religiose soppresse 1012; data from 1515 onwards kindly provided by Paolo Malanima.

Pistoia: ASFi, CRS 184, nn.5–6; 198, nn.23–5; 188, nn.18-27, 33; ASPt, Opera di S.Jacopo 9–10, 407–8, 413–14, 425–7, 430, 432, 434, 435bis, 436–36bis, 439–41, 443, 505, 764

Saragossa: Zulaica Palacios 1994; Hamilton 1936.

Utrecht: Posthumus 1964.

Varese: Giampaolo 1954.

Volterra: BCV, Croce nera, Conventi soppressi 72-3, 80, 82, 92, 97, 98; BCV, G' 146; ASFi, Compagnie religiose soppresse da Pietro Leopoldo 2949, 2962.

8 Conclusion

Prisoner's dilemmas caused by decentralised rent-seeking, and coordination failures caused by jurisdictional fragmentation, posed the most significant constraint on pre-modern growth. Prisoner's dilemmas arose from individuals' unwillingness to commit themselves not to use military, political or economic power in exchange for the future benefits of peace and lower factor and product prices; coordination failures arose where two or more agents found it hard to match policies which they both desired. Both conditions restricted markets and raised the costs of contracting. By enforcing pre-commitment to rules and by providing the legal and political framework to coordinate decentralised agents, pre-modern states mobilised scale economies in trade networks, in urban and rural manufacture, and in systems of food supply, raised the costs of collusion, and enforced clearer rules and procedures for legal and political dispute settlement. The main contribution by European states to pre-modern economic growth was thus the centralisation of government, the reduction of decentralised rent-seeking, and the creation of viable markets. With the exception of markets in food supply, however, pre-modern markets were the unintended consequence of attempts to extend state sovereignty rather than the outcome of deliberate political action.

Three factors caused levels of income and rates of Smithian growth to vary: first, opportunities to capture scale economies in industry (e.g. protoindustry) and distribution (e.g. fairs), which were a function of the state's capacity to overcome feudal decentralised rent-seeking in, and cartelization of, the 'public' transactional sphere (the 'market'); second, differences in macro-economic stability, that is, in the frequency and intensity of warfare, which Chapter 7 showed was the main cause of market disintegration; third, technological progress or innovation, which was a function of market size.

The first two factors were particularly important for static and dynamic efficiency. However, since most states (with the notable exception of England) could not avoid foreign warfare even if they had desired to, the nature of the political regime only affected the provision of public goods.

On this matter we need to distinguish more clearly than is usual for modern societies between the state's fiscal-cum-borrowing apparatus and its capacity to coordinate domestic markets. On the one hand, evidence from long-term government interest rates shows that England's self-imposed isolation from Continental politics during the late sixteenth and seventeenth centuries also increased the English monarchy's capacity for fiscal depredation, which elsewhere was kept in check by the threat of military invasion or civil war. The fifteenth-century English nationalist trope, which defined Continental monarchies as tyrannical because their rulers lacked formal constraints, is turned on its head by the discovery that discerning capitalist lenders trusted Continental 'tyrants' more than the government of the freeborn English. If we accept that a defining feature of a political system is its reliability and predictability, government interest rates show that in practical as against theoretical terms, absolutist regimes were every bit as 'constitutional' – that is, as institutionally and politically constrained – as parliamentary ones, even though the precise nature and dynamics of the constraints was different.

On the other hand, it is also clear that state interest rates measure the sophistication of the state's fiscal and financial regimes and not the country's potential for Smithian growth or its actual economic performance; to put it somewhat differently, constitutional constraints on state power to influence private property rights do not account for variations in growth and prosperity. This point is brought home forcefully by a comparison between interest rates on state debt (Figure 2.1) and on landed investments (Figure 3.1). This shows that the initial discrepancies between national rates on public debt, which reflect the regime's financial credibility, were far greater than on private returns to land, which reflect opportunities for investment. Both levels and trends in base rates show that early modern England was a constitutional but not an economic outlier; indeed, with a highly centralised and stable government and comparatively little domestic war, the country possessed clear-cut advantages in the provision of public goods compared with its Continental neighbours. By contrast, discussion of the Tuscan example suggests that urban-based republics paid the lowest interest rates on state debt but were also prone to serious market failures in manufacture and urban food supply.

The late medieval crisis was arguably a turning point for Smithian and technological growth associated with rise of more centralised states. The strongest evidence of the structural improvements caused by the crisis comes from the halving of base and state interest rates across much of Europe between 1300 and 1500, corroborated by evidence of growing market integration, rising urbanisation, increased technological diffusion, and better living standards. The crisis brought European economies closer to their technological frontier and established a new dynamic equilibrium, which initiated a centuries-long process of catch up in welfare and technology with the most advanced economy of the time,

Ming-Ching China (it is generally accepted that 'medieval', Song China was considerably more developed than medieval Europe).

However, the late medieval crisis also gave rise to different institutional equilibria based on the different claims to 'public' rents from production and trade prevailing in particular countries. Some institutional bundles provided more effective productive incentives than others, although for the moment we must remain agnostic about which of them promoted economic growth and technological innovation most efficiently. There are several reasons for caution. In the first place, we still know too little about levels and rates of growth in pre-modern economies to make very plausible claims about their causes. The large economic differences we observe between European countries at the dawn of the industrial age were largely the result of compounding very small differences in growth rates over very long periods of time. For example, the near doubling of GNP per head in England during the late Middle Ages was achieved at an annual rate of less than 0.4 per cent, and subsequent growth rates up to 1700 are unlikely to have been much higher.[1] Some answers to the question of how such small differences in growth could be caused by major differences in politico-institutional arrangements have been sketched here, but there is clearly much more work to be done in a comparative perspective and in terms of devising and improving ways of measuring changing levels and rates of growth. It will also be necessary to take more account of the macro-economic effects of domestic warfare, which appears to have caused the virtual collapse of markets and major economic setbacks over significant stretches of time, even though the gains to the English economy from the relative lack of domestic strife are hard to quantify.

A second reason for a degree of agnosticism about regime efficiency is that different sets of institutions may have been optimal under different economic conditions. Some may have been better at maximising current welfare than at stimulating the technological changes needed to increase welfare in the future. For example, Italian city-states were highly efficient modes of economic organisation in societies with highly fragmented jurisdictions, but were less effective than monarchies in coordinating markets over larger and politically more complex territories; their smaller scale may also have made it easier for vested economic interests to capture the political agenda. In addition, we need to consider whether different political regimes may have been effective solutions to different sets of political and welfare problems or different political constituencies, a possible example of the latter being the adoption of different systems of food supply because of their different distributional consequences. Both possibilities have been ignored by a one-size-fits-all approach to

---

1 Craig and Fisher 2000: Table 6.2.

political regimes that assumes a once-and-for-all ordinal ranking in terms of their outcomes.[2]

Finally, the presence of economies of scale and technological external-ities has important implications for institutional and economic path dependence that have yet to be explored. The suggestion that externalities in protoindustry and trading networks explain some of the lack of conver-gence between pre-modern economies, and that the striking absence of economic growth in Italy after 1500 was in no small part a consequence of the power of its cities and of its weak protoindustrial base, needs to be tested more extensively against the experience of other regions.[3]

Among the conclusions to be drawn from this book is thus the extent of our ignorance about the political economy of pre-modern societies. Simple analogies with present conditions simply will not do. To assume that pre-modern individuals were economically rational and that their actions can be examined with the tools of modern economics does not mean that pre-modern market structures were merely a more 'constrained' version of our own. Pre-modern markets, like modern capitalist markets, were the artefact of political and legal systems that were in turn the outcome of political negotiation and contestation. Just as we take it for granted that social demo-cratic 'social markets', Anglo-American market liberalism, and south-east Asian state capitalism are the product of different sets of institutions but are nonetheless all fundamentally capitalist in structure and inspiration, we may reasonably assume that feudal-tributary political economies were equally diverse, even though we are still far from understanding precisely how these differences shaped economic prospects in the past.

The arguments I have presented do however allow us to speculate about some of the institutional prerequisites for the transition from a feudal-trib-utary to a capitalist economy. Two preliminary points are in order. First, pre-modern intensive growth was not restricted to western Europe and Japan. Pre-modern living standards and per caput rates of growth in parts of south-east Asia, including southern China, for example, may well have equalled or surpassed those achieved in the most advanced European regions.[4] Second, Smithian growth was a necessary but not sufficient cause of the technological and organisational changes associated with modern industrialisation. Although the fact that pre-modern growth was a precon-dition for industrialisation is in a trivial sense true, the traditional chronicles which took the failure of non-European societies to industri-alise to infer that they had not undergone any intensive growth are now being increasingly questioned.

---

2   See Epstein (2000a), Introduction.

3   See Epstein 1998b: 101–8.

4   See the discussions by Gunder Frank 1998; Pomerantz 2000. For more traditional views of Chinese economic performance, see Maddison 1998.

The reason why Smithian growth and industrial growth are not causally linked is that industrialisation was first and foremost a technological revolution, and the interaction between market growth and the direction of technological change is not predetermined. In our current state of knowledge it seems entirely plausible that if, for example, pre-modern Europe and Asia started with different bundles of technology, they would also subsequently face different probabilities of inventing modern industrial machinism. The question of what caused the industrial revolution is therefore conceptually and empirically distinct from the question of what caused pre-modern, Smithian growth. Moreover, if we define capitalism as an economic system in which there is private ownership of the means of production, the majority of producers are separated from their means of production, and resources are allocated competitively through markets, it is clear that capitalism is fully compatible with Smithian growth but is neither conceptually nor empirically homologous to modern industrialisation. Although there are good reasons why commercial growth will also stimulate technological progress, strictly speaking the main motive force behind the rise of capitalism is political and market structure, whereas the main motive force for the rise of modern industry is technological change.

Feudalism was instead a system in which political power largely determined economic power and defined individual access to wealth. Resources were systematically allocated through decentralised political rent-seeking, while feudal markets excluded participants on grounds of status; even under republican states, not all subjects had equal rights to produce and trade. Property rights that distinguished between rights of usage and rights of jurisdiction and disposal were a source of legal ambiguity and contestation.[5] By contrast with capitalism, rent-seeking and property rights 'fuzziness' were fundamental features of the feudal system which systematically constrained both Smithian growth and technological progress.

For this reason, the transition from a feudal to a capitalist system of political economy required the creation at the same time of absolute property and of absolute sovereignty, that is, the confluence of distinct rights into single, autonomous subjects and into single, autonomous sovereign bodies. The establishment of capitalist markets and *individual* property rights required the centralisation of political sovereignty and the abolition of decentralised rent-seeking based on social class and privilege: in other words, the establishment of clear *state* property rights. Contrary to

---

5 What modern capitalist societies simply call *property*, that is, whole and undivided ownership, was under feudalism split into two distinctive elements: beneficial ownership, which included the right to sell, divide, rent and transfer through inheritance, and eminent domain, which was a hereditary right based upon immemorial possession that conveyed jurisdictional authority and rents, and which became increasingly commercialised from the fourteenth century onwards. Eminent domain was the main source of jurisdictional fragmentation and divided property rights under feudalism.

theories of natural rights and natural markets, the main precondition for both modern individualism based on self-autonomy and self-ownership and for the equality before law and market of the whole population was the rise of the modern state: the rise, that is, of a state with a division between legislative, executive and judicial powers, in which the jurisdictional boundaries between different centres of institutional power are strictly defined, and in which the possession of full and legitimate sovereignty empowers it to mediate between competing jurisdictions and to enforce collective agreements. These crucial institutional changes were achieved in England from the latter half of the seventeenth century and elsewhere in Europe in the course of the eighteenth and early nineteenth.[6]

6 For the argument that the modern, autonomous state was the main prerequisite of modern individualism, see for example Schnur 1963; Richet 1973; Tarello 1976: 15–42, 156–89; Brewer and Staves 1995; also Chapter 2 note 8 in this book. A similar claim is made by some Marxists (Meiksins Wood 1981).

Bibliography

Published primary sources

Agnoletti, A. M. E. (ed.) (1940) *Statuto dell'Arte della lana di Firenze (1317–1319)*, Florence.

Berti, F. and M. Guerrini (eds) (1980) *Empoli: statuti e riforme. Statuto e riforme del popolo di Santo Andrea (1416–1441). Statuto del comune di Empoli (1428)*, Empoli.

Berti, F. and M. Mantovani (eds) (1985) *Statuti di Figline: Statuti del comune di Figline Valdarno (1408). Patti fra il comune di Figline e il popolo di S. Maria al Tartigliese (1392)*, Figline.

Bonaini, F. (1857) 'Breve dell'Arte della Lana corretto nel MCCCV', in F. Bonaini (ed.) *Statuti della città di Pisa*, 3 vols, Florence, vol. 3: 645–760.

Bonora, G. (ed.) (1860) 'Statuta antiqua comunis Placentie', in G. Bonora (ed.) *Statuta varia civitatis Placentiae*, Parma.

Bruni, L. (1978) 'Panegyric to the city of Florence', in B. G. Kohl and R. G. Witt (eds) *The Earthly Republic. Italian Humanists on Government and Society*, Manchester, pp. 135–75.

Calamari, G. (ed.) (1927) *Lo statuto di Pescia del MCCCXXXIX*, Pescia.

Camerani Marri, G. (1963) 'Statuto di Castelfranco di Sopra (1394)', in G. Camerani Marri (ed.) *Statuti dei comuni di Castelfranco di Sopra (1394) e di Castiglione degli Ubertini (1397)*, Florence.

Casini, B. (1968) *Statuto del comune di Montopoli (1360)*, Florence.

Castellani, A. (1956) 'Ordinamenti dell'arte della lana di S.Gimignano (1334)', in A. Castellani (ed.) *Testi sangimignanesi del secolo XIII e della prima metà del secolo XIV*, Florence, pp. 93–137.

Castignoli, P. and P. Racine (eds) (1967) 'Statuta antiqua mercatorum Placentiae', in P. Castignoli and P. Racine (eds) *Corpus statutorum mercatorum Placentiae (secoli XIV–XVIII)*, Milan.

Codex (1547) *Codex statutorum magnifice communitatis atque die-caesis [sic] Alexandrinae ad Reipublicae utilitatem noviter excusi*, Alessandria.

Colombo, A. (1933) 'Gli "antichi statuti" di Vigevano (Liber statutorum veterum terrae Vigevani) con appendice', in R. Soriga (ed.) *Carte e statuti dell'agro ticinese*, Turin, pp. 292–508.

Conti, E. (ed.) (1981) *Le 'Consulte' e 'Pratiche' della Repubblica fiorentina nel Quattrocento, I. (1401) (Cancellierato di Coluccio Salutati)*, Pisa.

Contractus (1575) *Contractus datiorum Bergomi*, Brescia.

Day, J. (ed.) (1963) *Les douanes de Gênes, 1376–1377*, 2 vols, Paris.

Finazzi, G. (1876) 'Statutum vetus', in G. Finazzi (ed.) *Antiquae collationes statuti civitatis Pergami*, Turin, coll. 1921–2046.

Gherardi, A. (ed.) (1893) *I capitoli del comune di Firenze. Inventario e regesto*, 2, Florence.

Guasti, C. (ed.) (1866) *I capitoli del comune di Firenze. Inventario e regesto*, 1, Florence.

Guicciardini, F. (1951) *Ricordi*, ed. R. Spongano, Florence.

Machiavelli, N. (1960) *Il Principe e Discorsi sopra la prima deca di Tito Livio*, ed. S. Bertelli, introd. G. Procacci, Milan.

Magnani, G. (1963) 'Documenti inediti di vita economica medioevale. Lo statuto dei merciai di Pavia', *Bollettino storico pavese di storia patria*, new ser. 15: 79–88.

Masi, G. (ed.) (1934) *Statutum bladi Reipublicae Florentinae (1348)*, Milan.

Mor, C. G. (ed.) (1932) 'Statuta Burgi Sexii MCCCLXXXXVII', in C. G. Mor (ed.) *Statuti della Valsesia del sec. XIV. Valsesia, Borgosesia, Crevola, Quarona*, Milan.

Morandi, U. (ed.) (1966) *Statuto del comune di Montepulciano (1337)*, Florence.

Motta, E. (1892) 'Le lettere ducali dell'epoca viscontea nell'Archivio civico di Como. Regesti e documenti', *Periodico della società storica per la provincia e antica diocesi di Como* 9: 7–83.

Natale, A. R. (ed.) (1987) *Acta libertatis Mediolani. I Registri n.5 e n.6 dell'Archivio dell'Ufficio degli Statuti di Milano (Repubblica Ambrosiana 1447–1450)*, Milan.

Noto, A. (ed.) (1950) *Il Liber datii mercantie Communis Mediolani. Registro del secolo XV,* Milan.

Nuti, R. (1928) '*Un frammento di antico statuto dell'Arte della lana di Prato*', *Archivio storico pratese* 8: 11–28.

Odorici, F. (ed.) (1876) 'Statuta civitatis Brixiae', in *Monumenta historiae patriae, XVI Leges municipales,* 2 vols, Turin, vol.2.

Pacta (1722) 'Pacta, sive statuta datii mercantiae', in *Statuta civilia, et criminalia communitatis Leonati*, Brescia.

Pallastrelli, B. (ed.) (1869) *Statuta Artis lanificii civitatis et episcopatus Placentiae ab anno MCCCCXXXVI ad annum MCCCLXXXVI*, Parma.

Pancotti, V. (1925–30) *I paratici piacentini e i loro statuti*, 3 vols, Piacenza.

Patti (1782) *Patti di dedizione alla Serenissima Repubblica di Venezia. Privilegi, decreti, giudizi, terminazioni, ed altro raccolti a favore della spettabile Valle Seriana inferiore, territorio di Bergamo*, Bergamo.

Pezzati, G. (1842) 'Diario della ribellione della città d'Arezzo dell'anno 1502', *Archivio storico italiano*, 1st ser. 1: 213–26.

Piattoli, R. and R. Nuti (eds) (1947) *Statuti dell'Arte della lana di Prato (secoli XIV–XVIII)*, Florence.

Provigioni (1590) *Provigioni de' dacii di Cremona*, Cremona.

Roscoe, W. (1862) *The Life of Lorenzo de' Medici called the Magnificent*, 2 vols, London.

Sabbioneta Almansi, C. (ed.) (1970) *Statuti dell'Università e paratico dell'Arte del pignolato bombace e panno di lino [of Cremona]*, Cremona.

Santoro, C. (ed.) (1940) *La matricola dei mercanti di lana sottile di Milano*, Milan.

Sartini, F. (ed.) (1940) *Statuti dell'Arte dei rigattieri e linaioli di Firenze (1296–1340)*, Florence.

Statuta (1480) *Statuta Mediolani*, Milan, A. Suardi.

Statuta (1489) *Statuta communitatis Riperiae Benacensis*, Portese, B. Zanni.

Statuta (1508) *Statuta Brixiae*, Brescia, A. Britannicus.

Statuta (1557) *Statuta civitatis Brixiae cum reformationibus*, Brescia.

Statuta (1592) *Statuta civilia communitatis Leuci*, Milan.

Statuta (1625) *Statuta collegii mercatorum Papiae*, Pavia.

Statuta (1778–83) *Statuta populi et Communis Florentie publica auctoritate collecta et praeposita, anno salutis MCCCCXV*, Fribourg [Florence].

Statuti (1580?) *Statuti dei mercanti della città di Cremona*, Cremona.

Statuti (1891) *Statuti della società dei mercanti di Monza*, Monza.

Storti Storchi, C. (ed.) (1986) *Lo statuto di Bergamo del 1331*, Milan.

Vianello, C. A. (1951–2) 'Un incunabolo dell'emancipazione del proletariato: Lo Statuto dei battilana di Soncino del 1511', *Archivio storico lombardo*, 8th ser. 3: 202–8.

Volumen (1686) *Volumen statutorum et privilegiorum paratici et fori universitatis mercatorum civitatis et districtus Bergomi*, Bergamo.

von Liebenau, T. (1885–6) 'Le ordinazioni daziarie di Como nel XIV secolo (Da un codice lucernese)', *Periodico della società storica comense* 5: 205–94.

Secondary sources

Abel, W. (1980) *Agricultural Fluctuations in Europe. From the Thirteenth to the Twentieth Centuries*, Eng. trans. O. Ordish, London.

Abrams, P. and E. A. Wrigley (eds) (1978) *Towns in Societies. Essays in Economic History and Historical Sociology*, Cambridge.

Acemoglu, D and F. Zilibotti (1996) 'Was Prometheus unbound by chance? Risk, diversification, and growth', *Journal of Political Economy* 105, 4: 709–51.

Ades, A. F. and E. L. Glaeser. (1995) 'Trade and circuses: explaining urban giants', *Quarterly Journal of Economics* 110, 1: 195–227.

Albini, G. (1993) 'Contadini-artigiani in una comunità bergamasca: gandino sulla base di un estimo della seconda metà del '400', *Studi di storia medioevale e di diplomatica* 14: 111–92.

Alchian, A. and H. Demsetz (1973) 'The property right paradigm', *Journal of Economic History* 33, 1: 16–28.

Allegra, L. (1987) *La città verticale. Usurai, mercanti e tessitori nella Chieri del Cinquecento*, Milan.

Allen, R. C. (1995) *Enclosure and the Yeoman. The Agricultural Development of the South Midlands 1450–1850*, Oxford.

—— (1999) 'Tracking the agricultural revolution in England', *Economic History Review*, 2nd ser. 52, 2: 209–35.

Allix, A. (1922) 'The geography of fairs: illustrated by old-world examples', *Geographical Review* 12: 532–69.

Allmand, C. (1988) *The Hundred Years War. England and France at War c.1300–c.1450*, Cambridge.

Ammann, H. (1950–1) 'Die Friedberger Messen', *Rheinische Vierteljahrsblätter* 15–16: 192–255.

—— (1953) 'Die deutschen und schweizerischen Messen', in *La foire*, Brussels, pp. 149–73.

—— (1955) 'Die Nördlingen Messe im Mittelalter', in *Aus Verfassungs- und Landesgeschichte. Festschrift zum 70. Geburtstag von Th. Mayer*, 2 vols, Lindau-Konstanz, vol. 2, pp. 283–315.

—— (1970) *Die wirtschaftliche Stellung der Reichsstadt Nürnberg im Spätmittelalter*, Nürnberg.

Anderson, P. (1974) *Lineages of the Absolutist State*, London.

Annoni, A. (1970) 'I rapporti tra lo Stato di Milano e i popoli della Confederazione Elvetica nei secoli XV e XVI', *Archivio storico lombardo* 97: 287–312.

Antoni, T. (1982) 'Note sull'arte vetraria a Pisa fra il Tre e il Quattrocento', *Bollettino storico pisano* 51: 295–305.

Appleby, A. B. (1978) *Famine in Tudor and Stuart England*, Stanford.

Arneson, R. J. (1993) 'Socialism as the extension of democracy', in E. F. Paul, F. D. Miller Jr. and J. Paul (eds) *Liberalism and the Economic Order*, Cambridge/New York, pp. 145–71.

Ashton, R. (1960) *The Crown and the Money Market*, 1603–1640, Oxford.

Astill, G. and A. Grant (1988) 'The medieval countryside: efficiency, progress and change', in G. Astill and A. Grant (eds) *The Countryside of Medieval England*, Oxford, pp. 213–34.

Astill, G. and J. Langdon (eds) (1997) *Medieval Farming and Technology. The Impact of Agricultural Change in Northwest Europe*, Leiden/New York/Cologne.

Aston, T. H. and C. H. E. Philpin (eds) (1985) *The Brenner Debate. Agrarian Class Structure and Economic Development in Pre-Industrial Europe*, Cambridge.

Astorri, A. (1993) 'La Mercanzia fiorentina nella prima metà del XIV secolo: funzione economica e ruolo istituzionale', unpublished Ph.D. thesis, University of Florence.

Aubin, H. and W. Zorn (eds) (1971) *Handbuch der deutschen Wirtschafts- und Sozialgeschichte*, vol.1, Stuttgart.

Aylmer, G. A. (1957a) 'Attempts at administrative reform, 1625–40', *English Historical Review* 72: 229–59.

—— (1957b) 'The last years of purveyance, 1610–60', *Economic History Review*, 2nd ser. 8, 2: 310–22.

Aymard, M. (1978) 'La transizione dal feudalesimo al capitalismo', in R. Romano and C. Vivanti (eds) *Storia d'Italia 2, Dalla caduta dell'Impero romano al secolo XVIII*, 2 vols, Turin: vol. 2, pp. 1131–92.

Baehrel, R. (1961) *Une croissance. La Basse-Provence rurale de la fin du XVIe siècle à 1789*, Paris.

Bailey, M. (1988) 'The rabbit and the medieval East Anglian economy', *Agricultural History Review* 36: 1–20.

—— (1989) *A Marginal Economy? East Anglian Breckland in the Later Middle Ages*, Cambridge.

—— (1996) 'Demographic decline in late medieval England: some thoughts on recent research', *Economic History Review*, 2nd ser. 49, 1: 1–19.

—— (1998a) 'Peasant welfare in England, 1290–1348', *Economic History Review*, 2nd ser. 51, 2: 223–51.

—— (1998b) 'Historiographical essay; the commercialisation of the English economy, 1086–1500', *Journal of Medieval History* 24, 3: 297–311.

Ball, J. N. (1977) *Merchants and Merchandise. The Expansion of Trade in Europe 1500–1630*, London.

Banti, O. (1971) *Iacopo d'Appiano. Economia, società e politica del comune di Pisa al suo tramonto (1392–1399)*, Pisa.

Baratier, E. (1961) *La démographie provençale du XIIIe au XVIe siècle*, Paris.

Barbieri, G. (1938) *Economia e politica nel ducato di Milano (1386–1535)*, Milan.

Barzel, Y. (1989) *Economic Analysis of Property Rights*, Cambridge.

Bautier, R-H. (1953) 'Les foires de Champagne', in *La foire*, Brussels, pp. 97–145.

—— (1967) 'Les mutations agricoles des XIVe et XVe siècles et les progrès de l'élevage', *Bulletin philologique et historique* 1: 1–27.

Bean, R. (1971) 'War and the birth of the nation state', *Journal of Economic History* 33: 203–21.

Becker, G. S. (1983) 'A theory of competition among pressure groups for political influence', *Quarterly Journal of Economics* 98: 371–400.

Becker, G. and K. M. Murphy (1992) 'The division of labour, coordination costs and knowledge', *Quarterly Journal of Economics* 107, 4: 1137–60.

Beik, W. (1985) *Absolutism and Society in Seventeenth-Century France*, Cambridge.

Belfanti, C. M. (1986) 'Una geografia impositiva. Dazi, gabelle e contrabbandi fra Cinque e Settecento', in G. Taborelli (ed.) *Commercio in Lombardia*, 2 vols, Milan, vol. 2, pp. 121–33.

Beloch, K. J. (1937–61) *Bevölkerungsgeschichte Italiens*, 3 vols, Berlin/Leipzig.

Beltrami, D. (1961) *Forze di lavoro e proprietà fondiaria nelle campagne venete dei secoli XVII e XVIII*, Venice/Rome.

Benadusi, G. (1996) *A Provincial Elite in Early Modern Tuscany. Family and Power in the Creation of the State*, Baltimore/London.

Bentzien, U. (1990) *Bauernarbeit im Feudalismus. Landwirtschaftliche Arbeitsgeräte und -verfahren in Deutschland von der Mitte des ersten Jahrtausends u. Z. bis um 1800*, Vaduz.

Beonio Brocchieri, V. H. (1987) 'La manifattura rurale nella pars alpestris dello Stato di Milano tra XVI e XVII secolo', *Archivio storico lombardo,* 11th ser. 4: 9–46.

—— (1993) 'Artigiani, manifatture e protoindustrie fra città e campagna: la Lombardia del XVI secolo', *Studi di storia medioevale e di diplomatica* 14: 193–209.

—— (1995) '"Piazza universale di tutte le professioni del mondo": Structures économiques et familiales dans les campagnes de la Lombardie entre 16e et 17e siècle', unpublished Ph.D. thesis, Paris, École des Hautes Études en Sciences Sociales: 2 vols.

Berengo, M. (1974) 'La città di antico regime', *Quaderni storici* 9: 661–92.

Berg, M., P. Hudson and M. Sonenscher (eds) (1983a) *Manufacture in Town and Country Before the Factory*, Cambridge.

—— (1983b) 'Manufacture in town and country before the factory', in M. Berg, P. Hudson and M. Sonenscher (eds) *Manufacture in Town and Country Before the Factory*, Cambridge: 1–32.

Bergier, J. F. (1962) 'Taux de l'intérêt et crédit à court terme à Genève dans la seconde moitié du XVIe siècle', in *Studi in onore di Amintore Fanfani*, 5 vols, Milan, vol. 4, pp. 89–119.

—— (1963a) *Genève et l'économie européenne de la Renaissance*, Paris.

—— (1963b) 'Port de Nice, sel de Savoie et foires de Genève. Un ambitieux projet de la seconde moitié du XVe siècle', *Moyen Âge* 65: 857–65.

—— (1975) 'Le trafic à travers les Alpes et les liaisons transalpines du haut Moyen Age au XVII siècle', in *Le Alpi e l'Europa*, Bari, vol.3, pp. 1–72.

—— (1980) '"De nundinis rehabendis frivola prosecutio". La politique commerciale de Genève devant la crise des foires de Lyon (1484–1494)', in *Lyon et l'Europe, hommes et sociétés. Mélanges d'histoire offerts à Richard Gascon*, 2 vols, Lyon, vol. 1, pp. 33–46.

—— (1985) 'Le trafic à travers les Alpes et les liaisons alpines du haut moyen âge au XVIIe siècle', in J. F. Bergier *et al. Le Alpi e l'Europa, 3. Economia e transiti*, Bari, pp. 1–72.

Berman, H. J. (1983) *Law and Revolution. The Formation of the Western Legal Tradition*, Cambridge, Mass./London.

Bersani, P. (1992) 'L'arte della lana a Piacenza nel XV secolo', *Studi di storia medievale e diplomatica* 12–13: 121–34.

Berthe, M. (1984) *Famines et épidémies dans les campagnes navarraises à la fin du Moyen Age*, Paris.

Berti, M. (1980) *Commercio all'ingrosso e al minuto dei panni di lana a Pisa nei primi decenni della dominazione fiorentina*, Pisa.

Beveridge, W. H. (1929) 'A statistical crime of the seventeenth century', *Journal of Economic and Business History* 1, 4: 503–33.

Biadi, L. (1859) *Storia della città di Colle in Val d'Elsa*, Florence.

Biasibetti, E. (1976–7) 'Ricerche sui prezzi dei cereali a Milano (1475–1599)', Unpublished M.A. thesis, University of Milan.

Biller, P. P. A. (1980) 'Birth-control in the West in the thirteenth and early fourteenth centuries', *Past and Present* 94: 3–26.

Birell, J. (1969) 'Peasant craftsmen in the national forest', *Agricultural History Review* 17: 91–107.

Bisson, T. N. (1986) *The Medieval Crown of Aragon. A Short History*, Oxford.

Black, A. (1984) *Guilds and Civil Society in European Political Thought from the Twelfth Century to the Present*, London.

Black, J. W. (1988) 'The limits of ducal authority: a fifteenth-century treatise on the Visconti and their subject cities', in P. Denley and C. Elam (eds) *Florence and Italy. Renaissance Studies in Honour of Nicolai Rubinstein*, London, pp. 149–60.

Black, R. (1993) 'Piero de' Medici and Arezzo', in A. Beyer and B. Boucher (eds) *Piero de' Medici 'il Gottoso' (1416–1489). Art in the Service of the Medici*, Stuttgart, pp. 21–38.

—— (1996) 'Lorenzo and Arezzo', in M. Mallett and N. Mann (eds) *Lorenzo the Magnificent. Culture and Politics*, London, pp. 217–34.

Blanchard, I. S. W. (1986) 'The Continental European cattle trades, 1400–1600', *Economic History Review*, 2nd ser. 39: 427–60.

—— (1992) 'Introduction', in Blanchard, A. Goodman and J. Newman (eds) *Industry and Finance in Early Modern History. Essays Presented to George Hammersley to the Occasion of His 74th Birthday*, Stuttgart, pp. 13–26.

Blasquez, A. (1996) 'Foires et marchés ruraux en Castille à l'époque moderne, approche et problématique: le cas de la province de Guadalajara', in C. Desplat (ed.) *Foires et marchés dans les campagnes de l'Europe médiévale et moderne*, Toulouse, pp. 105–28.

Bloch, M. (1970) [1931] *French Rural History*, Eng. trans. J. Sondheimer, London.

Blockmans, W. (1987) 'Stadt, Region und Staat: ein Dreiecksverhältnis. Der Kasus der Niederlande im 15. Jahrhundert', in F. Seibt and W. Eberhard (eds) *Europa 1500. Integrationsprozesse im Widerstreit: Staaten, Regionen, Personenverbände, Christenheit*, Stuttgart, pp. 211–26.

—— (1988) 'Princes conquérants et bourgeois calculateurs. Le poids des réseaux urbains dans la formation des états', in N. Bulst and J-P. Genet (eds) *La ville, la bourgeoisie et la genèse de l'état moderne (XIIe –XVIIIe siècles)*, Paris, pp. 167–81.

—— (1989) 'Voracious states and obstructing cities: an aspect of state formation in pre-industrial Europe', *Theory and Society* 18: 733–55.

—— (1993) 'The economic expansion of Holland and Zeeland in the fourteenth–sixteenth centuries', in E. Aerts, B. Henau, P. Janssens and R. van Uytven (eds) *Studia Historica Oeconomica. Liber Amicorum Herman van der Wee*, Leuven, pp. 41–58.

—— (1997) 'The impact of cities on state formation: three contrasting territories in the Low Countries, 1300–1500', in P. Blickle (ed.) *Resistance, Representation, and Community*, Oxford, pp. 256–71.

Bognetti, G. P. (1927) 'Per la storia dello stato visconteo (Un registro di decreti della cancelleria di Filippo Maria Visconti e un trattato segreto con Alfonso d'Aragona)', *Archivio storico lombardo* 54: 237–357.

Bois, G. (1984) *The Crisis of Feudalism: Economy and Society in Eastern Normandy*, Eng. trans. J. Birell, Cambridge.

Bolton, J. L. (1980) *The Medieval English Economy 1150–1500*, London.

Bonney, R. (1981) *The King's Debts: Finance and Politics in France, 1589–1661*, Oxford.

—— (ed.) (1995a) *Economic Systems and State Finance*, Oxford.

—— (1995b) 'Revenues', in R. Bonney (ed.) *Economic Systems and State Finance*, Oxford: 423–506.

—— (ed.) (1999) *The Rise of the Fiscal State in Europe c.1200–1815*, Oxford.

Boone, M. (1995) 'Les toiles de lin des Pays-bas bourguignons sur le marché anglais (fin XIVe–XVIe siècles)', *Publication du Centre Européen d'études bourguignonnes (XIVe –XVIe s.)* 35: 61–81.

—— (1997) 'Destroying and reconstructing the city: the inculcation and arrogation of princely power in the Burgundian-Habsburg Netherlands (14th –16th centuries)', in M. Gosman, A. van der Jagt, and J. Veenstra (eds) *The Propagation of Power in the Medieval West*, Groningen, pp. 1–33.

Boone, M. and W. Prevenier (eds) (1993) *Drapery Production in the Late Medieval Low Countries: Markets and Strategies for Survival (14th–16th Centuries)*, Leuven-Apeldoorn.

Boorsch, S. and N. M. Orenstein (1997) 'Introduction', in S. Boorsch and N. M. Orenstein (eds) *The Print in the North. The Age of Albrecht Dürer and Lucas van Leyden*, New York, pp. 3–12.

Borlandi, F. (1949) 'Note per la storia della produzione e del commercio di una materia prima. Il guado nel Medio Evo', in *Studi in onore di Gino Luzzatto*, 2 vols Milan, vol. 1, pp. 297–324.

—— (1953) '"Futainiers" et futaines dans l'Italie du Moyen Age', in *Hommage à Lucien Febvre. Éventail de l'histoire vivante*, 2 vols, Paris, 2: 133–40.

Boserup, E. (1965) *The Conditions of Agricultural Growth*, London.

Bossenga, G. (1991) *The Politics of Privilege. Old Regime and Revolution in Lille*, Cambridge.

—— (1997) 'Rights and citizens in the Old Regime', *French Historical Studies* 20, 2: 217–43.

Botticini, M. (1998) 'The choice of agrarian contracts in 1427 Tuscany: risk sharing, moral hazard, or capital market imperfections?', mimeo, Department of Economics, Boston University.

Bowsky, W. M. (1970) *The Finance of the Commune of Siena*, 1287–1355, Oxford.

—— (1981) *A Medieval Italian Commune. Siena Under the Nine, 1287–1355*, Berkeley/London/Los Angeles.

Braddick, M. J. (1993) 'An English military revolution?', *Historical Journal* 36: 765–75.

—— (1994) *Parliamentary Taxation in Seventeenth-Century England. Local Administration and Response*, Woodbridge.

—— (1996) *The Nerves of the State. Taxation and the Financing of the English State, 1558–1714*. Manchester/New York.

Bratchel, M. E. (1995) *Lucca 1430–1494. The Reconstruction of an Italian City-Republic*, Oxford.

Braudel, F. (1982) *Civilization and Capitalism, 2. The Wheels of Commerce*, London/New York.

Braunstein, P. (1979) 'Les foires de Chalon: un entre-deux dans l'histoire du commerce européen (Note critique)', *Annales E.S.C.* 34, 1: 172–9.

Brennan, G. and J. M.Buchanan (1980) *The Power to Tax. Analytical Foundations of a Fiscal Constitution*, Cambridge.

Brenner, R. (1976) 'Agrarian class structure and economic development in pre-industrial Europe', *Past and Present* 70: 30–75.

—— (1982) 'The agrarian roots of European capitalism', *Past and Present* 97: 16–113; repr. in T. H. Aston and C. H. E. Philpin (eds) *The Brenner Debate. Agrarian Class Structure and Economic Development in Pre-Industrial Europe*, Cambridge, pp. 213–327.

—— (1997) 'Property relations and the growth of agricultural productivity in late medieval and early modern Europe', in A. Bhaduri and R. Skarstein (eds) *Economic Development and Agricultural Productivity*, Cheltenham/Lyme, pp. 9–41.

Bresard, M. (1914) *Les foires de Lyon aux XVe et XVIe siècles*, Paris.

Bresc, H. (1983) 'La draperie catalane au miroir sicilien, 1300–1460', *Acta mediaevalia historica et archaeologica* 4: 107–27.

Brewer, J. (1990) *The Sinews of Power. War, Money and the English State, 1688–1783*, Cambridge, Mass./London.

Brewer, J. and S. Staves (eds) (1995) *Early Modern Conceptions of Property*, London/New York.

Bridbury, A. R. (1955) *England and the Salt Trade in the Later Middle Ages*, Oxford.

—— (1962) *Economic Growth. England in the Later Middle Ages*, London.

—— (1982) *Medieval English Clothmaking. An Economic Survey*, London.

—— (1986) 'Dr Rigby's reply: a comment', *Economic History Review,* 2nd ser. 39, 3: 417–22.

Britnell, R. H. (1978) 'English markets and royal administration before 1200', *Economic History Review,* 2nd ser. 31, 2: 183–96.

—— (1979) 'King John's early grants of markets and fairs', *English Historical Review* 94: 90–6.

—— (1981) 'The proliferation of markets in England 1200–1349', *Economic History Review,* 2nd ser. 34, 2: 209–21.

—— (1986) *Growth and decline in Colchester, 1300–1525*, Cambridge.

—— (1989) 'England and northern Italy in the early fourteenth century: the economic contrasts', *Transactions of the Royal Historical Society,* 5th ser. 39: 167–83.

—— (1993) *The Commercialisation of English Society 1000–1350*, Cambridge.

Brown, A. (1991) 'City and citizen: changing perceptions in the fifteenth and sixteenth centuries', in A. Molho, K. Raaflaub, and J. Emlen (eds) *City States in Classical Antiquity and Medieval Italy*, Stuttgart.

—— (1992) *The Medici in Florence: The Exercise and Language of Power*, Florence/Perth.

Brown, J. C. (1982) *In the Shadow of Florence. Provincial Society in Renaissance Pescia*, Oxford.

Brucker, G. (1977) *The Civic World of Early Renaissance Florence*, Princeton.

Brugaro, A. (1912) 'L'artigianato pisano nel medio evo (1000–1406)', *Studi storici* 20: 377–453.

Brunt, L. and E. Cannon (1999) 'A grain of truth in medieval interest rates? Re-examining the McCloskey-Nash hypothesis', *Bristol Economics Discussion Papers* 98 (462).

Bruwier, M. (1983) 'La foire de Mons aux XIVe et XVe siècles (1355–1465)', *Publications du Centre européen d'Études bourguignonnes* 23: 83–93.

Buchinsky, M. and B. Polak (1993) 'The emergence of a national capital market in England, 1710–1880', *Journal of Economic History*, 53, 1: 1–24.

Bückling, G. (1907) *Die Bozener Märkte bis zum Dreissigjahrigenkriege*, Leipzig.

Bueno de Mesquita, D. M. (1941) *Giangaleazzo Visconti Duke of Milan (1351–1402). A Study in the Political Career of an Italian Despot*, Cambridge.

—— (1960) 'Ludovico Sforza and his vassals', in E. F. Jacob (ed.) *Italian Renaissance Studies*, London, pp. 184–216.

—— (1988) 'The Sforza prince and his state', in P. Denley and C. Elam (eds) *Florence and Italy. Renaissance Studies in Honour of Nicolai Rubinstein*, London, pp. 161–72.

Bulst, N. (1988) 'Zum Problem städtischer und territorialer Kleider-, Aufwands- und Luxusgesetzgebung in Deutschland (13.-Mitte 16. Jahrhundert)', in A. Gouron and A. Rigaudière (eds) *Renaissance du pouvoir législatif et genèse de l'État*, Montpellier, pp. 29–57.

Bur, M. (1978) 'Note sur quelques petites foires de Champagne', in *Studi in memoria di Federigo Melis*, 5 vols, Naples, vol. 1, pp. 254–67.

Caenegem, R. C. van (1995) *An Historical Introduction to Western Constitutional Law*, Cambridge.

Calabria, A. (1991) *The Cost of Empire. The Finances of the Kingdom of Naples in the Time of Spanish Rule*, Cambridge.

Cameron, R. (1989) *A Concise Economic History of the World*, Oxford.

Cammarosano, P. (1988) 'Il sistema fiscale delle città toscane', in S. Gensini (ed.) *La Toscana nel secolo XIV. Caratteri di una civiltà regionale*, Pisa, pp. 201–13.

Campbell, B. M. S. (ed.) (1991) *Before the Black Death. Studies in the 'Crisis' of the Early Fourteenth Century*, Manchester.

—— (1995) 'Progressiveness and backwardness in thirteenth- and early four-teenth-century English agriculture: the verdict of recent research', in J.-M. Duvosquel and E. Thoen (eds) *Peasants and Townsmen in Medieval Europe. Studia in Honorem Adriaan Verhulst*, Ghent, pp. 541–59.

—— (1997a) 'Matching supply to demand: crop production and disposal by English demesnes in the century of the Black Death', *Journal of Economic History* 57, 4: 827–58.

—— (1997b) 'Economic rent and the intensification of English agriculture, 1086–1350', in G. Astill and J. Langdon (eds) *Medieval Farming and Technology. The Impact of Agricultural Change in Northwest Europe*, Leiden/New York/Cologne, pp. 225–49.

—— (1998) 'Constraint or constrained? Changing perspectives on medieval English agriculture', *NEHA-Jaarboek* 61: 15–35.

—— (2000) 'The sources of tradable surpluses: English agricultural exports 1250–1350', in N. Hybel and A. Landen (eds) *The Emergence of Large-Scale Trade in Northern Europe 1150–1400*, Toronto.

Campbell, B. M. S. and M. Overton (eds) (1991) *Land, Labour and Livestock. Historical Studies in European Agricultural Productivity*, Manchester/New York.

—— (1993) 'A new perspective on medieval and early modern agriculture: six centuries of Norfolk farming *c*.1250–*c*.1850', *Past and Present* 141: 38–105.

Carboni, M. (1995) *Il debito della città. Mercato del credito fisco e società a Bologna fra Cinque e Seicento*, Bologna.

Carlotto, N. (1993) *La città custodita. Politica e finanza a Vicenza dalla caduta di Ezzelino al vicariato imperiale (1259–1312)*, Milan.

Carrère, C. (1976) 'La draperie en Catalogne et en Aragon au XVe siècle', in M. Spallanzani (ed.) *Produzione commercio e consumo dei panni di lana (nei secoli XII–XVIII)*, Florence: 475–510.

Carus-Wilson, E. M. (1950–51) 'Trends in the export of English woollens in the fourteenth century', *Economic History Review*, 2nd ser. 3, 1–3: 162–79.

Caso, A. (1981) 'Per la storia della società milanese: i corredi nuziali nell'ultima età viscontea e nel periodo della Repubblica Ambrosiana (1433–1450) dagli atti del notaio Protaso Sansari', *Nuova rivista storica* 65: 521–51.

Cassandro, M. (1978) 'Note per una storia delle fiere', in *Studi Melis* 1978: vol. 1, pp. 239–54.

—— (1991) 'Commercio, manifatture e industria', in G. Cherubini (ed.) *Prato storia di una città, I. Ascesa e declino del centro medievale (dal Mille al 1494)*, 2 vols, Florence, vol. 1, pp. 395–477.

Castagneto, P. (1996) *L'Arte della Lana a Pisa nel Duecento e nei primi decenni del Trecento. Commercio, industria e istituzioni*, Naples.

Cate, J. L. (1938) 'The Church and market reform in England during the reign of Henry III', in J. L. Cate and E. N. Anderson (eds) *Medieval and Historiographical Essays in Honour of James Westfall Thompson*, Chicago, pp. 27–65.

Cauchies, J. M. and G. Chittolini (eds) (1990) *Milano e Borgogna. Due stati principeschi tra medioevo e Rinascimento*, Rome.

Cavalcabò, A. (1952–3) 'Le vicende storiche di Viadana (secoli XII–XV)', *Bollettino storico cremonese* 18: 159–216.

Cenedella, C. (1990) 'Proprietà terriera ed imprenditorialità a Milano nel secondo Quattrocento: La famiglia del patrizio Ambrogio Alciati', *Studi di storia medioevale e di diplomatica* 11: 199–256.

Chanaud, R. (1980) 'La foire aux ovins de Briançon: deux siècles d'échanges avec le Piémont (XIVe–XVe siècle)', *Cahiers d'histoire (Lyon)* 25: 227–55.

—— (1983) 'Le mouvement du trafic transalpin d'après un journal du péage de Briançon (1368–1369)', *Bulletin philologique et historique du Comité des travaux historiques et scientifiques (108e Congrès des sociétés savantes)*, Grenoble, pp. 105–20.

—— (1984) 'Les acheteurs de la foire aux ovins de Briançon (1385–1406)', *Bollettino storico-bibliografico subalpino* 82: 192–217.

Chartres, J. A. (1985) 'The marketing of agricultural produce', in J. Thirsk (ed.) *The Agrarian History of England and Wales*, Vol.2. 1640–1750, Cambridge, pp. 406–501.

—— (1995) 'Market integration and agricultural output in seventeenth, eighteenth, and early nineteenth-century England', *Agricultural History Review* 43: 117–38.

—— (1996) 'Foires et marchés en Angleterre de 1500 à 1850', in C. Desplat *Foires et marchés dans les campagnes de l'Europe médiévale et moderne*, Toulouse: 153–75.

Cherubini, G. (1981) 'Le campagne italiane dall' XI al XV secolo', in O. Capitani, R. Manselli, G. Cherubini, A. I. Pini and G. Chittolini, *Comuni e signorie: istituzioni, società e lotte per l'egemonia*, Storia d'Italia ed. G. Galasso, vol. 4, Turin, pp. 265–448.

Chevalier, B. (1982) *Les bonnes villes de France du XIVe au XVIe siècle*, Paris.

Chevet, J-M. (1996) 'National and regional corn markets in France from the sixteenth to the nineteenth century', *Journal of European Economic History* 25, 3: 681–703.

Chiappa Mauri, L. (1985) 'Riflessioni sulle campagne lombarde del Quattro-Cinquecento', *Nuova rivista storica* 69: 123–30.

—— (1986) 'Le merci di Lombardia. Le produzioni agricole e agroalimentari', in G. Taborelli (ed.) *Commercio in Lombardia*, 2 vols, Milan: vol. 1, pp. 119–44.

—— (1990a) *Paesaggi rurali di Lombardia*, Bari.

—— (1990b) 'Le trasformazioni nell'area lombarda', in S. Gensini (ed.) *Le Italie del tardo Medioevo*, Pisa: 409–32.

—— (1997) *Terra e uomini nella Lombardia medievale*, Bari.

Chittolini, G. (1978) 'I capitoli di dedizione delle comunità lombarde a Francesco Sforza: motivi di contrasto fra città e contado', in *Felix olim Lombardia. Studi di storia padana in onore di G.Martini*, Milan, pp. 673–93.

—— (1979) *La formazione dello Stato regionale e le istituzioni del contado. Secoli XIV e XV*, Turin.

—— (1982) 'Governo ducale e poteri locali', in *Gli Sforza* 1982: 27–42.

—— (1983) 'Le terre sepa-rate nel ducato di Milano in età sforzesca', in *Milano nell'età di Ludovico il Moro*, 2 vols, Milan, vol.1, pp. 115–28.

—— (1987) 'La città europea tra Medioevo e Rinascimento', in P. Rossi (ed.) *Modelli di città. Strutture e funzioni politiche*, Turin, pp. 371–92.

—— (1988) 'La pianura irrigua lombarda fra Quattrocento e Cinquecento', *Annali dell'Istituto 'Alcide Cervi'* 10: 207–21.

—— (1989) 'Cities, "city-states", and regional states in north-central Italy', *Theory and Society* 18: 689–706.

—— (1990) 'Di alcuni aspetti della crisi dello stato sforzesco', in J.M. Cauchies and G. Chittolini (eds) *Milano e Borgogna. Due stati principeschi tra medioevo e Rinascimento*, Rome: 21–34.

—— (ed.) (1992) *Metamorfosi di un borgo. Vigevano in età visconteo-sforzesce*, Milan.

—— (1994) 'Organizzazione territoriale e distretti urbani nell'Italia del tardo medioevo', in G. Chittolini, and D. Willoweit (eds) *L'organizzazione del territorio in Italia e Germania: secoli XIII–XIV*, Bologna.: 7–26.

—— (1995) 'Centri minori e città fra Medioevo e Rinascimento', in P. Nencini (ed.) *Colle di Val d'Elsa: diocesi e città fra '500 e '600*, Castelfiorentino, pp. 11–37.

—— (1996) *Città, comunità e feudi negli stati dell'Italia centro-settentrionale (XIV–XVI secolo)*, Milan.

Chittolini, G., A. Molho and P. Schiera (eds) (1994) *Origini dello Stato. Processi di formazione statale in Italia fra medioevo ed età moderna*, Bologna.

Chittolini, G. and D. Willoweit (eds) (1991) *Statuti città territori in Italia e Germania tra medioevo ed età moderna*, Bologna.

—— (eds) (1994) *L'organizzazione del territorio in Italia e Germania: secoli XIII–XIV*, Bologna.

Chorley, P. (1997) 'The evolution of the woollen', in N. B. Harte (ed.) *The New Draperies in the Low Countries and England, 1300–1800*, Oxford, pp. 7–34.

Ciccone, A. and K. Matsuyama (1996) 'Start-up costs and pecuniary externalities as barriers to economic development', *Journal of Development Economics* 49: 33–59.

Cipolla, C. M. (1963a) 'The economic policies of governments: the Italian and Iberian peninsulas', in M. M. Postan, E. E. Rich and E. Miller (eds) *Cambridge Economic History of Europe, III. Economic Organization and Policies in the Middle Ages*, Cambridge, pp. 397–429.

—— (1963b) 'Currency depreciation in medieval Europe', *Economic History Review* 2nd ser. 15, 4: 413–22.

—— (1975) *Storia economica dell' Europa pre-industriale*, 2nd ed., Bologna.

Cipolla C. M., R. S. Lopez and H. A. Miskimin. (1964) 'Economic depression of the

Renaissance?', *Economic History Review,* 2nd ser. 16: 519–29.

Clark, G. (1987) 'Productivity growth without technical change in European agriculture before 1850', *Journal of Economic History* 47, 2: 419–32.

—— (1988) 'The cost of capital and medieval agricultural technique', *Explorations in Economic History* 25: 265–94.

—— (1996) 'The political foundations of modern economic growth: England, 1540–1800', *Journal of Interdisciplinary History* 26: 4, 563–88.

Clark, P. (1981) 'English country towns 1500–1800', in P. Clark (ed.) *Country Towns in Pre-Industrial England,* Leicester, pp. 1–43.

Clerici, T. (1982–83) 'Il mercato comasco nel 1429 e 1434 dagli atti di Francesco de Cermenate', *Archivio storico lombardo* 108–9: 85–171.

Coates, B. E. (1965) 'The origin and distribution of markets and fairs in medieval Derbyshire', *Derbyshire Archaeological Journal* 85: 92–111.

Cohen, G. A. (1978) *Karl Marx's Theory of History. A Defence,* Oxford.

Cohn, H. (1965) *The Government of the Rhine Palatinate in the Fifteenth Century,* Oxford.

Collins, J. B. (1988) *Fiscal Limits of Absolutism. Direct Taxation in Early Seventeenth-Century France,* Berkeley/Los Angeles.

Colombo, D. (1988) 'La società vigevanese', *Annali di storia pavese* 16–17: 197–204.

Comba, R. (1988a) *Contadini, signori e mercanti nel Piemonte medievale,* Bari.

—— (1988b) 'Industria rurale e strutture agrarie: il paesaggio del Pinerolese nella prima metà del XV secolo', *Annali dell'Istituto 'Alcide Cervi'* 10: 187–205.

—— (1988c) 'Vasellame in legno e ceramica di uso domestico nel basso Medioevo', in Comba, *Contadini, signori e mercanti nel Piemonte medievale,* Bari: 111–24.

Comba, R., and G. Sergi (1977) 'Piemonte meridionale e viabilità alpina: note sugli scambi commerciali con la Provenza dal XIII al XV secolo', *Provence historique* 27: 123–35.

Combes, J. (1958) 'Les foires en Languedoc au moyen âge', *Annales E.S.C.* 13, 2: 231–59.

Coniglio, G. (1958) *Mantova. La storia,* 2 vols, Mantua.

Conklin, J. (1998) 'The theory of sovereign debt and Spain under Philip II', *Journal of Political Economy* 106, 3: 483–513.

Connell, W. J. (1991) 'Clientelismo e Stato territoriale. Il potere fiorentino a Pistoia nel XV secolo', *Società e storia* 14: 504–31.

Contamine, P. (1980) *La guerre au Moyen Âge,* Paris.

Coornaert, E. (1957) 'Charactères et mouvement des foires internationales au Moyen Age et au XVIe siècle', in *Studi in onore di Armando Sapori,* 2 vols, Milan, vol.1, pp. 355–71.

Coornaert, E. (1961) *Les Français et le commerce international à Anvers, fin du XVe–XVIe siècles,* 2 vols, Paris.

Corrao, P. (1980) 'L'apprendista nella bottega artigiana palermitana (secc.XIV–XVII)', in *I mestieri. Atti del II Congresso internazionale di studi antropologici siciliani (26–29 marzo 1980),* Palermo, pp. 137–44.

Corritore, R. P. (1993) 'Il processo di "ruralizzazione" in Italia nei secoli XVII–XVIII. Verso una regionalizzazione', *Rivista di storia economica,* new ser. 10, 3: 353–86.

—— (1995) 'Una fondamentale discontinuità padana: la linea dell'Oglio (secoli XVI–XVIII)', in *La Lombardia spagnola. Nuovi indirizzi di ricerca,* Milan.

Cortesi, M. (ed.) (1984) *Statuti rurali e statuti di valle. La provincia di Bergamo nei secoli XIII–XVIII,* Bergamo

Cortonesi, A. (1995) 'Note sull'agricoltura italiana fra XIII e XIV secolo', in *Europa* 1995: 87–128.

Cotts Watkins, S. and J. Menken (1985) 'Famines in historical perspective', *Population and Development Review* 11: 647–75.

Cova, A. (1991) 'Banchi e monti pubblici a Milano nei secoli XVI e XVII', in D. Puncuh (ed.) *Banchi pubblici, banchi privati e monti di pietà nell'Europa preindustriale. Amministrazione, tecniche operative e ruoli economici,* Genoa, pp. 327–39.

Craig, L. A. and D. Fisher (2000) *The European Macroeconomy: Growth and Integration,* Cheltenham.

Cristini, L. (1987) 'Aspetti dell'economia e della società a Torno nel XV secolo dagli atti del notaio Maxolo de Margaritis', unpublished M.A. thesis, University of Milan.

Crotti Pasi, R. (1984) 'Note sul mondo artigianale pavese alla fine del medioevo: il paratico dei tessitori di tela di Pavia e del suo principato', *Bollettino storico pavese di storia patria,* new ser. 36: 22–72.

Davis, R. W. (ed.) (1995) *The Origins of Modern Freedom in the West,* Stanford Calif./Cambridge.

Daviso di Charvensod, M. C. (1961) *I pedaggi delle Alpi occidentali nel medio evo,* Turin.

Day, J. (1999) *Money and Finance in the Age of Merchant Capitalism,* Oxford.

Day, W. R. (1999) 'The early development of the Florentine economy: local and regional market networks, c. 1100–1275', unpublished Ph.D. thesis, London School of Economics.

De Long, D. J. and A. Shleifer (1992) 'Princes and merchants: city growth before the Industrial Revolution', mimeo, Department of Economics, Harvard University.

de Maddalena, A. (1950) *Prezzi e aspetti di mercato in Milano durante il secolo XVII,* Milan.

De Roover, R. (1953) *L'évolution de la lettre de change XIVᵉ–XVIIIᵉ siècles,* Paris.

—— (1956) 'The development of accounting prior to Luca Pacioli according to the account books of medieval merchants', in A. C. Littleton and B. S. Yamey (eds) *Studies in the History of Accounting,* London, pp. 114–74.

—— (1963) *The Rise and Decline of the Medici Bank 1397–1494,* Cambridge, Mass.

Del Panta, L. (1980) *Le epidemie nella storia demografica italiana (secoli XIV–XIX),* Turin.

Del Panta, L., M. Livi Bacci, G. Pinto, and G. Sonnino (1996) *La popolazione italiana dal Medioevo a oggi,* Rome/Bari.

Della Bordella, P. L. (1984) *L'arte della lana in Casentino: storia dei lanifici,* Cortona.

Denley, P. and C. Elam (eds) (1988) *Florence and Italy. Renaissance Studies in Honour of Nicolai Rubinstein,* London.

Dent, J. (1973) *Crisis in Finance. Crown, Financiers and Society in Seventeenth Century France,* Newton Abbot.

Derville, A. (1987) 'Dîmes, rendements du blé et "révolution agricole" dans le Nord de la France au moyen âge', *Annales E.S.C.* 42, 6: 1411–32.

Desai, M. (1991) 'The agrarian crisis in medieval England: a Malthusian tragedy or a failure of entitlements?', *Bulletin of Economic Research* 43, 3: 223–58.

DeSoignie, R. R. (1976) 'The fairs of Nîmes: evidence on their function, importance, and demise', in W. C. Jordan, B. McNab and T. F. Ruiz (eds) *Order and Innovation in the Middle Ages. Essays in Honor of J. R. Strayer*, Princeton, pp. 195–205.

Desplat, C. (ed.) (1996) *Foires et marchés dans les campagnes de l'Europe médiévale et moderne*, Toulouse.

Desportes, P. (1979) *Reims et les Rémois aux XIIIe et XIVe siècles*, Paris.

de Vries, J. (1974) *The Dutch Rural Economy in the Golden Age 1500–1700*, New Haven/London.

—— (1984) *European Urbanization 1500–1800*, London.

—— (1992) 'The labour market', *Economic and Social History in the Netherlands* 4: 55–78.

—— (1994) 'The industrial revolution and the industrious revolution', *Journal of Economic History* 54, 2: 249–70.

—— (1996) 'The transition to capitalism in a land without feudalism', mimeo, Department of History, Berkeley.

de Vries, J. and A. W. van der Woude (1997) *The First Modern Economy. Success, Failure, and Perseverance of the Dutch Economy, 1500–1815*, Cambridge.

de Waal, A. (1990) 'A re-assessment of entitlement theory in the light of the recent famines in Africa', *Development and Change* 21: 469–90.

Deyon, P. and Ph. Guignet (1980) 'The royal manufactures and economic and technological progress in France before the industrial revolution', *Journal of European Economic History*, 9: 611–32.

Diaz, F. (1989) 'L'articolazione del Principato mediceo e la prospettiva di un raffronto', in C. H. Smyth and G. C. Garfagnini (eds) *Florence and Milan. Comparisons and Relations*, 2 vols, Florence, vol. 2, pp. 157–68.

Dickson, P. G. M. (1967) *The Financial Revolution in England. A Study in the Development of Public Credit, 1688–1756*, London.

Dini, B. (1984) *Arezzo intorno al 1400. Produzioni e mercato*, Arezzo.

—— (1986) 'Le vie di comunicazione del territorio fiorentino alla metà del Quattrocento', in *Mercati e consumi: organizzazione e qualificazione del commercio in Italia dal XII al XX secolo*, Bologna, pp. 285–96.

—— (1990a) 'L'industria tessile italiana nel tardo Medioevo', in S. Gensini (ed.) *Le Italie del tardo Medioevo*, Pisa, pp. 321–59.

—— (1990b) 'Il viaggio di un mercante fiorentino in Umbria alla fine del Trecento', *Miscellanea storica della Valdelsa* 96: 81–104.

—— (1993) 'L'industria serica in Italia. Secc.XIII–XV', in S. Cavaciocchi (ed.) *La seta in Europa, sec.XII–XX*, Florence, pp. 91–123.

di Raimondo, G. (1975–6) 'Ricerche sulla storia dei prezzi fra '400 e '500: I mastri delle "Quattro Marie"', unpublished M.A. thesis, University of Milan.

Dobb, M. (1946) *Studies in the Development of Capitalism*, London.

Dollinger, P. (1964) *La Hanse (XIIe–XVIIe siècles)*, Paris.

Dowd, D. F. (1961) 'The economic expansion of Lombardy, 1300–1500: a study in political stimuli to economic change', *Journal of Economic History* 21, 2: 143–60.

Drobak, J. N. and J. V. C. Nye (eds) (1997) *The Frontiers of the New Institutional Economics*, San Diego/London.

Dubois, H. (1976) *Les foires de Chalon et le commerce dans la vallée de la Sâone à la fin du Moyen Âge (vers 1280–vers 1430)*, Paris.

Dubois, H. (1982) 'Le commerce et les foires au temps de Philippe Auguste', in R. H. Bautier (ed.) *La France de Philippe Auguste. Le temps des mutations*, Paris, pp. 687–709.

—— (1988) 'L'essor médiévale', in J. Dupâquier (ed.) *Histoire de la population française, 1. Des origines à la Renaissance*, Paris, pp.207–66.

Dufourcq, C.-E. and J. Gautier Dalché (1976) *Histoire économique et sociale de l'Espagne chrétienne au Moyen Age*, Paris.

Duval, M. (1981) 'Foires et marchés en Bretagne sous le règne de Jean V (1399–1442)', *Annales de Normandie* 31: 336.

Dyer, A. (1990) *Decline and Growth in English Towns 1400–1640*, London/ Basingstoke.

Dyer, C. (1989a) *Standards of Living in the Later Middle Ages. Social Change in England, c.1200–1520*, Cambridge.

—— (1989b) 'The consumer and the market in the later Middle Ages', *Economic History Review* 2nd ser. 42: 305–27.

—— (1998) 'Did the peasants really starve in medieval England?', in M. Carlin and J. T. Rosenthal (eds) *Food and Eating in Medieval Europe*, London/Rio Grande, pp. 53–71.

Eggertsson, T. (1990) *Economic Behavior and Institutions*, Cambridge.

Elliott, J. H. (1992) 'A Europe of composite monarchies', *Past and Present* 137: 48–71.

Elster, J., and R. Slagstad (eds) (1988) *Constitutionalism and Democracy*, Cambridge.

Emigh, R. J. (1997) 'The spread of sharecropping in Tuscany: the political economy of transaction costs', *American Sociological Review* 62, 2: 423–42.

Endemann, T. (1964) *Markturkunde und Markt in Frankreich und Burgund vom 9. bis 11. Jahrhundert*, Konstanz.

Endrei, W. and W. von Stromer. (1974) 'Textiltechnische und hydraulische Erfindung und ihre Innovatoren im Mitteleuropa im 14.–15. Jahrhundert (die Seidenzwirnmühle)', *Technikgeschichte* 41.

Epstein, S. R. (1989) 'The textile industry and the foreign cloth trade in late medieval Sicily (1300–1500): a "colonial relationship"?', *Journal of Medieval History* 15: 141–83.

—— (1991) 'Cities, regions and the late medieval crisis: Sicily and Tuscany compared', *Past and Present* 130: 3–50.

—— (1992) *An Island For Itself. Economic Development and Social Change in Late Medieval Sicily*, Cambridge.

—— (1993) 'Manifatture tessili e strutture politico-istituzionali nella Lombardia tardo-medievale. Ipotesi di ricerca', *Studi di storia medioevale e diplomatica* 14: 55–89.

—— (1994) 'Storia economica e storia istituzionale dello stato', in G. Chittolini, A. Molho and P. Schiera (eds) *Origini dello Stato. Processi di formazione statale in Italia fra medioevo ed età moderna*, Bologna: 97–111.

—— (1995a) 'Dualismo economico, pluralismo istituzionale in Italia nel Rinascimento', *Revista d'història medieval* 5: 63–77.

—— (1995b) 'Freedom and growth: the European miracle?', in E. V. Barker (ed.) *LSE on Freedom*, London, pp. 165–81.

—— (1996a) 'Taxation and social representation in Italian territorial states', in M. Boone and W. Prevenier (eds) *Finances publiques et finances privées au bas moyen âge*, Leuven-Apeldoorn, pp. 101–15.

—— (1996b) 'Stato territoriale ed economia regionale nella Toscana del Quattrocento', in R. Fubini (ed.) *La Toscana al tempo di Lorenzo il Magnifico. Politica Economia Cultura Arte*, 3 vols, Pisa, vol. 3, pp. 869–90.

—— (1998a) 'Craft guilds, apprenticeship, and technological change in pre-industrial Europe', *Journal of Economic History* 53, 3: 684–713.

—— (1998b) 'Italy', in T. Scott (ed.) *The Peasantries of Europe from the Fourteenth to the Eighteenth Century*, London, pp. 75–110.

—— (1998c) 'Nuevas aproximaciones a la historia urbana de Italia: el Renacimiento temprano', *Història* 58, 2: 417–38.

—— (ed.) (2000a) *Town and Country in Europe, 1300–1750*, Cambridge.

—— (2000b) 'The rise and fall of Italian city-states', in M. H. Hansen (ed.) *City-State Cultures in World History*, Copenhagen.

—— (2000c) 'Market structures', in W. Connell and A. Zorzi (eds) *Florentine Tuscany: Structures and Practices of Power*, Cambridge, pp. 90–121.

Ertman, T. (1997) *Birth of the Leviathan. Building States and Regimes in Medieval and Early Modern Europe*, Cambridge.

Espejo, C. and J. Paz. (1908) *Las antiguas ferias de Medina del Campo*, Valladolid.

Europa (1995) *Europa en los umbrales de la crisis: 1250–1350. XXI Semana de Estudios Medievales, Estella, 18–22 julio 1994*, Pamplona.

Everitt, A. (1967) 'The marketing of agricultural produce', in J. Thirsk (ed.) *The Agrarian History of England and Wales, IV. 1500–1640*, Cambridge, pp. 466–592.

Fanfani, A. (1933) 'Le arti di Sansepolcro dal XIV al XVI secolo', *Rivista internazionale di scienze sociali* 41: 140–57.

—— (1935) *Un mercante del Trecento*, Milan.

—— (1940) *Indagini sulla 'rivoluzione dei prezzi'*, Milan.

Farmer, D. L. (1991) 'Marketing the produce of the countryside, 1200–1500', in E. Miller (ed.) *The Agrarian History of England and Wales, III. 1350–1500*, Cambridge, pp. 324–430.

Fasano Guarini, E. (1976) 'Città soggette e contadi nel dominio fiorentino tra Quattro e Cinquecento: il caso pisano', in M. Mirri (ed.) *Ricerche di storia moderna I*, Pisa, pp. 1–94.

—— (1991) 'Gli statuti delle città soggette a Firenze tra '400 e '500: riforme locali e interventi centrali', in G. Chittolini and D. Willoweit (eds) *Statuti città territori in Italia e Germania tra Medioevo ed Età moderna*, Bologna, pp. 69–124.

—— (1994) 'Centro e periferia, accentramento e particolarismi: dicotomia o sostanza degli Stati in età moderna', in G. Chittolini, A. Molho and P. Schiera (eds) *Origini dello Stato. Processi di formazione statale in Italia fra medioevo ed età moderna*, Bologna, pp. 147–76.

Fazio, I. (1990) 'I mercati regolati e la crisi settecentesca dei sistemi annonari', *Studi storici* 31, 3: 655–92.

—— (1993) *La politica del grano. Annona e controllo del territorio in Sicilia nel Settecento*, Milan.

Feder, G., R. E. Just, and D. Zilberman (1985) 'Adoption of agricultural innovation in developing countries: a survey', *Economic Development and Cultural Change* 34: 255–98.

Federico, G. (1999) 'On the economic causes and effects of the Italian Risorgimento: market integration in the 19th century', paper presented at the conference on *Historical Market Integration: Performance and Efficiency of Markets in the Past*, Venice, 17–20 December 1999.

Feenstra, R. (1953) 'Les foires aux Pays Bas septentrionaux', in *La foire*, Brussels, pp. 209–39.

Felloni, G. (1977) 'Italy', in C. Wilson and G. Parker (eds) *An Introduction to the Sources of European Economic History 1500–1800, 1. Western Europe*, London, pp. 1–36.

Fennell Mazzaoui, M. (1967–68) 'The emigration of Veronese textile artisans to

Bologna in the thirteenth century', *Atti e memorie dell'Accademia di agricoltura, scienze e lettere di Verona*, 6th ser. 18–19: 275–322.

—— (1972) 'The cotton industry of northern Italy in the late Middle Ages: 1150–1450', *Journal of Economic History* 32, 1: 262–86.

—— (1981) *The Italian Cotton Industry in the Later Middle Ages 1100–1600*, Cambridge.

—— (1984) 'Artisan migration and technology in the Italian textile industry in the late Middle Ages (1100–1500)', in R. Comba, G. Piccinni and G. Pinto (eds) *Strutture familiari epidemie migrazioni nell'Italia medievale*, Naples, pp. 519–34.

—— (1987) 'La diffusione delle tecniche tessili del cotone nell'Italia dei secoli XII–XVI', in *Tecnica e società nell'Italia dei secoli XII–XVI*, Pistoia, pp. 157–71.

Fiumi, E. (1943) *L'utilizzazione dei lagoni boraciferi della Toscana nell'industria medievale*, Florence.

—— (1948) *L'impresa di Lorenzo de' Medici contro Volterra (1472)*, Florence.

—— (1956) 'Sui rapporti economici tra città e contado nell'età comunale', *Archivio storico italiano* 114: 16–68.

—— (1961) *Storia economica e sociale di San Gimignano*, Florence.

—— (1977) *Fioriture e decadenza dell'economia fiorentina*, Florence.

Fogel, R. (1992) 'Second thoughts on the European escape from hunger: famines, chronic malnutrition, and mortality', in S. R. Osmani (ed.) *Nutrition and Poverty*, Oxford, pp. 243–86.

—— (1994) 'The relevance of Malthus for the study of mortality today: long-run influences on health, mortality, labour force participation, and population growth', in K. Lindahl-Kiessling and H. Landberg (eds) *Population, Economic Development, and the Environment*, Oxford, pp. 231–84.

Fontaine, L. (1996) *History of Pedlars in Europe*, Eng. trans. V. Whittaker, Cambridge.

Fossati, F. (1914a) 'Rapporti fra una "terra" e i suoi signori (Vigevano e i duchi di Milano nel secolo XV)', *Archivio storico lombardo* 41: 109–86.

—— (1914b) 'Un problema di storia vigevanese', *Archivio storico lombardo* 41: 757–78.

Foster, A. D. and M. R. Rosenzweig (1995) 'Learning by doing and learning from others: human capital and technical change in agriculture', *Journal of Political Economy* 103, 6: 1176–1209.

Fournial, E. (1967) *Les villes et l'économie d'échange en Forez aux XIIIe et XIVe siècles*, Paris.

—— (1982) 'Lettres comtales instituant les foires de Montbrison (1308, 1399, 1400, 1410, 1438)', *Bulletin de la Diana* 47: 279–95.

Fourquin, G. (1964) *Les campagnes de la région parisienne à la fin du Moyen Âge du milieu du XIIIe siècle au début du XVIe siècle*, Paris.

—— (1972) *Les soulèvements populaires au Moyen Age*, Paris.

—— (1979) *Histoire économique de l'Occident médiéval*, 3rd ed., Paris.

Franceschi, F. (1988) 'Criminalità e mondo del lavoro: il tribunale dell'Arte della lana a Firenze nei secoli XIV e XV', *Ricerche storiche* 18: 551–90.

—— (1989) 'I tedeschi e l'Arte della Lana a Firenze fra Tre e Quattrocento', in M. Del Treppo (ed.) *Dentro la città. Stranieri e realtà urbane nell'Europa dei secoli XII–XVI*, Naples, pp. 257–78.

—— (1993) *Oltre il 'Tumulto'. I lavoratori fiorentini dell'Arte della Lana fra il Tre e il Quattrocento*, Florence.

—— (1994) 'Istituzioni e attività economica a Firenze: considerazioni sul governo del settore industriale (1350–1450)', in *Istituzioni e società in Toscana nell'età moderna. Atti delle giornate di studio dedicate a Giuseppe Pansini*, Rome, pp. 76–117.

Franceschini, G. (1948–9) 'Invito ai senesi nuovi sudditi del duca di Milano di partecipare alla fiera di Sant'Abbondio a Como', *Archivio storico lombardo*, 5th ser. 1: 223–4.

Frangioni, L. (1983) *Milano e le sue strade. Costi di trasporto e vie di commercio dei prodotti milanesi alla fine del Trecento,* Bologna.

—— (1986a) 'Le merci di Lombardia. Produzioni artigianali di grande serie e produzioni pregiate', in G. Taborelli (ed.) *Commercio in Lombardia*, 2 vols, Milan: vol. 1, pp. 56–118.

—— (1986b) 'Storia del commercio e storia dei trasporti. Strade, mezzi, uomini e itinerari', in G. Taborelli (ed.) *Commercio in Lombardia*, 2 vols, Milan: vol. 2, pp. 25–71.

—— (1992) *Milano e le sue misure. Appunti di metrologia lombarda fra Tre e Quattrocento,* Naples.

Friedman, D. (1977) 'A theory of the size and shape of nations', *Journal of Political Economy* 85: 59–77.

Friel, I. (1995) *The Good Ship. Ships, Shipbuilding and Technology in England 1200–1520,* Baltimore.

Fryde, E. B. and M. M. Fryde (1963) 'Public credit, with special reference to north-western Europe', in M. M. Postan, E. E. Rich and E. Miller (eds) *Cambridge Economic History of Europe, III. Economic Organization and Policies in the Middle Ages,* Cambridge, pp. 430–553.

Fubini, R. (ed.) (1977) *Lorenzo de' Medici. Lettere, I (1460–1474),* Florence.

Galloway, J. (2000) 'Town and country in England, 1300–1570', in S. R. Epstein (ed.) *Town and Country in Europe, 1350–1750,* Cambridge.

Galloway, P. R. (1986) 'Differentials in demographic responses to annual price variations in pre-revolutionary France: a comparison of rich and poor areas in Rouen, 1681 to 1797', *European Journal of Population* 2: 269–305.

—— (1988) 'Basic patterns in annual variations in fertility, nuptiality, mortality and prices in pre-industrial Europe', *Population Studies* 42: 275–302.

—— (1993) 'Short-run population dynamics among the rich and poor in European countries, rural Jutland, and urban Rouen', in D. S. Reher and R. S. Schofield (eds) *Old and New Methods in Historical Demography,* Oxford, pp. 84–108.

—— (1994) 'Secular changes in the short-term preventive, positive, and temperature checks to population growth in Europe, 1460 to 1909', *Climatic Change* 26: 3–63.

Gambetta, D. (ed.) (1988) *Trust. Making and Breaking Cooperative Relations,* Oxford.

Gandilhon, R. (1940) *Politique économique de Louis XI,* Rennes.

Gardner, B. D. and R. D. Pope (1978) 'How is scale and structure determined in agriculture?', *American Journal of Agricultural Economics* 60, May: 295–302.

Gascon, R. (1971) *Grand commerce et vie urbaine au XVIe siècle. Lyon et ses marchands, environs de 1520 – environs de 1580,* 2 vols, Paris.

Gasson, R. and B. Hill (1984) *Farm Tenure and Performance,* Wye.

Gellner, E. (1988) 'Introduction', in J. Baechler, J. A. Hall and M. A. Mann (eds) *Europe and the Rise of Capitalism,* Oxford, pp. 1–6.

Genet, J. P. (1995) 'Le développement des monarchies d'Occident est-il une conséquence de la crise?', in *Europa* 1995: 63–86.

Genet, J.-P. and M.Le Mené (eds) (1987) *Genèse de l'Etat moderne. Prélèvement et redistribution,* Paris.

Génicot, L. (1973) 'Les grands villes d'Occident en 1300', in *Économies et sociétés au moyen âge. Mélanges offerts à Edouard Perroy*, Paris, pp.199–219.

Gensini, S. (ed.) (1990) *Le Italie del tardo Medioevo*, Pisa.

Giampaolo, L. (1954) *La cronaca varesina di Giulio Tatto (1540–1620) e i prezzi dei grani e del vino sul mercato di Varese dal 1525 al 1620*, Varese.

Gilissen, J. (1953) 'La notion de la foire à la lumière comparative', in *La foire*, Brussels, pp. 323–33.

Gilpin, R. (1981) *War and Change in International Politics*, Cambridge.

Ginatempo, M. (1993) 'Dietro un'eclissi: considerazioni sulle città minori dell'Italia centrale', in S.Gensini (ed.) *Italia 1350–1450: Tra crisi e trasformazione*, Pistoia, pp. 35–76.

—— (1996) 'Gerarchie demiche e sistemi urbani nell'Italia bassomedievale: una discussione', *Società e storia* 72: 347–83.

—— (1997) 'Le città italiane, XIV–XV secolo', in *Poderes públicos en la Europa medieval: principados, reinos y coronas, 23 Semana de estudios medievales. Estella, 22–26 julio 1996:* , Estella, pp. 149–209.

Ginatempo, M. and L. Sandri (1990) *L'Italia delle città. Il popolamento urbano tra Medioevo e Rinascimento (secoli XIII–XVI)*, Florence.

Glaeser, E. L., H. D. Kallal, J. A. Scheinkman and A. Shleifer (1992) 'Growth in cities', *Journal of Political Economy* 100, 6: 1126–52.

Glasscock, R. E. (1976) 'England *circa* 1334', in H. C. Darby (ed.) *A New Historical Geography of England Before 1600*, Cambridge, pp. 136–85.

Gli Sforza (1982) *Gli Sforza a Milano e in Lombardia e i loro rapporti con gli Stati italiani ed europei (1450–1535)*, Milan.

Glick, T. F. (1970) *Irrigation and Society in Medieval Valencia*, Cambridge, Mass.

Goldberg, P. J. P. (1992) *Women, Work, and Life Cycle in a Medieval Economy. Women in York and Yorkshire c.1300–1520*, Oxford.

Goldthwaite, R. (1976) 'I prezzi del grano a Firenze dal XIV al XVI secolo', *Quaderni storici* 28: 5–36

—— (1993) *Wealth and the Demand for Art in Italy, 1300–1600*, Baltimore.

Goodfellow, P. (1987) 'Medieval markets in Northamptonshire', *Northamptonshire Past and Present* 7: 305–24.

Goubert, P. (1970) *Louis XIV and Twenty Million Frenchmen*, trans. A. Carter, London.

Grafton, A. (1997) *Commerce with the Classics: Ancient Books and Renaissance Readers*, Ann Arbor.

Grantham, G. W. (1993) 'Divisions of labour: agricultural productivity and occupational specialization in pre-industrial France', *Economic History Review*, 2nd ser. 46, 3: 478–502.

—— (1997a) 'Espaces privilégiés: productivité agraire et zones d'approvisionnement des villes dans l'Europe préindustrielle', *Annales HSS* 52, 3: 695–725.

—— (1997b) 'The French cliometric revolution: a survey of cliometric contributions to French economic history', *European Review of Economic History*, 1, 3: 353–405.

—— (1999) 'Contra Ricardo: on the macroeconomics of pre-industrial economies', *European Review of Economic History* 3, 2: 199–232.

Greci, R. (1983) 'Luoghi di fiera e di mercato nelle città medievali dell'Italia padana', in *Studi in onore di Gino Barbieri. Problemi e metodi di storia ed economia*, 2 vols, Salerno, vol. 2, pp. 943–66.

Greengrass, M. (1991)(ed.) *Conquest and Caolescence. The Shaping of the State in Early Modern Europe*, London.

Grillo, P. (1993) '"Vicus Lanificius Insignis". Industria laniera e strutture sociali del borgo lariano di Torno nel XV secolo', *Studi di storia medioevale e di diplomatica* 14: 91–110.

—— (1994) 'Le origini della manifattura serica in Milano (1400–1450)', *Studi storici* 35: 897–916.

—— (1995) *Le strutture di un borgo medievale. Torno, centro manifatturiero nella Lombardia viscontea*, Florence.

Grohmann, A. (1969) *Le fiere del Regno di Napoli in età aragonese*, Naples.

—— (1981) *Città e territorio tra Medioevo ed Età moderna (Perugia, secc.XIII–XVI)*, 2 vols, Perugia.

Gual Camarena, M. (1976) 'Orígenes y expansión de la industria textil lanera catalana en la edad media', in M. Spallanzani (ed.) *Produzione commercio e consumo dei panni di lana (nei secoli XII–XVIII)*, Florence: 511–24.

Gual, J. M. (1982) 'Bases para el estudio de las ferias murcianas en la Edad Media', *Miscelanea medieval murciana* 9: 9–55.

Gualazzini, U. (1950–1) 'Preliminari osservazioni sugli Statuti cremonesi del 1339', *Bollettino storico cremonese*, 2nd ser. 17: 3–167.

Guarducci, A. (ed.) (1988) *Prodotto lordo e finanza pubblica. Secoli XIII–XIX*, Florence.

Guérin, I. (1960) *La vie rurale en Sologne aux XIVe et XVe siècles*, Paris.

Guidi, G. (1981) *Il governo della città-repubblica di Firenze del primo Quattrocento*, 4 vols, Florence.

Gunder Frank, A. (1998) *ReOrient: Global Economy in the Asian Age*, London.

Gutmann, M. P. (1980) *War and Rural Life in the Early Modern Low Countries*, Princeton.

Hadenius, A. (1992) *Democracy and Development*, Cambridge.

Haldon, J. (1993) *The State and the Tributary Mode of Production*, London.

Hall, J. A. (1985) *Powers and Liberties. The Causes and Consequences of the Rise of the West*, Oxford.

Hamilton, E. (1936) *Money, Prices and Wages in Valencia, Aragon, and Navarre, 1351–1500*, Cambridge, Mass.

Hare, J. N. (1999) 'Growth and recession in the fifteenth-century economy: the Wiltshire textile industry and the countryside', *Economic History Review* 2nd ser. 52, 1: 1–26.

Harriss, G. L. (1963) 'Aids, loans and benevolences', *Historical Journal* 6: 1–19.

—— (1975) *King, Parliament, and Public Finance in Medieval England to 1369*, Oxford.

Harte, N. B. (ed.) (1997) *The New Draperies in the Low Countries and England, 1300–1800*, Oxford.

Harte, N. B. and K. G. Ponting (eds) (1983) *Cloth and Clothing in Medieval Europe. Essays in Memory of Professor E. M. Carus-Wilson*, London.

Harvey, B. F. (1991) 'Introduction: the "crisis" of the early fourteenth century', in B. M. S. Campbell (ed.) *Before the Black Death. Studies in the 'Crisis' of the Early Fourteenth Century*, Manchester, pp. 1–24.

Harvey, P. D. A. (1991) *Medieval Maps*, Toronto/Buffalo.

Hasse, E. (1885) 'Geschichte der Leipziger Messen', *Preisschriften Fürstliche Jablonowski'schen Gesellschaft zu Leipzig* 25: 1–516.

Hatcher, J. (1970) *Economy and Society in the Duchy of Cornwall 1300–1500*, Cambridge.

Hatcher, J. (1973) *English Tin Production and Trade before 1550*, Oxford.

—— (1994) 'England in the aftermath of the Black Death', *Past and Present* 144: 3–35.

—— (1996) 'The great slump of the mid-fifteenth century', in R. Britnell and J. Hatcher (eds) *Progress and Problems in Medieval England. Essays in Honor of Edward Miller*, Cambridge, pp. 237–72.

Hayek, F. A. (1973) *Law, Legislation and Liberty, 1. Rules and Order*, Chicago.

Heers, J. (1961) *Gênes au XVᵉ siècle: Activité économique et problèmes sociaux*, Paris.

—— (1976) 'La mode et les marchés des draps de laine: Gênes et la montagne à la fin du Moyen Age', in M. Spallanzani, (ed.) *Produzione commercio e consumo dei panni di lana (nei secoli XII–XVIII)*, Florence, pp. 199–220.

Henderson, J. (1994) *Piety and Charity in Late Medieval Florence*, Oxford.

Henning, F.-W. (1991) *Deutsche Wirtschafts- und Sozialgeschichte im Mittelalter und in der frühen Neuzeit*, Paderborn.

Henshall, N. (1992) *The Myth of Absolutism. Change and Continuity in Early Modern European Monarchy*, New York/London.

Herlihy, D. (1964) 'Direct and indirect taxation in Tuscan urban finance, c.1200–1400', in *Finances et comptabilités urbaines du XIIIᵉ au XVIᵉ siècles*, Brussels, pp. 385–405.

—— (1965) 'Population, plague and social change in rural Pistoia, 1201–1430', *Economic History Review*, 2nd ser. 18, 2: 225–44.

—— (1967) *Medieval and Renaissance Pistoia. The Social History of an Italian Town, 1200–1430*, New Haven, Conn./London.

—— (1968) 'Santa Maria Impruneta: a rural commune in the late Middle Ages', in N. Rubinstein (ed.) *Florentine Studies. Politics and Society in Renaissance Florence*, London, pp. 242–76.

—— (1978) 'The distribution of wealth in a Renaissance community: Florence 1427', in P. Abrams and E. A. Wrigley (eds) *Towns in Societies. Essays in Economic History and Historical Sociology*, Cambridge, pp. 131–58.

—— (1982) 'Demography', in J. R. Strayer (ed.) *Dictionary of the Middle Ages*, New York, vol. 4, pp. 136–48.

—— (1987) 'Outline of population developments in the Middle Ages', in B. Herrmann and R. Sprandel (eds) *Determinanten der Bevölkerungsentwicklung im Mittelalter*, Weinheim, pp. 1–23.

—— (1997) *The Black Death and the Transformation of the West*, Cambridge, Mass./London.

Herlihy, D. and C. Klapisch Zuber (1985) *Tuscans and Their Families. A Study of the Florentine Catasto of 1427*, New Haven/London.

Hibbert, A. B. (1963) 'The economic policy of towns', in M. M. Postan, E. E. Rich and E. Miller (eds) *Cambridge Economic History of Europe, III. Economic Organization and Policies in the Middle Ages*, Cambridge, pp. 155–229.

Hicks, D. L. (1986) 'Sources of wealth in Renaissance Siena: businessmen and landowners', *Bullettino senese di storia patria* 103: 9–42.

Hicks, J. R. (1969) *A Theory of Economic History*, Oxford.

Hildebrandt, R. (1992) 'The effects of empire: changes in the European economy after Charles V', in I. Blanchard, A. Goodman and J. Newman (eds) *Industry and Finance in Early Modern History. Essays Presented to George Hammersley to the Occasion of his 74th Birthday*, Stuttgart, pp. 58–76.

Hilton, R. H. (1965) 'Rent and capital formation in feudal society', in *2nd International Conference of Economic History (Aix-en-Provence, 1962)*, 5 vols, Paris, vol. 2, pp. 33–68.

—— (1975) *The English Peasantry in the Late Middle Ages. The Ford Lectures for 1973 and Related Studies*, Oxford.

—— (1985) 'Medieval market towns and simple commodity production', *Past and Present* 109: 3–23.

—— (1992) *English and French Towns in Feudal Society. A Comparative Study*, Cambridge.

Hilton, R. H. and T. H. Aston (eds) (1984) *The English Rising of 1381*, Cambridge.

Hirschmann, A. O. (1970) *Exit, Voice and Loyalty*, Cambridge, Mass.

—— (1977) *The Passions and the Interests. Political Arguments for Capitalism Before its Triumph*, Princeton.

Hoffman, P. (1996) *Growth in a Traditional Society. The French Countryside, 1450–1815*, Princeton.

Hoffman, P. T. and K. Norberg (eds) (1994) *Fiscal Crises, Liberty, and Representative Government, 1450–1789*, Stanford.

Hohenberg, P. M. and L. H. Lees. (1985) *The Making of Urban Europe, 1000–1950*, Cambridge, Mass./London.

—— (1989) 'Urban decline and regional economies: Brabant, Castile, and Lombardy, 1550–1750', *Comparative Studies in Society and History* 31: 439–61.

Holbach, R. (1993) 'Some remarks on the role of "putting-out" in Flemish and northwest European cloth production', in M. Boone and W. Prevenier (eds) *Drapery Production in the Late Medieval Low Countries. Markets and Strategies for Survival (14th–16th Centuries)*, Leuven/Apeldoorn.

—— (1994) *Frühformen von Verlag und Grossbetrieb in der gewerblichen Production (13.–16. Jahrhundert)*, Stuttgart.

Holmes, C. (1992) 'Parliament, liberty, taxation and property', in J. H. Hexter (ed.) *Parliament and Liberty from the Reign of Elizabeth to the English Civil War*, Stanford, pp. 122–54.

Holton, R. H. (1953) 'Marketing structure and economic development', *Quarterly Journal of Economics* 67: 344–61.

Homer, S. and R. Sylla. (1991) *A History of Interest Rates*, 3rd ed., New Brunswick/London.

Hoppenbrouwers, P. (1997) 'Agricultural production and technology in the Netherlands, *c.*1000–1500', in G. Astill and J. Langdon (eds) *Medieval Farming and Technology. The Impact of Agricultural Change in Northwest Europe*, Leiden/New York/Cologne, pp. 89–114.

Hoppenbrouwers, P. (2000) 'Town and country in Holland, 1300–1550', in S.R. Epstein (ed.) *Town and Country in Europe, 1350–1750*, Cambridge.

Hoshino, H. (1980) *L'Arte della Lana in Firenze nel basso medioevo. Il commercio della lana e il mercato dei panni fiorentini nei secoli XIII–XV*, Florence.

—— (1983) 'The rise of the Florentine woollen industry in the fourteenth century', in N. B. Harte and K. G. Ponting (eds) *Cloth and Clothing in Medieval Europe. Essays in Memory of Professor E.M. Carus-Wilson*, London, pp. 183–200.

Howell, M. C. (1986) *Women, Production, and Patriarchy in Late Medieval Cities*, Chicago/London.

Hoyle, R. W. (1998) 'Taxation and the mid-Tudor crisis', *Economic History Review*, 2nd ser. 51, 4: 649–75.

Hume, D. (1993a) [1777] *Selected Essays*, ed. S. Copley and A. Edgar, Oxford.

—— (1993b) 'Of civil liberty', in Hume, *Selected Essays*, ed. S. Copley and A. Edgar, Oxford: 49–56.

—— (1993c). 'That politics may be reduced to a science', in Hume, *Selected Essays*, ed. S. Copley and A. Edgar, Oxford: 13–23.

Hurstfield, J. (1955) 'The profits of fiscal feudalism', *Economic History Review* 2nd ser. 8, 1: 53–61.

Huvelin, P. (1897) *Essai historique sur le droit des marchés et des foires*, Paris.

Hymer, S. and S. Resnick (1969) 'A model of an agrarian economy with nonagricultural activities', *American Economic Review*, 59: 493–506.

Iradiel Murugarren, P. (1974) *Evolución de la industria textil castellana en los siglos XIII–XVI. Factores de desarrollo, organización y costes de la producción en Cuenca*, Salamanca.

Irsigler, F. (1971) 'Köln, die Frankfurter Messen und die Handelsbeziehungen mit Oberdeutschland im 15. Jahrhundert', *Mitteilungen aus dem Stadtarchiv von Köln* 60: 341–429.

Jacoby, D. (1993) 'Raw materials for the glass industries of Venice and the Terraferma, about 1370 – about 1460', *Journal of Glass Studies* 35: 65–90.

Jacopetti, N. I. (1965) *Monete e prezzi a Cremona dal XVI al XVIII secolo*, Cremona.

Jansen, H. P. H. (1978) 'Holland's advance', *Acta Historiae Neerlandicae* 10: 1–19.

Jardine, L. (1996) *Worldly Goods. A New History of the Renaissance*, London.

Jeannin, J. (1987) 'Il concetto di protoindustrializzazione e la sua utilizzazione per la storia dell'industria in Europa alla fine del Medioevo', *Quaderni storici* 22: 275–85.

Jesse, W. (1928) *Der Wendische Münzverein*, Lübeck.

Jones, D. W. (1978) 'Production, consumption, and the allocation of labor by a peasant in a periodic marketing system', *Geographical Analysis*, 10: 13–30.

Jones, E. L. (1981) *The European Miracle*, Cambridge.

—— (1988) *Growth Recurring. Economic Change in World History*, Oxford.

Jones, P. (1978) 'Economia e società nell'Italia medievale: la leggenda della borghesia', in R. Romano and C. Vivanti (eds) *Storia d'Italia. Annali*, 2 vols, Turin, pp. 185–372.

Jordan, W. C. (1996) *The Great Famine. Northern Europe in the Early Fourteenth Century*, Princeton.

Kaeuper, R. W. (1973) *Bankers to the Crown. The Riccardi of Lucca and Edward I*, Princeton.

—— (1988) *War, Justice and Public Order. England and France in the Later Middle Ages*, Oxford.

Käsler, D. (1988) *Max Weber. An Introduction to His Life and Work*, Oxford.

Kedar, B. Z. (1976) *Merchants in Crisis. Genoese and Venetian Men of Affairs and the Fourteenth Century Depression*, New Haven/London.

Keene, D. and V. Harding (1987) *Historical Gazetteer of London before the Great Fire, 1. Cheapside*, Cambridge, microfiche.

Kellenbenz, H. (1963) 'Industries rurales en Occident de la fin du Moyen Age au XVIIIe siècle', *Annales E.S.C.* 18: 833–82.

—— (1982) 'Oberdeutschland und Mailand zur Zeit der Sforza', in *Gli Sforza a Milano e in Lombardia e i loro rapporti con gli Stati italiani ed europei (1450–1535)*, Milan, pp. 193–225.

—— (1983) 'The fustian industry of the Ulm region in the fifteenth and early sixteenth centuries', in N. B. Harte and K. G. Ponting (eds) (1983) *Cloth and Clothing in Medieval Europe. Essays in Memory of Professor E.M. Carus-Wilson*, London, pp. 259–77.

—— (1986) 'Wirtschaft und Gesellschaft Europas 1350–1650', in W. Fischer, J.A. van Houtte, H. Kellenbenz, I. Mieck and F. Vittinghoff (eds) *Handbuch der Europäischen Wirtschafts- und Sozialgeschichte*, 3, Stuttgart, pp. 1–386.

Kelley, D. R. (1981) *The Beginning of Ideology. Consciousness and Society in the French Reformation*, Cambridge.

Kiessling, R. (1996) 'Markets and marketing, town and country', in B. Scribner (ed.) *Germany. A New Social and Economic History, I. 1450–1630*, London/New York, pp. 145–80.

Kindleberger, C. P. (1991) 'The economic crisis of 1619 to 1623', *Journal of Economic History* 51, 1: 149–75.

Kitsikopoulos, H. (2000) 'Standards of living and capital formation in pre-plague England: a peasant budget model', *Economic History Review* 2nd ser., 53 (2): 237–61.

Kleineke, H. (1997) *Towns and Trade in Southern England c. (1400). A Database*, mimeo, Centre for Metropolitan History, Institute of Historical Research, London.

Knotter, A. (1994) 'Problems of the family economy: peasant economy, domestic production and labour markets in pre-industrial Europe', *Economic and Social History in the Netherlands*, 6.

Koenigsberger, H. G. (1978) 'Monarchies and parliaments in early modern Europe. Dominium regale or dominium politicum et regale', *Theory and Society* 5: 191–217.

—— (1995a) 'Parliaments and estates', in R.W. Davis (ed.) *The Origins of Modern Freedom in the West*, Stanford Calif./Cambridge, pp. 135–77.

—— (1995b) 'Parliaments in the sixteenth century and beyond', in R. W. Davis (ed.) *The Origins of Modern Freedom in the West*, Stanford Calif./Cambridge, pp. 269–312.

Koppe, W. (1952) 'Die Hansen und Frankfurt am Main im 14. Jahrhundert', *Hansische Geschichtsblätter* 71: 30–49.

Körner, M. (1993–4) 'Das System der Jahrmärkte und Messen in der Schweiz im periodischen und permanenten Markt 1500–1800', *Jahrbuch für Regionalgeschichte und Landeskunde* 19: 13–34.

—— (1995) 'Public credit', in R. Bonney (ed.) *Economic Systems and State Finance*, Oxford, pp. 507–38.

Kowaleski, M. (1995) *Local Markets and Regional Trade in Medieval Exeter*, Cambridge.

—— (2000) 'The expansion of the south-western fisheries in late medieval England', *Economic History Review*, 2nd ser. 53.

Kreutz, B. M. (1973) 'Mediterranean contributions to the medieval mariner's compass', *Technology and Culture* 14: 367–83.

Krugman, P. (1991) *Geography and Trade*, Leuven/Cambridge, Mass.

Krugman, P. and A. J. Venables (1996) 'Integration, specialization, and adjustment', *European Economic Review* 40: 959–67.

Kussmaul, A. (1990) *A General View of the Rural Economy of England, 1538–1840*, Cambridge.

Labrousse, E. (1933) *Esquisse du mouvement des prix et des revenus en France au XVIIIe siècle*, 2 vols, Paris.

Ladero Quesada, M. A. and M. Gonzalez Jimenez (1979) *Diezmo ecclesiastico y producción de cereales en el reino de Sevilla (1408–1503)*, Seville.

Ladero Quesada, M. L. (1982) 'Las ferias de Castilla. Siglos XII a XV', *Cuadernos de historia de España* 67–8: 269–347.

Landes, D. (1997) *The Wealth and Poverty of Nations. Why Some are So Rich and Some So Poor*, New York.

Lane, F. C. (1958) 'Economic consequences of organized violence', *Journal of*

Economic History 18, 4.

—— (1975) 'The role of governments in economic growth in early modern times', *Journal of Economic History* 35, 1: 8–17.

Langdon, J. (1986) *Horses, Oxen and Technological Innovation. The Use of Draught Animals in English Farming from 1066–1500*, Cambridge.

Langton, J. and G. Hoppe (1983) *Town and Country in the Development of Early Modern Western Europe*, Norwich.

Larsimont Pergameni, E. (1948–9) 'Censimenti milanesi dell'età di Carlo V. Il censimento del 1545–1546', *Archivio storico lombardo,* 8th ser. 1: 168–209.

Le Mené, M. (1982) *Les campagnes angevines à la fin du Moyen Age (vers 1350 – vers 1530) . Étude économique*, Nantes.

Le Roy Ladurie, E. (1966) *Les paysans de Languedoc*, 2 vols, Paris.

Leone, A. (1956) 'Lineamenti di una storia delle corporazioni in Sicilia nei secoli XIV–XVII', *Archivio storico siciliano,* 3rd ser. 2: 82–100.

—— (1983) *Profili economici della Campania aragonese*, Naples.

Lerner, F. (1971) 'Die Reichsstadt Frankfurt und ihre Messen im Verhältnis zu Ost- und Südosteuropa im Zeitraum von 1480 bis 1630', in I. Bog (ed.) *Aussenhandel Ostmitteleuropas* 1450–1650, Cologne/Vienna, pp. 147–84.

Lesger, C. M. (1994) 'Urban systems and economic development in Holland during the later Middle Ages and the early modern period', in *Proceedings, XI International Economic History Congress, Milan. Recent doctoral research in economic history*, Milan, pp. 69–79.

Leverotti, F. (1989) 'Dalla famiglia stretta alla famiglia larga. Linee di evoluzione e tendenze della famiglia rurale lucchese (secoli XIV–XV)', *Studi storici* 30: 171–202.

Levi, M. (1988) *Of Rule and Revenue*, Berkeley/Los Angeles.

Livi Bacci, M. (1990) *Population and Nutrition. An Essay on European Demographic History*, Cambridge.

Lloyd, T. H. (1991) *England and the German Hanse 1157–1611. A Study of Their Trade and Commercial Diplomacy*, Cambridge.

Lombard-Jourdan, A. (1970) 'Y a-t-il une protohistoire urbaine en France?', *Annales* E.S.C. 25, 5: 1121–42.

—— (1982) 'Les foires aux origines des villes', *Francia* 10: 429–48.

—— (1984) 'Fairs', in J. R .Strayer (ed.) *Dictionary of the Middle Ages*, New York, vol. 4, pp. 582–90.

Lombardo, G. (2000) 'Guilds in Early Modern Sicily', unpublished Ph.D. Thesis, London School of Economics and Political Science.

Long, P. O. (1991) 'Invention, authorship, "intellectual property," and the origin of patents: notes toward a conceptual history', *Technology and Culture* 32, 4: 846–84.

Lopez, R. S. (1953) 'The Origin of the Merino Sheep', *The Joshua Starr Memorial Volume: Studies in History and Philology*, New York, pp. 161–8.

—— (1971) *The Commercial Revolution of the Middle Ages, 950–1350*, New Haven.

Lot, F. and R. Fawtier (1958) *Histoire des institutions françaises au Moyen Âge*, 2 vols, Paris.

Luzzati, M. (1962–3) 'Note di metrologia pisana', *Bollettino storico pisano:* 191–220.

—— (1973) *Una guerra di popolo. Lettere private del tempo dell'assedio di Pisa (1494–1509)*, Pisa.

Luzzatto, G. (1955) 'Vi furono fiere a Venezia?', in Luzzatto, *Studi di storia economica veneziana*, Venice, pp. 201–9.

—— (1958) *Breve storia economica dell'Italia medievale*, Turin.

—— (1963) *Il debito pubblico della Repubblica di Venezia dagli ultimi decenni del XII secolo alla fine del XV*, Milan/Varese.

—— (1965) *Breve storia economica dell'Italia medievale*, Turin.

Macfarlane, A. (1987) *The Culture of Capitalism*, Oxford.

Mackay, A. (1977) *Spain in the Middle Ages. From Frontier to Empire, 1000–1500*, Basingstoke/London.

—— (1987) 'Existieron aduanas castellanas en la frontera con Portugal en el siglo XV?', in *Actas de II jornades luso-espanholes da história medieval*, Porto, pp. 3–21.

Maddicott, J. R. (1975) *The English Peasantry and the Demands of the Crown, 1294–1341*, Oxford.

Maddison, A. (1998) *Chinese Economic Performance in the Long Run*, Paris.

Mainoni, P. (1982) *Mercanti lombardi tra Barcellona e Valenza nel basso medioevo*, Bologna.

—— (1983) 'L'attività mercantile e le casate milanesi nel secondo Quattrocento', in G. Bologna (ed.) *Milano nell'età di Ludovico il Moro*, 2 vols, Milan, vol. 2, pp. 575–84.

—— (1984) 'Il mercato della lana a Milano dal XIV al XV secolo. Prime indagini', *Archivio storico lombardo*, 11th ser. 1: 20–43.

—— (1992) '"Viglaebium opibus primum". Uno sviluppo economico nel Quattrocento lombardo', in G. Chittolini (ed.) *Metamorfosi di un borgo. Vigevano in età visconteo-sforzesce*, Milan: 193–266.

—— (1993) 'Politiche fiscali, produzione rurale e controllo del territorio nella signoria viscontea (secoli XIV–XV)', *Studi di storia medioevale e di diplomatica* 13: 25–54.

—— (1994a) *Economia e politica nella Lombardia medievale. Da Bergamo a Milano fra XIII e XV secolo*, Cavallermaggiore.

—— (1994b) 'La seta a Milano nel XV secolo: aspetti economici e istituzionali', *Studi storici* 35: 871–96.

Malanima, P. (1982) *La decadenza di un'economia cittadina. L'industria di Firenze nei secoli XVI–XVIII*, Bologna.

—— (1983) 'La formazione di una regione economica: la Toscana nei secoli XIII–XV', *Società e storia* 6: 229–69.

—— (1990) *Il lusso dei contadini. Consumi e industrie nelle campagne toscane del Sei e Settecento*, Bologna.

—— (1996) 'Teoria economica regionale e storia: il caso della Toscana (XIII–XVI secolo)', in Lo *sviluppo economico regionale in prospettiva storica. Atti dell'incontro interdisciplinare, Milano 18–19 maggio 1995*, Milan, pp. 133–48.

—— (1998) 'Italian cities 1300–1800: a quantitative approach', *Rivista di storia economica*, 14, 2: 91–126.

Mann, M. (1986) *The Sources of Social Power, 1. A History of Power From the Beginning to A.D.1760*, Cambridge.

—— (1989) 'European development: approaching a historical explanation', in J. Baechler, J. A. Hall and M. A. Mann (eds) *Europe and the Rise of Capitalism*, Oxford, pp. 6–19.

Małowist, M. (1972) 'Les changements dans la structure de la production et du commerce du drap au cours du XIVe et XVe siècle', in Małowist, *Croissance et régression en Europe XIVe–XVIIe siècles*, Paris, pp. 53–62.

Marciani, C. (1965) 'Le relazioni tra l'Adriatico orientale e l'Abruzzo nei secoli XV,

XVI e XVII', *Archivio storico italiano* 123: 14–47.

Marcucci, R. (1906) 'Sull'origine della fiera di Senigallia', *Archivio storico italiano*, 5th ser. 28: 31–49.

Margairaz, D. M. (1988) *Foires et marchés dans la France pré-industrielle*, Paris.

Martines, L. (1968) *Lawyers and Statecraft in Renaissance Florence*, Princeton.

Martinez Sopena, P. (1996) 'Foires et marchés ruraux dans les pays de la couronne de Castille et de Léon du Xe au XIIIe siècle', in C. Desplat (ed.) *Foires et marchés dans les campagnes de l'Europe médiévale et moderne*, Toulouse, pp. 47–70.

Martini, G. (1980) 'L'*Universitas Mercatorum* di Milano e i suoi rapporti col potere politico (secoli XIII–XV)', in *Studi di storia medievale e moderna per Ernesto Sestan, I. Medioevo*, 2 vols, Florence, vol.1, pp. 219–58.

Mas-Latrie, R. de (1866) 'Le droit de marque ou de représailles au moyen age', *Bibliothèque de l'École des Chartes*, 27: 529–77.

Masschaele, J. (1997) *Peasants, Merchants and Markets. Inland Trade in Medieval England, 1150–1350*, London/New York.

Massetto, G. (1990) 'Le fonti del diritto nella Lombardia del Quattrocento', in J. M. Cauchies and G. Chittolini (eds) *Milano e Borgogna. Due stati principeschi tra medioevo e Rinascimento*, Rome, pp. 49–65.

Mate, M. (1982) 'The impact of war on the economy of Canterbury Cathedral priory, 1294–1340', *Speculum*, 57, 4: 761–78.

—— (1991) 'The agrarian economy of south-east England before the Black Death: depressed or buoyant?', in B. M. S. Campbell (ed.) *Before the Black Death. Studies in the 'Crisis' of the Early Fourteenth Century*, Manchester, pp. 79–109.

Mathias, P. and P. K. O'Brien (1976) 'Taxation in Britain and France, 1715–1810: a comparison of the social and economic incidence of taxes collected for the central government', *Journal of European Economic History* 5: 601–50.

Mauro, F. and G. Parker (1977) 'Spain', in C. Wilson and G. Parker (eds) *An Introduction to the Sources of European Economic History 1500–1800, 1. Western Europe*, London, pp. 37–62.

Mayhew, N. J. (1995) 'Population, money supply, and the velocity of circulation in England, 1300–1700', *Economic History Review*, 2nd ser. 48, 3: 238–57.

Mazzi, M. S. and S. Raveggi (1983) *Gli uomini e le cose nelle campagne fiorentine del Quattrocento*, Florence.

McCutcheon, K. L. (1939) 'Yorkshire fairs and markets to the end of the eighteenth century', *Thoresby Society* 39: 1–177.

McIntosh, A., M. L. Samuels and M. Beskin (1986) *Linguistic Atlas of Late Medieval English*, 4 vols, Aberdeen.

McNeill, W. H. (1954) *Past and Future*, Chicago.

Meiksins Wood, E. (1981) 'The separation of the economic and the political in capitalism', *New Left Review* 127: 66–95.

Melis, F. (1964) 'Werner Sombart e i problemi della navigazione nel Medio Evo', in G.Barbieri *et al. L'opera di Werner Sombart nel centenario della nascita*, Milan, pp. 85–149.

—— (1984) *I vini italiani nel Medioevo*, ed. A. Affortunati Parrini, Florence.

—— (1989) *Industria e commercio nella Toscana medievale*, ed. B. Dini, introd. M. Tangheroni, Florence.

—— (1991) *L'azienda nel medioevo*, ed. M. Spallanzani, introd. M. del Treppo, Florence.

Mendels, F. (1972) 'Proto-industrialisation: the first phase of the industrialisation process?' *Journal of Economic History* 32: 241–61

Meroni, U. (1957) '"Cremona fedelissima". Studi di storia economica e amministrativa di Cremona durante la dominazione spagnola, II', *Annali della Biblioteca governativa e della Libreria civica di Cremona* 10: 1–157.

Mestayer, M. (1963) 'Les prix du blé et de l'avoine à Douai de 1329 à 1793', *Revue du Nord* 45: 157–76.

Miani, G. (1964) 'L'économie lombarde aux XIVe et XVe siècle: Une exception à la règle?', *Annales E.S.C.* 19, 3: 569–79.

Michaud-Fréjaville, F. (1996) 'Belles foires et marchés du Berry (XIVe–XVIe s.)', in C. Desplat (ed.) *Foires et marchés dans les campagnes de l'Europe médiévale et moderne*, Toulouse, pp. 85–104.

Miller, J. A. (1999) *Mastering the Market. The State and Grain Trade in Northern France, 1700–1860*, Cambridge.

Miller, E. (1963) 'The economic policies of governments. France and England', in M. M. Postan E. E. Rich and E. Miller (eds) *Cambridge Economic History of Europe, III. Economic Organization and Policies in the Middle Ages*, Cambridge, pp. 290–339.

—— (1975) 'War, taxation and the English economy in the late thirteenth and early fourteenth centuries', in J. M. Winter (ed.) *War and Economic Development. Essays in Memory of David Joslin*, Cambridge, pp. 11–31.

—— (1991) 'Introduction: land and people', in E. Miller (ed.) *The Agrarian History of England and Wales, III: 1350–1500*, Cambridge, pp. 1–33.

Miller, E. and J. Hatcher (1995) *Medieval England. Towns, Commerce and Crafts 1086–1348*, London/New York.

Miller, J. (ed.) (1990) *Absolutism in Seventeenth Century Europe*, Basingstoke.

Millward, C. (1989) *A Biography of the English Language*, Fort Worth.

Mineo, E. I. (1997) 'Città e società urbana nell'età di Federico III: le élites e la sperimentazione istituzionale', *Archivio storico siciliano*, 4th ser. 23: 109–49.

Mira, G. (1937) 'Provvedimenti viscontei e sforzeschi sull'arte della lana in Como (1335–1535)', *Archivio storico lombardo*, new ser. 2: 345–402.

—— (1939) *Aspetti dell'economia comasca all'inizio dell'età moderna*, Como.

—— (1941) 'I prezzi dei cereali a Como dal 1512 al 1658', *Rivista internazionale di scienze sociali*, 3rd ser. 12: 195–211.

—— (1955) *Le fiere lombarde nei secoli XIV–XVI. Prime indagini*, Como.

—— (1957) 'Il fabbisogno di cereali in Perugia e nel suo contado nei secoli XIII–XIV', in *Studi Sapori, Studi in onore di Armando Sapori*, 2 vols, Milan: vol. 1, pp. 507–17.

—— (1958) 'L'organizzazione fieristica nel quadro dell'economia della "Bassa" lombarda alla fine del Medioevo e nell'età moderna', *Archivio storico lombardo*, 8th ser. 8: 289–300.

—— (1961) 'Prime indagini sulle fiere umbre nel Medioevo', in *Studi in onore di Epicarmo Corbino*, Milan, pp. 539–62.

Mitterauer, M. (1967) 'Jahrmärkte im Nachfolge antiker Zentralorte', *Mitteilungen des Instituts für Oesterreichische Geschichtsforschung* 75: 237–321.

—— (1971) 'La continuité des foires et la naissance des villes', *Annales E.S.C.* 28, 4: 711–34.

Moioli, A. (1986) 'La deindustrializzazione della Lombardia nel secolo XVII', *Archivio storico lombardo*, 11th ser. 3: 167–203.

Mokyr, J. (1990) *The Lever of Riches. Technological Creativity and Economic Progress*, Oxford/New York.

Molho, A. (1979) 'Cosimo de' Medici: *Pater Patriae* or padrino?', *Stanford Italian Review* (Spring): 5–33.

—— (1987) 'L'amministrazione del debito pubblico a Firenze nel quindicesimo secolo', in *I ceti dirigenti nella Toscana del Quattrocento*, Monte Oriolo, pp. 191–208.

—— (1993) 'Tre città-stato e i loro debiti pubblici. Quesiti e ipotesi sulla storia di Firenze, Genova e Venezia', in S. Gensini (ed.) *Italia 1350–1450: tra crisi, trasformazione, sviluppo*, Pistoia, pp. 185–215.

—— (1994a) *Marriage Alliance in Late Medieval Florence*, Cambridge, Mass./London.

—— (1994b) 'Lo Stato e la finanza pubblica. Un'ipotesi basata sulla storia tardomedievale di Firenze', in G. Chittolini, A. Molho and P. Schiera (eds) *Origini dello Stato. Processi di formazione statale in Italia fra medioevo ed età moderna*, Bologna, pp. 225–80.

Mollat, M. and P. Wolff (1970) *Ongles bleus Jacques et Ciompi. Les revolutions populaires en Europe au XIVe et XVe siecles*, Paris.

Moore, B. Jr. (1966) *The Social Origins of Dictatorship and Democracy*, Boston.

Moore, E. W. (1985) *The Fairs of Medieval England. An Introductory Study*, Toronto.

Mosley, W. H. (ed.) (1978) *Nutrition and Human Reproduction*, Baltimore.

Muendel, J. (1981) 'The distribution of mills in the Florentine countryside during the late Middle Ages', in J. A. Raftis (ed.) *Pathways to Medieval Peasants*, Toronto, pp. 83–115.

Munro, J. H. (1984) 'Mint outputs, money, and prices in late-medieval England and the Low Countries', in E. van Cauwenberghe and F. Irsigler (eds) *Münzprägung, Geldumlauf und Wechselkurse/Minting, Monetary Circulation and Exchange Rates*, Trier, pp. 31–122.

—— (1991) 'Industrial transformations in the north-west European textile trades, c.1290–c.1340: economic progress or economic crisis?', in B. M. S. Campbell (ed.) *Before the Black Death. Studies in the 'Crisis' of the Early Fourteenth Century*, Manchester, pp. 110–48.

—— (1997) 'The origin of the English "new draperies": the resurrection of an old Flemish industry, 1270–1570', in N. B. Harte (ed.) *The New Draperies in the Low Countries and England, 1300–1800*, Oxford, pp. 35–128.

Musset, L. (1976) 'Foires et marchés en Normandie à l'époque ducale', *Annales de Normandie* 26: 2–23.

Muzzi, O. (1995) 'Attività artigianali e cambiamenti politici a Colle val d'Elsa prima e dopo la conquista fiorentina', in R. Ninci (ed.) *La società fiorentina nel Basso Medioevo. Per Elio Conti*, Rome, pp. 21–54.

Nader, H. (1990) *Liberty in Absolutist Spain. The Habsburg Sale of Towns, 1516–1700*, Baltimore/London.

Nairn, T. (1997) 'Sovereignty after the election', *New Left Review* 224: 3–18.

Najemy, J.M. (1982) *Corporatism and Consensus in Florentine Electoral Politics, 1280–1400*, Chapel Hill, N.C.

Nerlove, M. (1958) *The Dynamics of Supply: Estimation of Farmers' Response to Prices*, Baltimore.

Neumann, M. (1865) *Geschichte des Wuchers in Deutschland*, Halle.

Nicholas, D. (1971) *Town and Countryside: Social, Economic, and Political Tensions in Fourteenth-Century Flanders*, Bruges.

Noordegraaf, L. (1992) 'Internal trade and internal trade conflicts in the Northern Netherlands: autonomy, centralism and state formation in the pre-industrial era', in S. Groenveld and M. Wintle (eds) *State and Trade. Government and the Economy in Britain and the Netherlands since the Middle Ages*, Walburg Pers/Zutphen, pp. 12–23.

North, D. C. (1981) *Structure and Change in Economic History*, New York.

—— (1990) 'A transaction cost theory of politics', *Journal of Theoretical Politics* 2, 4: 355–67.

—— (1991) 'Institutions, transactions costs, and the rise of merchant empires', in J. D. Tracy (ed.) *The Political Economy of Merchant Empires*, Cambridge, pp. 22–40.

—— (1995) 'The paradox of the West', in R. W. Davis (ed.) *The Origins of Modern Freedom in the West*, Stanford Calif./Cambridge, pp. 7–34.

North, D. C. and R. P. Thomas (1973) *The Rise of the Western World*, Cambridge.

North, D. C. and B. Weingast (1989) 'Constitutions and commitment: evolution of institutions governing public choice in seventeenth-century England', *Journal of Economic History*, 49, 4: 803–32.

O'Brien, P. K. (1982) 'European economic development: the contribution of the periphery', *Economic History Review*, 2nd ser. 35, 1: 1–18.

—— (1988) 'The political economy of British taxation, 1660–1815', *Economic History Review*, 2nd ser. 41, 1: 1–32.

O'Brien, P. K. and P. A. Hunt (1999) 'England, 1485–1815', in R. Bonney (ed.) *The Rise of the Fiscal State in Europe c.1200–1815*, Oxford, pp. 53–100.

Occhipinti, E. (1992) 'Le relazioni tra Vigevano e Milano nel corso del Trecento', in G. Chittolini (ed.) *Metamorfosi di un borgo. Vigevano in età visconteo-sforzesce*, Milan, pp. 31–42.

Ogilvie, S. C. (1997) *State Corporatism and Proto-Industry. The Württemberg Black Forest, 1580–1797*, Cambridge.

Ogilvie, S. C. and M. Cerman (eds) (1996) *European Proto-Industrialization*, Cambridge.

Olson, M. (1965) *The Logic of Collective Action. Public Goods and the Theory of Groups*, Cambridge, Mass.

—— (1982) *The Rise and Decline of Nations. Economic Growth, Stagflation, and Social Rigidities*, New Haven/London.

—— (1991) 'Autocracy, democracy and prosperity', in R. J. Zeckhauser (ed.) *Strategy and Choice*, Cambridge, Mass., pp. 131–57.

Oman, C. (1906) *The Great Revolt of 1381*, Oxford (repr. 1968).

Ormrod, W. M. (1990) *The Reign of Edward III. Crown and Political Society in England, 1327–1377*, London.

—— (1995) 'The West European monarchies in the later Middle Ages', in R. Bonney (ed.) *Economic Systems and State Finance*, Oxford, pp. 123–62.

Otsuka, K., H. Chuma and Y. Hayami (1992) 'Land and labour contracts in agrarian economies: theories and facts', *Journal of Economic Literature* 30: 1965–2018.

Outhwaite, R. B. (1966) 'The trials of foreign borrowing: the English crown and the Antwerp money market in the mid-sixteenth century', *Economic History Review*, 2nd ser. 19, 2: 289–305.

—— (1971) 'Royal borrowing in the reign of Elizabeth I: the aftermath of Antwerp', *English Historical Review* 339: 251–63.

—— (1981) 'Dearth and government intervention in English grain markets, 1590–1700', *Economic History Review*, 2nd ser. 34, 4: 389–406.

Overton, M. (1996) *Agricultural Revolution in England. The Transformation of the*

Agrarian Economy 1500–1850, Cambridge.

Owen Hughes, D. (1983) 'Sumptuary law and social relations in Renaissance Italy', in J. Bossy (ed.) *Disputes and Settlements. Law and Human Relations in the West*, Cambridge, pp. 69–100.

Paganini, C. (1971–3) 'Premesse a una rilettura degli statuti dei mercanti di Pavia', *Archivio storico lombardo*, 9th ser. 10: 478–513.

Pagliazzi, P. (1939) 'Caratteristiche di gestione di una azienda del medioevo', *Rassegna volterrana* 10–11: 1–45.

Palermo, L. (1990) *Mercati del grano a Roma tra Medioevo e Rinascimento, I. Il mercato distrettuale del grano in età comunale*, Rome.

Palliser, D. M. (1988) 'Urban decay revisited', in J. A. F. Thomson (ed.) *Towns and Townspeople in the Fifteenth Century*, Gloucester, pp. 1–21.

—— 2000) 'Towns and the English state, 1066–1500', in D. M. Palliser and J. R. Maddicott (eds) *The Medieval State: Essays Presented to James Campbell*, London/Rio Grande, pp. 127–45.

Palliser, D. M. and A. C. Pinnock. (1971) 'The markets of medieval Staffordshire', *North Staffordshire Journal of Field Studies* 11: 49–63.

Pelham, R. A. (1938) 'The trade relations of Birmingham during the Middle Ages', *Transactions and Proceedings of the Birmingham Archaeological Society* 62: 32–40.

—— (1945–6) 'The cloth markets of Warwickshire during the later Middle Ages', *Transactions and Proceedings of the Birmingham Archaeological Society* 66: 131–41.

Penn, S. A. C. and C. Dyer (1990) 'Wages and earnings in late medieval England: evidence from the enforcement of the labour laws', *Economic History Review*, 2nd ser. 43, 3: 356–76.

Pérez Pérez, C. (1982) 'La feria de San Miguel de Lérida. Privilegio dado par Jaime I para su fundación', in *Jaime I y la su época. X Congreso de Historia de la Corona de Aragón*, 5 vols, Zaragoza, vols 3–5, pp. 247–51.

Perol, C. (1994) 'Cortona. Une cité-état aux marches de la Toscane XVe–XVIe siècles', unpublished Ph.D. thesis, University of Paris, Paris X-Nanterre.

Persson, K. G. (1984) 'Consumption, labour and leisure in the late Middle Ages', in D. Menjot (ed.) *Manger et boire au Moyen Age*, Nice, vol. 1, pp. 211–23.

—— (1988) *Pre-Industrial Economic Growth. Social Organization and Technological Progress in Europe*, Oxford.

—— (1991) 'Labour productivity in medieval agriculture: Tuscany and the "Low Countries"', in B. M. S. Campbell and M. Overton (eds) *Land, Labour and Livestock. Historical Studies in European Agricultural Productivity*, Manchester/New York, pp. 124–43.

—— (1993) 'Was there a productivity gap between fourteenth-century Italy and England?', *Economic History Review*, 2nd ser. 46, 1: 105–14.

—— (1996) 'The seven lean years, elasticity traps, and intervention in grain markets in pre-industrial Europe', *Economic History Review*, 2nd ser. 49, 4: 692–714.

—— (1999) *Grain Markets in Europe, 1500–1900. Integration and Deregulation*, Cambridge.

Petralia, G. (1987) '"Crisi" ed emigrazione dei ceti eminenti a Pisa durante il primo dominio fiorentino. L'orizzonte cittadino e la ricerca di spazi esterni', in *I ceti dirigenti nella Toscana del Quattrocento*, Monte Oriolo, pp. 291–352.

Pezzolo, L. (1990) *L'oro dello Stato. Società, finanza e fisco nella Repubblica veneta del secondo '500*, Treviso.

—— (1994) 'La finanza pubblica', in A. Tenenti and U. Tucci (eds) *Storia di Venezia, VI. Dal Rinascimento al Barocco*, Rome, pp. 713–73.

—— (1995) 'Elogio della rendita. Sul debito pubblico degli Stati italiani nel Cinque e Seicento', *Rivista di storia economica*, new ser. 12: 3, 283–330.

—— (2001) 'Economic policy, finance and war', in S. R. Epstein (ed.) *State and Society in Italy, 1350–1550*, Oxford/Rhode Island.

Piccinni, G. (1982) '*Seminare, fruttare raccogliere'. Mezzadri e salariati sulle terre di Monte Oliveto Maggiore (1374–1430)*, Milan.

—— (1985) 'Le donne della mezzadria toscana delle origini', *Ricerche storiche* 15: 130–55.

Pini, A. I. (1984) 'La fiera d'agosto a Cesena dalla sua istituzione alla definitiva regolamentazione (1380–1509)', *Nuova rivista storica* 68: 175–89.

Pinto, G. (1978) *Il Libro del Biadaiolo. Carestie e annona a Firenze dalla metà del '200 al 1348*, Florence.

—— (1981) 'I livelli di vita dei salariati cittadini nel periodo successivo al tumulto dei Ciompi (1380–1430)', in *Il tumulto dei Ciompi. Un momento di storia fiorentina ed europea*, Florence, pp. 161–98.

—— (1982) *La Toscana nel tardo medio evo. Ambiente, economia rurale, società*, Florence.

—— (1985) 'Appunti sulla politica annonaria in Italia fra XIII e XV secolo', in *Aspetti della vita economica medievale. Atti del convegno nel X anniversario della morte di Federigo Melis*, Florence, pp. 624–43.

—— (1987) 'Commercio del grano e politica annonaria nella Toscana del Quattrocento: la corrispondenza dell'Ufficio fiorentino dell'Abbondanza negli anni 1411–1412', in *Studi di storia economica toscana nel Medioevo e nel Rinascimento in memoria di Federigo Melis*, Pisa, pp.257–83

—— (1994) 'Borgo Sansepolcro: profilo di un centro minore della Toscana tra Medioevo e prima età moderna', in L. Borgia *et al.* (eds) *Studi in onore di Arnaldo d'Addario*, Lecce.

—— (1995a) 'Lineamenti d'economia volterrana fra XIII e XVI secolo', in *Volterra dagli albori comunali alla rivolta antifrancese*, Volterra.

—— (1995b) 'Popolazione e comportamenti demografici in Italia (1250–1348)', in *Europa* 1995: 37–62.

Piola Caselli, F. (1991) 'Banchi privati e debito pubblico pontificio a Roma tra Cinquecento e Seicento', in D. Puncuh (ed.) *Banchi pubblici, banchi privati e monti di pietà nell'Europa preindustriale. Amministrazione, tecniche operative e ruoli economici*, Genoa, pp. 461–95.

Pirenne, H. (1963) *Histoire économique et sociale du Moyen Age*, ed. H. Werveke, Paris.

Pistarino, G. (1986) 'I porti di Milano. Venezia, Genova, Pisa', in G. Taborelli (ed.) *Commercio in Lombardia*, 2 vols, Milan: vol. 2, pp. 86–92.

Ploss, E. E. (1973) *Ein Buch von alten Farben. Technologie der Textilfarben im Mittelaletr mit einem Ausblick auf die festen Farben*, 3rd ed., Munich.

Poehlmann, E. (1993) 'Economic growth in late medieval England: a challenge to the orthodoxy of decline', M.Sc. dissertation, London School of Economics.

Poignant, S. (1932) *La foire de Lille. Contribution à l'étude des foires flamandes au Moyen Age*, Lille.

Polanyi, K. (1944) *The Great Transformation*, New York/Toronto.

Pollard, S. (1997) *Marginal Europe. The Contribution of the Marginal Lands Since the Middle Ages*, Oxford.

Pomerantz, K. (2000) *The Great Divergence: China, Europe, and the Making of the Modern World Economy*, Princeton.

Poni, C. (1990) 'Per la storia del distretto industriale serico di Bologna (secoli XVI–XIX)', *Quaderni storici* 25, 1: 93–167.

Poos, L. (1991) *A Rural Society after the Black Death. Essex 1350–1525*, Cambridge.

Postan, M. M. (1952) 'The trade of medieval Europe: the North', in M. Postan and E. E. Rich (eds) *The Cambridge Economic History of Europe*, Cambridge, vol. 2, pp. 119–255.

—— (1967) 'Investment in medieval agriculture', *Journal of Economic History* 27, 4: 576–87.

—— (1973) *Essays on Medieval Agriculture and General Problems of the Medieval Economy*, Cambridge.

Postan, M. M., E. E. Rich and E. Miller (eds) (1963) *Cambridge Economic History of Europe, III. Economic Organization and Policies in the Middle Ages*, Cambridge.

Postan, M. M. and J. Z. Titow (with statistical notes by J. Longden) (1958–9) 'Heriots and prices on Winchester manors', *Economic History Review*, 2nd ser. 11, 4: 392–417.

Posthumus, N. W. (1964) *Inquiry into the History of Prices in Holland*, II, Leiden.

Postles, D. (1987) 'Markets for rural produce in Oxfordshire, 1086–1350', *Midland History* 12: 14–26.

—— (1989) 'Cleaning the medieval arable', *Agricultural History Review* 37: 130–43.

Pounds, N. J. G. (1973) *An Historical Geography of Europe 450BC–AD1330*, Cambridge.

—— (1974) *An Economic History of Medieval Europe*, London.

Pouzol, M. (1968) 'Les foires de Champagne à Lagny au Moyen Age', *Cèrcle d'Etudes Archéologiques et Historiques du Pays de Lagny* 7: 1–18.

Prak, M. (1995) 'Le regioni nella prima età moderna', *Proposte e ricerche: Economia e società nella storia dell'Italia centrale* 35: 7–40.

Prestwich, M. (1972) *War, Politics and Finance under Edward I*, London.

Prou, M. (1926) 'Une ville-marché au XIIe siècle. Étampes (Seine-et-Oise)', in *Mélanges d'histoire offerts à Henri Pirenne*, Brussels, pp. 379–89.

Przeworski, A. and F. Limongi (1993) 'Political regimes and economic growth', *Journal of Economic Perspectives* 7, 1: 51–69.

Pult Quaglia, A. M. (1990) *'Per provvedere ai popoli'. Il sistema annonario nella Toscana dei Medici*, Florence.

Puncuh, D. (ed.) (1991) *Banchi pubblici, banchi privati e monti di pietà nell'Europa preindustriale. Amministrazione, tecniche operative e ruoli economici*, Genoa.

Putnam, R. (1993) *Making Democracy Work. Civic Traditions in Modern Italy*, Princeton.

Quian, Y. and B. R. Weingast (1997) 'Federalism as a commitment to preserving market incentives', *Journal of Economic Perspectives* 11, 4: 83–92.

Racine, P. (1977) 'Ville et contado dans l'Italie communale: l'exemple de Plaisance', *Nuova rivista storica* 61: 273–90.

Radeff, A. (1991) 'Grandes et petites foires du Moyen Âge au XXe siècle. Conjoncture générale et cas vaudois', *Nuova rivista storica* 75: 329–48.

Rausch, W. (1969) *Handel an der Donau, I: Geschichte der Linzer Märkte im Mittelalter*, Linz.

Ravallion, M. (1987) *Markets and Famines*, Oxford.

—— (1997) 'Famines and economics', *Journal of Economic Literature* 35, 3: 1205–42.

Razi, Z. (1980) *Life, Marriage and Death in a Medieval Parish: Economy, Society and*

Demography in Halesowen, 1270–1400, Cambridge.

—— (1993) 'The myth of the immutable English family', *Past and Present* 140: 3–44.

Reed, C. G. (1973) 'Transactions costs and differential growth in seventeenth century western Europe', *Journal of Economic History* 33, 2: 177–90.

Reinicke, C. (1989) *Agrarkonjunktur und technisch-organisatorische Innovationen auf dem Agrarsektor im Spiegel niederrheinischer Pachtverträge 1200–1600*, Cologne/Vienna.

Reininghaus, W. (1981) *Die Entstehung der Gesellengilden im Spätmittelalter*, Wiesbaden.

Reynolds, S. (1977) *Introduction to the History of English Medieval Towns*, Oxford.

Richard, J. (1983) 'La "reconstruction" et les créations de foires et de marchés dans le Duché de Bourgogne, au temps des Ducs Valois', *Publications du Centre européenne d'études bourguignonnes* 23: 35–42.

Richet, D. (1973) *La France moderne: l'esprit des institutions*, Paris.

Riddle, J. M. (1991) 'Oral contraceptives and early-term abortifacients during Classical Antiquity and the Middle Ages', *Past and Present* 132: 3–32.

Rigby, S. H. (1986) 'Late medieval urban prosperity: the evidence of the lay subsidies', *Economic History Review* 2nd ser. 39, 3: 411–16.

Riu, M. (1983) 'The woollen industry in Catalonia in the later Middle Ages', in N. B. Harte and K. G. Ponting (eds) *Cloth and Clothing in Medieval Europe. Essays in Memory of Professor E.M. Carus-Wilson*, London, pp. 205–29.

Rogowski, R. (1987) 'Structure, growth, and power: three rationalist accounts', in R. H. Bates (ed.) *Towards a Political Economy of Development. A Rational Choice Perspective*, Berkeley/Los Angeles/London, pp. 300–30.

Romani, M. A. (1975) *Nella spirale di una crisi. Popolazione, mercato e prezzi a Parma tra Cinque e Seicento*, Milan.

—— (1986) 'L'annona e il mercato dei grani. Un commercio a libertà vigilata', in G. Taborelli (ed.) *Commercio in Lombardia*, 2 vols, Milan: vol. 2, pp. 103–17.

Romano R. (1974) 'La storia economica. Dal secolo XIV al Settecento', in R. Romano and C. Vivanti (eds) *Storia d'Italia 2, Dalla caduta dell'Impero romano al secolo XVIII*, 2 vols, Turin: vol. 2, pp. 1811–1913.

Romano, R. and C. Vivanti (eds) (1974) *Storia d'Italia 2, Dalla caduta dell'Impero romano al secolo XVIII*, Turin.

—— (eds) (1978) *Storia d'Italia. Annali* 1, Turin.

Romer, P. M. (1990) 'Endogenous technological change', *Journal of Political Economy* 98, 5, Part II: S71–102.

—— (1994) 'The origins of endogenous growth', *Journal of Economic Perspectives* 8, 1: 3–22.

Roncière, C. M. de la (1968) 'Indirect taxes or "gabelles" at Florence in the fourteenth century. The evolution of tariffs and problems of collection', in N. Rubinstein (ed.) *Florentine Studies. Politics and Society in Renaissance Florence*, London, pp. 140–91.

—— (1976) *Florence centre économique régional au XIVe siècle*, 5 vols, Aix-en-Provence.

Rondoni, G. (1877) *Memorie storiche di Samminiato al Tedesco con documenti inediti e le notizie degli illustri samminiatesi*, San Miniato.

Root, H. L. (1989) 'Tying the king's hand: credible commitment and royal fiscal policy during the ancien regime', *Rationality and Society*, 1, 2: 240–58.

Rosenberg, J. (1994) *The Empire of Civil Society. A Critique of the Realist Theory of*

International Relations, London.

Rosenthal, J-L. (1992) *The Fruits of Revolution*, Cambridge.

—— (1993) 'Credit markets and economic change in southeastern France 1630–1788', *Explorations in Economic History* 30: 129–57.

—— (1998) 'The political economy of absolutism reconsidered', in R. Bates *et al. Analytic Narratives*, Princeton, pp. 64–108.

Roseveare, H. G. (1988) 'Government financial policy and the money market in late seventeenth century England', in A. Guarducci (ed.) *Prodotto lordo e finanza pubblica. Secoli XIII–XIX*, Florence: 703–35.

—— (1991) *The Financial Revolution 1660–1760*, Harlow.

Rossini, E. and G. Zalin. (1985) *Uomini, grani e contrabbandi sul Garda tra Quattrocento e Seicento*, Verona.

Roveda, E. (1988) 'Allevamento e transumanza nella pianura lombarda: i berga-maschi nel Pavese tra '400 e '500', *Bollettino della società pavese di storia patria*, new ser. 40: 13–34.

—— (1989) 'I boschi nella pianura lombarda del Quattrocento', *Studi storici* 30: 1013–30.

Roveda, L. (1948) 'Note economico-sociali su costituzioni di dote della fine del Medio Evo', *Bollettino della Società pavese di storia patria*, new ser. 2: 97–109.

Rubinstein, N. (1966) *The Government of Florence under the Medici (1434 to 1494)*, Oxford.

—— (ed.) (1968) *Florentine Studies. Politics and Society in Renaissance Florence*, London.

Rucquoi, A. (1987) *Valladolid en la Edad Media*, 2 vols, Valladolid.

Ruiz Martin, F. (1975) 'Crédito y banca, comercio y transportes en la época del capitalismo mercantil', in *Actas de las I jornadas de metodologia aplicada a las ciencias históricas. III. Historia moderna*, Santiago de Compostela, pp. 723–49.

Russell, J. C. (1972) *Medieval Regions and their Cities*, Newton Abbott.

Rutenburg, V. (1988) 'A proposito del prodotto lordo fiorentino, un progetto d'im-posta del primo Quattrocento', in A. Guarducci (ed.) *Prodotto lordo e finanza pubblica. Secoli XIII–XIX*, Florence, pp. 864–70.

Saba, F. (1986) 'Le forme dello scambio. I mercati rurali', in G. Taborelli (ed.) *Commercio in Lombardia*, 2 vols, Milan: vol. 1, pp. 176–85.

Sahlins, P. (1989) *Boundaries: The Making of France and Spain in the Pyrenees*, Berkeley/Los Angeles/Oxford.

Sakellariou, E. (1996) 'The kingdom of Naples under Aragonese and Spanish rule. Population growth, and economic and social evolution in the late fifteenth and early sixteenth centuries', unpublished Ph.D. thesis, University of Cambridge.

Samsonowicz, H. (1971) 'Les foires en Pologne au XVe et XVIe siècle sur la toile de fond de la situation économique en Europe', in I. Bog (ed.) *Aussenhandel Ostmitteleuropas 1450–1650*, Cologne/Vienna, pp. 246–59.

Sanchez León, P. (2000) 'Town and country in Castile, 1400–1650', in S. R. Epstein (ed.) *Town and Country in Europe, 1350–1750*, Cambridge.

Sapori, A. (1955) 'Una fiera in Italia alla fine del Quattrocento. La fiera di Salerno del 1478', in Sapori, *Studi di storia economica. Secoli XIII–XIV–XV*, 3rd ed., 2 vols, Florence, vol. 1, pp. 443–74.

Savagnone, G. (1892) *Le maestranze siciliane e le origini delle corporazioni artigiane nel Medio Evo*, Palermo.

Sawyer, P. H. (1981) 'Fairs and markets in early medieval England', in N. Skyum-

Nielsen and N. Lund (eds) *Danish Medieval History: New Currents*, Copenhagen, pp. 153–68.

—— (1986) 'Early fairs and markets in England and Scandinavia', in B. L. Anderson and A. J. H. Latham (eds) *The Market in History*, Beckenham, pp. 59–76.

Scarfe, N. (1965) 'Markets and fairs in medieval Suffolk: a provisional list', *Suffolk Review* 3, 1: 4–11.

Scarlata, M. (1986) 'Mercati e fiere nella Sicilia aragonese', in *Mercati e consumi. Organizzazione e qualificazione del commercio in Italia dal XII al XX secolo*, Bologna, pp. 477–94.

Scharf, G. P. (1996) 'Borgo San Sepolcro a metà del Quattrocento: istituzioni e società (1440–1460)', unpublished M.A. thesis, Università degli Studi di Milano.

Schiff, M. and C. E. Montenegro (1997) 'Aggregate agricultural supply response in developing countries: a survey of selected issues', *Economic Development and Cultural Change* 45, 2: 393–410.

Schnur, R. (1963) *Individualismus und Absolutismus*, Berlin.

Schofield, P. R. (1997) 'Dearth, debt and the local land market in a late thirteenth-century village community', *Agricultural History Review* 45, 1: 1–17.

Schofield, R. S. (1965) 'Geographical distribution of wealth in England 1334–1649', *Economic History Review*, 2nd ser. 18: 483–510.

—— (1988) 'Taxation and the political limits of the Tudor state', in C. Cross, D. Loades and J. J. Scarisbrick (eds) *Law and Government under the Tudors. Essays presented to Sir Geoffrey Elton*, Cambridge, pp. 227–55.

Schremmer, E. (1972) 'Standortausweitung der Warenproduktion im langfristigen Wirtschaftswachtum. Zur Stadt-Land-Arbeitsteilung im Gewerbe des 18. Jahrhunderts', *Vierteljahrschrift für Sozial- und Wirtschaftsgeschichte* 59: 1–40.

Schulze, W. (1995) 'The emergence and consolidation of the "tax state". I. The sixteenth century', in R. Bonney (ed.) *Economic Systems and State Finance*, Oxford: 261–80.

Sclafert, T. (1926) *Le Haut-Dauphiné au Moyen Age*, Paris.

—— (1959) *Cultures en Haute-Provence. Réboisements et pâturages au Moyen Age*, Paris.

Scott, T. (1996) 'Economic landscapes', in R. S. Scribner (ed.) *Germany. A New Social and Economic History, I. 1450–1630*, London/New York: 1–32.

Scott, T. (1997) *Regional Identity and Economic Change. The Upper Rhine, 1450–1600*, Oxford.

Scott, T. and B. Scribner (1996) 'Urban networks', in R. S. Scribner (ed.) *Germany. A New Social and Economic History, I. 1450–1630*, London/New York: 113–43.

Scribner, R. S. (ed.) (1996) *Germany. A New Social and Economic History, I. 1450–1630*, London/New York.

Scully, G. W. (1992) *Constitutional Environments and Economic Growth*, Princeton.

Sella, D. (1978) 'Per la storia della coltura e della lavorazione del lino nello Stato di Milano durante il secolo XVII', in *Felix olim Lombardia. Studi di storia padana dedicati dagli allievi a Giuseppe Martini*, Milan, pp. 791–803.

Sen, A. (1981) *Poverty and Famines. An Essay on Entitlement and Deprivation*, Oxford.

Seneca, F. (1967) 'Sulle fiere udinesi di S. Caterina e S. Canciano alla fine del Quattrocento', *Archivio veneto* 82: 15–28.

Sereni, E. (1959–60) 'Mercato nazionale e accumulazione capitalistica nell'Unità italiana', *Studi storici* 1: 513–68

—— (1981) 'Note di storia dell'alimentazione nel Mezzogiorno: I Napoletani da "mangiafoglia" a "mangiamaccheroni"', in Sereni, *Terra nuova e buoi rossi e altri saggi per una storia dell'agricoltura europea*, Turin, pp. 292–371.

Sesma Muñoz, J. A. (1995) 'Produción para el mercado, commercio y desarrollo mercantil en espacios interiores (1250–1350): el modelo del sur de Aragon', in *Europa* 1995: 205–46

Siermann, C. L. J. (1998) *Politics, Institutions and the Economic Performance of Nations*, Cheltenham.

Silini, G. (1992) *E viva a Sancto Marcho! Lovere al tempo delle guerre d'Italia*, Bergamo.

Silva, P. (1910) 'Intorno all'industria e al commercio della lana in Pisa', *Studi storici* 19: 329–400.

Silver, M. (1983) 'A non-neo Malthusian model of English land value, wages, and grain yield before the Black Death', *Journal of European Economic History* 12, 3: 631–50.

Sivéry, G. (1973) *Structures agraires et vie rurale dans le Hainaut à la fin du Moyen Age*, Lille.

—— (1976) 'Les profits de l'éleveur et du cultivateur dans le Hainaut à la fin du Moyen Âge', *Annales E.S.C.* 31, 3: 604–30.

Smith, A. (1976) [1776]. *An Inquiry into the Nature and Causes of the Wealth of Nations*, ed. E. Cannan, Chicago.

Smith, R. H. T. (1979) 'Periodic market-places and periodic marketing: review and prospect', *Progress in Human Geography* 3: 471–505.

Smith, R. M. (1984) 'Some issues concerning families and their property in rural England 1250–1800', in R. M. Smith (ed.) *Land, Kinship and Life-Cycle*, Cambridge, pp. 1–86.

—— (1991) 'Demographic developments in rural England, 1300–48: a survey', in B. M. S. Campbell (ed.) *Before the Black Death. Studies in the 'Crisis' of the Early Fourteenth Century*, Manchester, pp. 25–78.

Sneller, Z. W. (1936) *Deventer, die Stadt der Jahrmärkte*, Weimar.

Sokoloff, K. (1988) 'Inventive activity in early industrial America: evidence from patent records, 1790–1846', *Journal of Economic History* 48, 4: 813–50.

Solazzi, G. (1952–3) 'Gli statuti di Viadana del secolo XIV', *Bollettino storico cremonese* 18: 3–156.

Solomou, S. and W. Wu (1999) 'Weather effects on European agricultural output 1850–1913', *European Review of Economic History* 3, 3: 351–74.

Sortor, M. (1993) 'Saint-Omer and its textile trades in the later Middle Ages: a contribution to the proto-industrialization debate', *American Historical Review* 98: 1475–99.

Spallanzani, M. (ed.) (1976) *Produzione commercio e consumo dei panni di lana (nei secoli XII–XVIII)*, Florence.

Sprandel, R. (1964) 'Die Ausbreitung des deutschen Handwerks im mittelalterlichen Frankreich', *Vierteljahrschrift für Sozial- und Wirtschaftsgeschichte* 51: 66–100.

—— (1969) 'La production du fer au Moyen Age', *Annales E.S.C.* 24, 2: 305–21.

—— (1971) 'Gewerbe und Handel', in H. Aubin and W. Zorn (eds) *Handbuch der deutschen Wirtschafts- und Sozialgeschichte*, vol. 1, Stuttgart, pp. 335–57.

Spruyt, H. (1994) *The Sovereign State and Its Competitors. An Analysis of Systems Change*, Princeton.

Spufford, P. (1988) *Money and its Use in Medieval Europe*, Cambridge.

Stabel, P. (1997) *Dwarf Among Giants. The Flemish Urban Network in the Late Middle Ages*, Leuven/Apeldoorn.

Stone, D. (1997) 'The productivity of hired and customary labour: evidence from

Wisbech Barton in the fourteenth century', *Economic History Review*, 2nd ser. 50, 4: 640–56.

Storti Storchi, C. (1984) 'Statuti viscontei di Bergamo', in M. Cortesi (ed.) *Statuti rurali e statuti di valle. La provincia di Bergamo nei secoli XIII–XVIII*, Bergamo, pp. 51–92.

—— (1988) 'Lo statuto quattrocentesco di Crema', in M. Cortesi (ed.) *Crema 1185. Una contrastata autonomia politica e territoriale*, Cremona, pp. 155–79.

—— (1990) 'Aspetti generali della legislazione statutaria lombarda in età viscontea', in *Legislazione e società nell'Italia medievale. Per il VII centenario degli statuti di Albenga (1288)*, Bordighera, pp. 55–70.

—— (1992) 'Statuti e decreti. Cenni sulla legislazione vigevanese nel Trecento', in G. Chittolini (ed.) *Metamorfosi di un borgo. Vigevano in età visconteo-sforzesce*, Milan, pp. 43–54.

Stromer, W. von (1976) 'Die oberdeutschen Geld- und Wechselmärkte. Ihre Entwicklung vom Spätmittelalter bis zum Dreißigjährigen Krieg', *Scripta Mercaturae* 1: 23–49.

—— (1977) 'Innovation und Wachstum im Spätmittelalter. Die Erfindung der Drahtmühle', *Technikgeschichte* 44: 65–74.

—— (1978) *Die Gründung der Baumwollindustrie im Mitteleuropa. Wirtschaftspolitik im Spätmittelalter*, Stuttgart.

—— (1986) 'Gewerbereviere und Protoindustrien im Spätmittelalter und Frühneuzeit', in H. Pohl (ed.) *Gewerbe- und Industrielandschaften vom Spätmittelalter bis ins 20. Jahrhundert*, Stuttgart, pp. 39–111.

Studi Melis (1978) *Studi in memoria di Federigo Melis*, 5 vols, Naples.

Studi Sapori (1957) *Studi in onore di Armando Sapori*, 2 vols, Milan.

Stumpo, E. (1988) 'Reddito nazionale e debito pubblico. La finanza pubblica in Piemonte nella seconda metà del secolo XVII', in A. Guarducci (ed.) *Prodotto lordo e finanza pubblica. Secoli XIII–XIX*, Florence, pp. 653–702.

Sugden, R. (1986) *The Economics of Rights, Co-operation and Welfare*, Oxford.

Sussman, N. (1998) 'The late medieval bullion famine reconsidered', *Journal of Economic History* 58, 1: 126–54.

Sutton, A. F. (1989) 'The early linen and worsted industry of Norfolk and the evolution of the London Mercers' Company', *Norfolk Archaeology* 40: 201–25.

Swanson, H. (1999) *Medieval British Towns*, Houndmills/London.

Sweezy, P. (1950) 'A critique [of Dobb 1946]', *Science and Society*. Reprinted in R. H. Hilton (ed.) (1978) *The Transition from Feudalism to Capitalism*, London, pp. 33–56.

Taborelli, G. (ed.) (1986) *Commercio in Lombardia*, 2 vols, Milan.

Tagliabue, L. (1991–92) 'Aspetti di vita economico-sociale a Monza dagli atti del notaio Andreolo de Polla (1442–1451)', unpublished M.A. thesis, Facoltà di Lettere e Filosofia, University of Milan.

Tangheroni, M. (1973) *Politica, commercio, agricoltura a Pisa nel Trecento*, Pisa.

—— (1978) 'Di alcuni accordi commerciali tra Pisa e Firenze in materia di cereali', in *Studi in memoria di Federigo Melis*, 5 vols, Naples: vol. 2, pp. 211–20.

—— (1988) 'Il sistema economico della Toscana nel Trecento', in S.Gensini (ed.) *La Toscana nel secolo XIV. Caratteri di una civiltà regionale*, Pisa, pp. 41–66.

Tarello, G. (1976) *Storia della cultura giuridica moderna, I. Assolutismo e codificazione del diritto*, Bologna.

TeBrake, W. H. (1988) 'Land drainage and public environmental policy in medieval Holland', *Environmental Review* 12(Fall): 75–93.

Teisseyre-Sallmann, L. (1990) 'Hiérarchie et complémentarité dans un réseau urbain régional. Le Bas-Languedoc oriental et cévenol aux XVIIe et XVIIIe siècles', *Histoire économique et société* 9: 337–64.

't Hart, M. (1989) 'Cities and statemaking in the Dutch republic, 1580–1680', *Theory and Society* 18: 663–87.

—— (2000) 'Town and country in the Netherlands, 1550–1750', in S. R. Epstein (ed.) *Town and Country in Europe, 1300–1750*, Cambridge.

Thoen, E. (1988) *Landbouwekonomie en bevolking in Vlaanderen gedurende de late Middeleeuwen en het begin van de Moderne Tijden. Testregio: de kasselrijen van Oodenaarde en Aalst (eind 13de – eerste helft 16de eeuw)*, Ghent, 2 vols.

—— (1990) 'Technique agricole, cultures nouvelles et économie rurale en Flandre au bas Moyen Age', in *Plantes et cultures novelles en Europe occidentale, au Moyen Age et à l'époque moderne*, Flaran, pp. 51–67.

—— (1994) 'Die Koppelwirtschaft im flämischen Ackerbau vom Hochmittelalter bis zum 16. Jahrhundert', in A. Verhulst and Y. Morimoto (eds) *Economie rurale et économie urbaine au moyen âge*, Gent/Fukuoka, pp. 135–53.

—— (1997) 'The birth of "the Flemish husbandry": agricultural technology in medieval Flanders', in G. Astill and J. Langdon (eds) *Medieval Farming and Technology. The Impact of Agricultural Change in Northwest Europe*, Leiden, New York/Cologne.

Thoen, E. and I. Devos (1999) 'Pest in de zuidelijke Nederlanden tijdens de Middeleuwen en de Moderne Tijden. Een status quaestionis over de ziekte in haar sociaal-economische context', in *La peste aux Pays-Bas: considérations médico-historiques 650 ans après la Peste Noire*, Brussels, pp. 19–43.

Thoen, E. and H. Soly (eds) (1999) *Labour and Labour Markets Between Town and Countryside (Middle Ages – 19th Century)*, Brussels.

Thomas, J. (1996) 'Foires et marchés ruraux en France à l'époque moderne', in C. Desplat (ed.) *Foires et marchés dans les campagnes de l'Europe médiévale et moderne*, Toulouse, pp. 177–207.

Thompson, I. A. A. (1994a) 'Castile: polity, fiscality, and fiscal crisis', in P. T. Hoffman and K. Norberg (eds) *Fiscal Crises, Liberty, and Representative Government, 1450–1789*, Stanford: 140–80.

—— (1994b) 'Castile: absolutism, constitutionalism, and liberty', in P. T. Hoffman and K. Norberg (eds) *Fiscal Crises, Liberty, and Representative Government, 1450–1789*, Stanford: 181–225.

Thomson, J. K. J. (1983) 'Variations in industrial structure in pre-industrial Languedoc', in M. Berg, P. Hudson and M. Sonenscher (eds) *Manufacture in Town and Country Before the Factory*, Cambridge, pp. 61–91.

—— (1996) 'Proto-industrialization in Spain', in S. C. Ogilvie and M. Cerman (eds) (1996) *European Proto-Industrialization*, Cambridge, pp. 85–101.

Tilly, C. (1990) *Coercion, Capital, and European States, AD990–1990*, Cambridge, Mass./Oxford.

Timbal, P.-C. (1958) 'Les lettres de marque dans le droit de la France médiévale', in *L'Étranger*, Brussels, pt. 2, pp. 108–38.

Tiraboschi, A. (1880) 'Cenni intorno alla valle Gandino ed ai suoi statuti', *Archivio storico lombardo* 7: 5–40.

Titow, J. Z. (1987) 'The decline of the fair of St. Giles, Winchester, in the thirteenth and fourteenth centuries', *Nottingham Medieval Studies* 31: 58–75.

214   *Bibliography*

Tits-Dieuaide, M.-J. (1975) *La formation des prix céréaliers en Brabant et en Flandre au XVe siècle*, Brussels.

—— (1981) 'L'évolution des techniques agricoles en Flandre et en Brabant du XIVe au XVIe siècle', *Annales ESC* 36, 3: 362–81.

—— (1984) 'Les campagnes flamandes du XIIIe au XVIIIe siècle, ou les succès d'une agriculture traditionnelle', *Annales ESC* 39, 3: 590–610.

—— (1987) 'L'évolution des prix du blé dans quelques villes d'Europe occidentale du XVe siècle au XVIIIe siècle', *Annales E.S.C.* 42, 3: 529–48.

Topolski, J. (1985) 'A model of east-central European continental commerce in the sixteenth and the first half of the seventeenth century', in A. Mączak, H. Samsonowicz and P. Burke (eds) *East-Central Europe in Transition from the Fourteenth to the Seventeenth Century*, Cambridge/Paris, pp. 128–39.

Toubert, P. (1976) 'Les statuts communaux et l'histoire des campagnes lombardes au XIVe siècle', in Toubert, *Études sur l'Italie médiévale (IXe–XIVe s.)*, London.

Tracy, J. D. (1985) *A Financial Revolution in the Habsburg Netherlands: "Renten" and "Renteniers" in the County of Holland, 1515–1566*, Berkeley/Los Angeles/London.

Tranchant, M. (1993) 'Navires et techniques de navigation en Atlantique à la fin du Moyen Age', M.A. diss., University of Poitiers.

Tupling, G. H. (1936) 'An alphabetical list of the markets and fairs of Lancashire recorded before the year 1701', *Transactions of the Lancashire and Cheshire Antiquarian Society* 51: 86–110.

Turnau, I. (1983) 'The diffusion of knitting in medieval Europe', in N. B. Harte and K. G. Ponting (eds) *Cloth and Clothing in Medieval Europe. Essays in Memory of Professor E. M. Carus-Wilson*, London, pp. 368–90.

Ugolini, P. (1985) 'La formazione del sistema territoriale e urbano della Valle Padana', in C. De Seta (ed.) *Storia d'Italia. Annali 8*, Turin, pp. 159–240.

Unger, R. W. (1978) 'The Netherlands herring fishery in the late Middle Ages: the false legend of Willem Beukels of Biervliet', *Viator* 9: 335–56.

—— (1980) *The Ship in the Medieval Economy 600–1600*, London.

—— (1983) 'Integration of Baltic and Low Countries grain markets, 1400–1800', in J. M. von Winter (ed.) *The Interactions of Amsterdam and Antwerp with the Baltic Region, 1400–1800*, Leiden, pp. 1–10.

Unwin, T. (1981) 'Rural marketing in medieval Nottinghamshire', *Journal of Historical Geography* 7: 231–51.

Usher, D. E. E. (1953) 'The medieval fair of St. Ives', in Usher, *Two Studies of Medieval Life*, Cambridge, pp. 1–83.

Valdéon Baruque, J. (1971) 'La crisis del siglo XIV en Castilla: revisión del problema', *Revista de la Universidad de Madrid, Estudios de História Economica II*, 79: 161–84.

Vandenbroeke, C. (1998) 'Macro-history in Flanders: a reconstruction of the gross regional product around 1560', *Journal of European Economic History* 28, 2: 359–66.

van der Wee, H. (1963) *The Growth of the Antwerp Market and the European Economy (Fourteenth-Sixteenth Centuries)*, 3 vols, Louvain.

—— (1977) 'Monetary, credit and banking systems', in E. E. Rich and C. H. Wilson (eds) *The Cambridge Economic History of Europe, V. The Economic Organization of Early Modern Europe*, Cambridge, pp. 290–393.

—— (1988) 'Industrial dynamics and the process of urbanization and de-urbanization in the Low Countries from the late middle ages to the eighteenth century.

A synthesis', in van der Wee (ed.) *The Rise and Decline of Urban Industries in Italy and in the Low Countries (Late Middle Ages – Early Modern Times)*, Louvain, pp.307–81.

van der Wee, H. and T. Peeters (1970) 'Un modèle dynamique de croissance inter-séculaire du commerce mondial (XIe–XVIIe siècles)', *Annales E.S.C.* 25, 1: 100–26.

van Houtte, J. A. (1940) 'La genèse du grand marché international d'Anvers à la fin du moyen âge', *Revue Belge de Philologie et d'Histoire* 19: 87–126.

—— (1966) 'The rise and decline of the market of Bruges', *Economic History Review,* 2nd ser. 19: 29–47.

—— (1977) *An Economic History of the Low Countries 800–1800*, London.

van Werveke, H. (1963) 'The economic policies of governments: the Low Countries', in M. M. Postan, E. E. Rich and E. Miller (eds) (1963) *Cambridge Economic History of Europe, III. Economic Organization and Policies in the Middle Ages*, Cambridge, pp. 340–60.

van Zanden, J. L. (1993) *The Rise and Decline of Holland's Economy. Merchant Capitalism and the Labour Market*, Manchester.

Varanini, G. M. (1976) 'Dal comune allo stato regionale', in N. Tranfaglia and M. Firpo (eds) *La Storia. I grandi problemi dal Medioevo all'Età contemporanea, II. Il Medioevo, 2. Popoli e strutture politiche*, Turin, pp. 693–724.

—— (1992) *Comuni cittadini e stato regionale. Ricerche sulla Terraferma veneta*, Verona.

—— (1994) 'L'organizzazione del distretto cittadino nell'Italia padana dei secoli XIII–XIV (Marca Trevigiana, Lombardia, Emilia)', in G. Chittolini and D. Willoweit (eds) (1994) *L'organizzazione del territorio in Italia e Germania: secoli XIII–XIV,* Bologna: 133–233.

—— (1997) 'Governi principeschi e nodello cittadino di organizzazione del territorio nell'Italia del Quattrocento', in G.Chittolini (ed.) *Principi e città alla fine del Medioevo*, San Miniato, pp. 95–127.

Venendaal, A. J. Jr. (1994) 'Fiscal crises and constitutional freedom in the Netherlands, 1450–1795', in P. T. Hoffman. and K. Norberg (eds) (1994) *Fiscal Crises, Liberty, and Representative Government, 1450–1789*, Stanford, pp. 96–139.

Ventura, A. (1964) *Nobiltà e popolo nella società veneta del '400 e '500*, Bari.

Verhulst, A. (1985) 'L'intensification et la commercialisation de l'agriculture dans les Pays-Bas méridionaux au XIIIe siècle', in *La Belgique rurale du Moyen Âge à nos jours. Mélanges offerts à Jean-Jacques Hoebanx*, Brussels, pp. 89–100.

—— (1990) 'The "agricultural revolution" of the Middle Ages reconsidered', in B. S. Bachrach and D. Nicholas (eds) *Law, Custom and the Social Fabric in Medieval Europe. Essays in Honor of Bryce Lyon*, Kalamazoo, pp. 17–28.

Verlinden, C. (1963) 'Markets and fairs', in M. M. Postan, E. E. Rich and E. Miller (eds) (1963) *Cambridge Economic History of Europe, III. Economic Organization and Policies in the Middle Ages*, Cambridge: 119–53.

Viazzo, P. P. (1989) *Upland Communities. Environment, Population and Social Structure in the Alps Since the Sixteenth Century*, Cambridge.

Waites, B. (1982) 'Medieval fairs and markets in north-east Yorkshire', *Ryedale Historian* 11: 3–10.

Waley, D. (1978) *The Italian City Republics*, 2nd ed., London.

Walford, C. (1883) *Fairs Past and Present. A Chapter in the History of Commerce*, London.

Walker, W. (1981) *Essex Markets and Fairs*, Chelmsford.

Wallerstein, I. M. (1974) *The Modern World-System*, 1, *Capitalist Agriculture and the*

Origins of the World-Economy in the Sixteenth Century, New York.

Walter, J. and R. Schofield (eds) (1989a) *Famine, Disease and the Social Order in Early Modern Society*, Cambridge.

—— (1989b) 'Famine, disease and crisis mortality in early modern society', in J. Walter and R. Schofield (eds) *Famine, Disease and the Social Order in Early Modern Society*, Cambridge, pp. 1–74.

Waters, D. W. (1968) 'Science and techniques of navigation in the Renaissance', in C. S. Singleton (ed.) *Art, Science and History in the Renaissance*, Baltimore, Md.

Watson, A. M. (1981) 'Towards denser and more continuous settlement: new crops and farming techniques in the early Middle Ages', in J. A. Raftis (ed.) *Pathways to Medieval Peasants*, Toronto, pp. 65–82.

—— (1983) *Agricultural Innovation in the Early Islamic World. The Diffusion of Crops and Farming Techniques, 700–1100*, Cambridge.

Watts, D. G. (1967) 'A model for the early fourteenth century', *Economic History Review*, 2nd ser. 20, 4: 543–7.

Weber, M.(1961) *General Economic History*, New York.

—— (1978) *Economy and Society*, ed. G. Roth and C. Wittich, 2 vols, Berkeley/Los Angeles/London.

Weinbaum, M. (1943) *British Borough Charters 1307–1640*, Cambridge.

Weingast, B. R. (1993) 'Constitutions as governance structures: the political foundations of secure markets', *Journal of Institutional and Theoretical Economics* 149, 1: 286–311.

—— (1995) 'The economic role of political institutions: market-preserving federalism and economic development', *Journal of Law, Economics, and Organization* 7, 1: 1–31.

—— (1997) 'The political foundations of limited government: parliament and sovereign debt in 17th- and 18th-century England', in J. N. Drobak and J. V. C. Nye (eds) (1997) *The Frontiers of the New Institutional Economics*, San Diego/London, pp. 213–46.

Weir, D. R. (1989) 'Markets and mortality in France, 1600–1789', in J. Walter and R. Schofield (eds) *Famine, Disease and the Social Order in Early Modern Society*, Cambridge, pp. 201–34.

—— (1995) 'Family income, mortality, and fertility on the eve of the demographic transition: a case study of Rosny-sur-Bois', *Journal of Economic History* 55, 1: 1–26.

Wielandt, F. (1971) 'Münzen, Gewichte und Masse bis 1800', in H. Aubin. and W. Zorn (eds) (1971) *Handbuch der deutschen Wirtschafts- und Sozialgeschichte*, vol. 1, Stuttgart, pp. 658–78.

Wiesner, M. E. (1986) *Working Women in Renaissance Germany*, New Brunswick, N.J.

Wolf, E. R. (1983) *Europe and the People Without History*, Berkeley/Los Angeles.

Wolff, P. (1954) *Commerce et marchands de Toulouse*, Paris.

—— (1976) 'Esquisse d'une histoire de la draperie en Languedoc du XIIe au début du XVIIe siècle', in M. Spallanzani (ed.) (1976) *Produzione commercio e consumo dei panni di lana (nei secoli XII–XVIII)*, Florence, pp. 435–62.

Wood, L. J. (1974) 'Population density and rural market provision', *Cahiers d'Études africaines* 14: 715–26.

Woude, A. van der, A. Hayami and J. de Vries (eds) (1990) *Urbanization in History. A Process of Dynamic Interactions*, Oxford.

Young, A. (1993) 'Invention and bounded learning by doing', *Journal of Political Economy* 101: 443–72.

—— (1998) 'Growth without scale effects', *Journal of Political Economy* 106, 1: 41–63.

Yun, B. (1994) 'Economic cycles and structural changes', in T. Brady, H. A. Oberman, and J. Tracy (eds) *Handbook of European History, 1400–1600. Late Middle Ages, Renaissance and Reformation*, Leiden/New York/Cologne, pp. 377–411.

Zanetti, D. (1964) *Problemi alimentari di una economia preindustriale. Cereali a Pavia dal 1398 al 1700*, Turin.

Zaninelli, S. (1969) 'Vita economica e sociale', in A. Bosisio and G. Vismara (eds) *Storia di Monza e della Brianza*, 3 vols, Milan.

Zanoni, L. (1911) *Gli Umiliati nei loro rapporti con l'eresia, l'industria della lana ed i Comuni nei secoli XII e XIII sulla scorta di documenti inediti*, Milan.

Zdekauer, L. (1920) *Fiera e mercato in Italia sulla fine del Medioevo*, Macerata.

Zelioli Pini, F. (1992) 'Economia e società a Lecco nel tardo medioevo. La famiglia de Molzio tra XIV e XV secolo', *Archivi di Lecco* 15, 4: 1–278.

Zilibotti, F. (1994) 'Endogenous growth and intermediation in an "archipelago" economy', *Economic Journal* 104: 462–73

Zorzi, A. (1990) 'Lo stato territoriale fiorentino (secoli XIV–XV). Aspetti giurisdizionali', *Società e storia* 13: 799–825.

Zug Tucci, H. (1978) 'Un aspetto trascurato del commercio medievale del vino', in *Studi in memoria di Federigo Melis*, 5 vols, Naples, vol. 3, pp. 311–48.

Zulaica Palacios, F. (1994) *Fluctuaciones economicas en un periodo de crisis. Precios y salarios en Aragon en la baja Edad Media (1300–1430)*, Zaragoza.

Zupko, R. E. (1977) *British Weights and Measures. A History from Antiquity to the Seventeenth Century*, Madison/London.

Index

Printed in the United States
by Baker & Taylor Publisher Services